DISCARD

D1510046

Adopting and Advocating for the Special Needs Child

362.734

Adopting and Advocating for the Special Needs Child

A Guide for Parents and Professionals

L. ANNE BABB and RITA LAWS

Foreword by Dorothy and Robert DeBolt

BERGIN & GARVEY
Westport, Connecticut • London

Library of Congress Cataloging-in-Publication Data

Babb, L. Anne (Linda Anne), 1957–
Adopting and advocating for the special needs child : a guide for parents and professionals / L. Anne Babb and Rita Laws ; foreword by Dorothy and Robert DeBolt.
p. cm.
Includes bibliographical references and index.
ISBN 0–89789–489–8 (alk. paper)
1. Special needs adoption—United States. 2. Older child adoption—United States. 3. Handicapped children—United States. 4. Adopted children—United States—Family relationships. 5. Adoptive parents—Services for—United States. 6. Adoption agencies—United States. I. Laws, Rita, 1956– . II. Title.
HV875.55.B33 1997
362.73′4—dc21 96–50474

British Library Cataloguing in Publication Data is available.

Copyright © 1997 by L. Anne Babb and Rita Laws

All rights reserved. No portion of this book may be reproduced, by any process or technique, without the express written consent of the publisher.

Library of Congress Catalog Card Number: 96–50474
ISBN: 0–89789–489–8

First published in 1997

Bergin & Garvey, 88 Post Road West, Westport, CT 06881
An imprint of Greenwood Publishing Group, Inc.

Printed in the United States of America

The paper used in this book complies with the Permanent Paper Standard issued by the National Information Standards Organization (Z39.48–1984).

10 9 8 7 6 5 4 3 2 1

To our parents,
Tom and Hanna Edwards and Sam and Nancy Laws,
whose love transformed us into child advocates.

Contents

Foreword

Occasionally a book appears which prompts your first thought to be, "Why didn't someone write this book sooner?" *Adopting and Advocating for the Special Needs Child* is certainly such a book. Remembering our own experiences in the adoption and rearing of special needs children beginning in the 1950s and continuing through the 1980s we would have certainly relished the wealth of knowledge and experience the authors have provided herein. That probably answers the question posed above—because this is a book that could only have been written by those who had both the practical *and* professional knowledge of children that the authors have accumulated. This was accomplished through years of personal experience with these "special kids." As a result, this is a very unique guide for both parents and professionals, a "how-to" that starts with the decision to adopt a special needs child and ends with information about launching these same children into adulthood.

The knowledge imparted in these chapters is of value not only to people directly involved in adoption but also to all those individuals who serve children. Educators could especially benefit from the insights so clearly presented in these pages. This is a book in which Dr. Babb and Dr. Laws show how these children, who some would call "unadoptable," can become happy and well-adjusted members of a family, of a classroom, and of society.

—Dorothy and Robert DeBolt
September, 1996

Acknowledgments

This book could not have been complete without the advice of mentors in special needs adoption: Joe Kroll and the North American Council on Adoptable Children; Bob and Dorothy DeBolt and Aask America; *Adoptive Families Magazine* editor Lynda Lynch, and all the folks at Adoptive Families of America who have supported our work for many years; and our dear friend DWe Williams, who read our manuscript from start to finish and gave us invaluable advice.

We appreciate Cheryl Reidy for reviewing and improving work on disclosure of information and transracial adoption; Adrienne Okin, for her advice on international adoption and English as a second language; Jim Cadwell of the Native American Child and Family Resource Center for his help with Native American issues and adoption history; and Peggy Soule for her generous sharing of the history of American photolisting.

Our special thanks to our advisers in higher education, Dr. LeRoy Cordray and Dr. Tom Neal; and to a politician who really puts kids first, the honorable Mark Seikel, Oklahoma House of Representatives. We also appreciate the support of the Oklahoma City Community Foundation, whose grant produced the seedling into which this book grew.

While this book was being written in our hearts, we were buoyed by the support and friendships of fellow members of Prodigy's on-line adoption community including Jody, Maggie, Jean, Curry, Patty, Sylvia, and Sharon. We are very grateful to Prodigy's management, ever supporting us in advocating for special needs adoption on-line.

Friends who gave us invaluable advice, feedback, and support as we wrote this book include Paul Mekaske, Bonnie Hagan, Jody McCollum, and Chuck and Nancy Diven. We also want to aknowledge the work Julie Agle did at The Family Tree in pioneering a multi-service agency that truly served the entire adoption triad. Much of what we learned went into the pages of this book.

Thanks, too, to our editors at Greenwood: Liz Murphy, who nurtured our dream of this book, and Lynn Taylor, who brought it to fruition.

To Dirk Babb, the fellow who tended the home fires in the Babb household and advised the Laws family on how to keep roof leaks from dousing theirs, thank you. And, last but not least, thanks to the little people who live in our homes and yell, "MOM!" They may not have made the writing of this book any easier, but they certainly inspired its contents.

Introduction

> Unlearn'd, he knew no schoolman's subtle art, no language but the language of the heart.
>
> —Alexander Pope

A few years and a few miles apart, the authors shared the same experience: We wanted to open our hearts and homes to special needs children, but it seemed as if no one could tell us how. Once we brought our children home, we were shocked to learn that adoption is not a one-time event, but a lifelong process—one for which we had been ill prepared.

This book is the result of a combined experience of 30 years of learning how to adopt children with special needs and raise them in ways that meet those needs. We have known from our earliest friendship that this book was meant to be. We wanted to help other people avoid the mistakes we've made and help them adopt. We hope it will result in the successful placements of more children who wait for what the rest of us take for granted—moms and dads.

LANGUAGE OF THE HEART

Throughout this book, we alternate between using *he* and *she* and between referring to adoptive *parents* (plural) or adoptive *parent* (singular). We also from time to time refer to adoptive parents as *adopters* and to birth parents as *original parents*. We refer to gay and lesbian adopters, and sometimes we write *partner* instead of *spouse.* We write about children as *he, she,* and *they.*

We intentionally use language as diverse as our families, not to be politically correct, but to communicate acceptance. Special needs adoption is not about anything if it is not about diversity. Though our personal religious and political beliefs are quite different, and remain an unending source of lively conversation, we have found commonality and friendship in a shared love and concern for children. We believe that all Americans, especially religious and political leaders, should work together for the good of children. And working for kids starts with using a language of the heart.

Our children come to us with feelings of abandonment, displacement, and a consuming lack of acceptance. Our belief is that, in special needs adoption, the rule should be love above all else, the goal to serve children, not political agendas.

PART I

GETTING STARTED

CHAPTER 1

Special Needs Adoption in the United States

> I figure, if I'm not perfect, why should I expect the child I adopt to be perfect?
>
> —Overheard at an adoption conference

WHAT IS SPECIAL NEEDS ADOPTION?

Special needs adoption refers to the adoption of children with mild to severe special needs such as mental, physical, and emotional disabilities. Other special needs include age, sibling status, race (in some states), and risk factors such as pre-natal exposure to drugs. Special needs children waiting to be adopted are referred to as waiting children and have usually spent some amount of time in foster care. About two-thirds are boys, many are sibling group members, and about half are members of minority groups. Roughly one-fourth of our nation's 500,000 foster children will need an adoptive parent or parents. Exact statistics, long promised by the federal government, have yet to materialize.

Under federal guidelines, children with special needs are those who cannot or should not be returned to their birth parents and who have a condition, history, or circumstances that make the child difficult to place without government assistance such as adoption assistance payments (AAP). Healthy Caucasian children under age six are usually not considered to have special needs; all other children, depending on federal and state definitions, may fall into the special needs category. These are the children who are waiting in line for a birthright most of society takes for granted: a permanent family. In the past, when death rates from poverty, illness, and drugs were much higher, such children were orphans. Today, these children are the "new orphans" whose original parents, while still living, are unable to care for them due to drug addiction, incarceration, abuse, or illness. Sadly, AIDS is taking us back in time by claiming lives and reviving the classic meaning of "orphan."

Waiting children are typically in the custody of a public or private adoption agency. Before 1980, these children were called "hard-to-place" or "unadoptable." Today, many adoption advocates claim that there is no such thing as an unadoptable child, only families who have not yet been found to adopt the children who wait. Even children who must be institutionalized due to severe medical, behavioral or emotional disabilities can benefit from having a loving, permanent, involved family that lives outside the institution.

CATEGORIES OF SPECIAL NEEDS

The following are explanations of the categories of special needs, including disabilities, age, sibling status, at-risk, and race and gender. A child's special needs may be in one or more of these categories, can range from mild to severe, and can be permanent, temporary, or correctable.

Disabilities

The disabilities category includes mental, physical, and emotional disabilities that can range from mild to severe. Mental disabilities refer to developmental delays, mental retardation, lags, and cognitive or learning problems. Physical disabilities include birth defects, physical limitations, diseases, and the after-effects of diseases and injuries. Emotional disabilities refer to behavioral problems and all types of mental and emotional illnesses.

Age

The age limit at which a child is considered to have special needs differs from one state to another (Gilles, 1992). One state, for example, defines age as a special need for African-American children over age two, other minorities over age five, and Caucasian children over age eight. This is simply a reflection of how quickly children of different races and ages are placed in that area. As minority race recruitment improves, these ages will be modified to reflect the fact that more families are available for minority race children. Since younger children are easier to place, the age of the onset of the special needs label will be adjusted upward.

Children who do not find adoptive homes "age-out" of the foster care system after their 18th birthday. Parents in the process of adopting a 17-year-old should not be concerned if the teen turns 18 before finalization. Depending on the state of residence, the legalities may change slightly, but the adoption process can continue.

Sibling Groups

Siblings groups are groups of siblings or half-siblings who must be placed together into adoption. Sibling groups of two members are called small sibling groups. All others are considered to be large sibling groups. Since small sibling groups of pre-school aged Caucasian children with mild to no disabilities are as easy to place as healthy white infants, such sibling groups do not fall into the special needs category unless other factors, such as disability, minority race, or risk factors are also present.

"At-Risk" Children

An at-risk child is one who, while currently healthy, is at risk of developing learning, emotional, behavioral, or physical disabilities in the future. Such children have been exposed to drugs (pre-natally or post-natally), abuse, neglect, or have genetic predispositions to mental illness or physical disabilities. Occasionally, at-risk children do not develop the problems that were predicted, but parents should not enter into at-risk placements hoping for miracles. Most often, the problems develop but their effect can be minimized by the presence of a loving, stable, and knowledgeable adoptive family.

Race and Gender

Some agencies consider minority race alone to be a special need, especially when the child is male, but other agencies do not. This does not mean that having a certain ethnicity or gender is a disability. It means that at this time in America adoption specialists have not recruited enough families to adopt our waiting minority race children, and especially the boys.

In all racial groups, males outnumber females, sometimes by as many as three to one. Sociologists point to complex factors to explain this phenomenon, but statistics show that fewer female children are available for adoption. Furthermore, adopting couples tend to prefer to adopt girls first. Interestingly, among parents by birth, there tends to be an equally strong desire to give birth to boys first.

TYPES OF ADOPTION

When an individual or couple decides to build a family through adoption, there are several options from which to choose. Prospective parents can work with a licensed public or private agency, do an independent or private adoption (no agency involvement), do an identified adoption (an open adoption either through an attorney or a licensed agency), or a foster child adoption. An adoption may be closed (no contact between birth and adoptive families), semi-open (limited and nonidentifying contact between birth and adoptive families), or open (complete identifying information shared between birth and adoptive families). The adoption may be domestic (U.S.) or international, of an infant or of an older child, of a healthy child, or a child or children with special needs. There are strengths and weaknesses to each kind of adoption, and it is up to the prospective adoptive parent to decide which type of adoption best suits his or her own situation. The basic types of adoption are discussed in the following sections. All information on costs, length of wait, and types of children available are estimates and individual experiences will vary.

Agency Adoption

There are two kinds of adoption agencies, public agencies and private agencies. Public agencies, supported by the taxpayer, exist in each of the 50 states and are either county-run or centrally located at the state level. Private agencies are licensed through the state. The two types of agency adoptions are discussed separately, along with their advantages and disadvantages.

Public Agency Adoption

Each of the 50 states operates a public child-placing agency. Public agencies usually place older children and children with special needs, although many also place minority-race infants and toddlers, as well as sibling groups. Occasionally a healthy infant can be adopted through a public agency. Public agencies offer pre-adoption counseling and training, adoptive home studies, adoption assistance payment contracts, or subsidies, and some post-placement services.

Public agencies and private agencies specializing in special needs placements are usually more flexible with regard to the requirements for prospective adoptive couples. They may allow older couples, large families, single parents, and parents with disabilities to adopt whereas a private agency might reject the same applicant. State agencies also usually offer photolisting books or other means of reviewing the children who are available for adoption, such as "matching" parties or attendance at adoption staffings. Prospective parents view these listings to search for children. Many states also offer an additional adoption exchange service that will list a family hoping to adopt a child. Social workers use these listings to facilitate matches.

Prospective adoptive parents should know that a growing number of state agency adoptions in the United States are accomplished by foster parents (fost-adopt), and that many states give preference to foster parents when a child becomes eligible for adoption. Thus, prospective adoptive parents may also want to consider becoming foster parents or enrolling in a state's fost-adopt program if they choose to adopt via their state agency.

Advantages. The advantages to public agency adoption are that the costs are minimal or nonexistent and the requirements for adoptive parents are flexible. As well, many states provide average to above-average post-finalization help to their adoptive families and organize helpful support groups for adoptive parents. Adoption Assistance Payments (AAP) and Medicaid are sometimes easier to negotiate when a child has been placed through the state's public (rather than a private) agency.

Disadvantages. Although state agencies place the majority of special needs children in the United States, many state adoption units are under staffed. Some families using state agencies complain that it takes eight or more months before the state will even begin an adoption homestudy, and that they waited years for a child. And, in spite of federal laws eliminating racial matching policies, in many states it continues to be difficult for families to adopt transracially through a state agency, even if a family has already adopted a child transracially from another source. Finally, adoptive parents in many states have complained that the state adoption agency failed to disclose all the available information about their adopted child, making it difficult for the parent to make good decisions about either adopting or raising the child.

The Children. Very few infants and toddlers who are not significantly disabled are placed through public agencies, except in cases of fost-adopt. The majority of children waiting to be placed through public agencies are school age, often with moderate to severe disabilities, and are of a minority race.

Approximate Waiting Time. Three to twelve months for the homestudy; one to five years for placement of a child.

The Cost. The major expenses incurred are in medical checkups for pre-adoptive parents and legal fees of finalizing the adoption, which can be reimbursed up to $2,000 per child after the placement.

Private Agency Adoption

Private agencies are privately owned or operated adoption agencies licensed by the state's licensor of child-placing or adoption agencies. Private agencies may be nonprofit or for-profit, religious or nonreligious. About half of all healthy white infants are placed through private agencies, along with some infants with special needs, healthy minority-race infants, and sometimes toddlers, sibling groups, or children with special needs or who are older at the time of placement. Many private adoption agencies also have one or more international adoption program.

A few innovative private agencies in the United States charge no fees for their services, and finance their operations solely through Purchase of Services and similar programs whereby adoption fees are paid or reimbursed, but the majority charge fees ranging from a few hundred dollars to over $20,000. The most expensive may involve international travel and services. The services such agencies offer are generally the same as those offered by the state agency: pre-placement counseling and training, placement oversight, adoption home studies, post-placement supervision, and sometimes post-finalization services.

Private adoption agencies can also arrange for the AAP of special needs children.

Advantages. At religious agencies, preference is given to same-faith applicants. Fees can sometimes be low or are negotiable, especially when the child is of minority race or has special needs. Private agencies are often willing to work with applicants who have been denied by the state agency, such as large families or those wishing to adopt transracially. Nondenominational private agencies will usually accept adoptive parents who have been divorced and, in some areas, those who are gay or lesbian. Many private agencies also offer open adoptions or semiopen adoptions, which can shorten the waiting time for prospective adoptive parents since many birth parents prefer open adoption. In international adoptions, once a family is approved and receives a referral, it is nearly always certain the family will receive the child. Foreign-born and U.S. waiting children are usually legally free for adoption, minimizing the risk of the child's referral being withdrawn.

Disadvantages. The requirements at religious agencies can be strict, the cost high, and the waiting time for infants as long as those at public agencies. International adoption usually requires adoptive parents to traverse a maze of bureaucratic red tape, often requires travel of one or both parents (sometimes for weeks), and involves language and cultural barriers. As well, internationally born children whose adoptions are finalized in a foreign country and who have never been in the custody of a U.S. licensed adoption agency are ineligible for adoption assistance regardless of their special needs.

The Children. Infants to age 18, with and without special needs.

Approximate Waiting Time. Two or three months for the adoption homestudy; one to five years for placement of a child.

The Cost. Private agencies, $0-$20,000. The average cost of a domestic non-special needs adoption is about $8,500.

Independent Adoption

Independent adoption is adoption made "independent" of an adoption agency. It may be facilitated by an attorney, doctor, or clergyman, or involve a direct link between the birth parents and adoptive parents. The majority of healthy infants are placed through independent adoption, according to Adoptive Families of America (*Adoption: How to Begin,* 1994). Independent special needs adoption is rare because by not using a licensed adoption agency, an adoptive couple forfeits the opportunity to obtain services later for their child if the parents discover that the child has special needs that were not noticeable at birth.

In some states independent adoption is illegal, so prospective adoptive parents should contact the adoption agency licensor in their state of residence to determine what laws apply. The costs may be higher in some regions than they are through licensed adoption agencies. In other areas, just the opposite is true. Most professional organizations recommend adoption through a licensed adoption agency.

Sometimes an independent adoption subsequently becomes an independent special needs adoption. In one case Rita worked with several years ago, a couple who had just finalized the independent adoption of a newborn baby (now eight months old) called to ask for help. They had just been told that their baby was HIV-infected. In their state, they were unable to obtain a Medicaid card or any adoption subsidy or assistance because the child had not been adopted through a licensed agency. Their income did not qualify them for a non adoption-related Medicaid card. After a struggle, they were finally able to have their baby accepted by their private health insurance company, but it was a difficult time.

In general, independent special needs adoption should be undertaken only in those cases where the adoptive family is aware of state and federal laws regarding eligibility for adoption assistance.

Advantages. The wait to adopt a healthy infant is usually shorter than with an agency and the prospective adoptive parent has more control than in other types of adoption. Parents can apply to more than one attorney or independent adoption facilitator at a time, and attorneys often have few or no requirements for adoptive parents other than the ability to pay the adoption fees required and completing the homestudy.

Disadvantages. Adoptive parents must undertake the paperwork and verifications normally undertaken by the adoption agency. Only one of four potential placements through independent adoption actually are successful, and the medical and other fees paid by the adoptive parents prior to the placement of the infant or child are not refunded (*Adoption: How to Begin,* 1994). Adoptive parents thus risk not only heartache, but the loss of thousands of dollars before finally being able to adopt a child. Independent adoption usually provides no counseling for adoptive or birth parents, resulting in the likelihood that original parents will enter adoption uninformed, increasing the risk of psychological and emotional damage.

Prospective adoptive parents may receive placement of a child prior to the termination of parental rights of the birth parents, which presents a legal and emotional risk to the adoptive parents. If an adoption falls through, adoptive parents must begin the adoption process all over again. And, in the event that a child develops a condition that was unknown at placement or is later found to have special needs, he or she is ineligible for adoption assistance by virtue of having been adopted through a source not licensed to place children.

The Children. Most of the children placed are healthy, Caucasian infants. Some mixed-race infants are also placed, and very few children with special needs.

Approximate Waiting Time. 1-7 years.

The Costs. \$3,500-\$30,000, plus costs of hospital birth if not covered by Medical Assistance or private insurance.

International or Transcultural Adoption

International adoption, comprising about 10 percent of all adoptions in the United States, refers to the adoption of children from countries outside the United States. International adoption began with the adoptions of Amerasian children fathered by American servicemen in Japan, Korea, and later, in Vietnam during the American occupations of these countries (Mason & Silberman, 1993). Private organizations, individuals such as Harry and Bertha Holt (founders of Holt International), and church groups sponsored early international adoptions. Today, most international adoptions are facilitated through licensed adoption agencies.

Special needs international adoption is relatively rare when the special needs are not minor or correctable, because it requires greater financial resources on the part of the adoptive family than a domestic special needs adoption. In rare cases internationally adopted children may receive adoption benefits such as state medical cards and state-funded (Title IV-B) subsidies, but the process is neither easy nor guaranteed.

International special needs adoption carries with it unique challenges such as language and cultural differences between adoptive parent and child. Adopting older children and sibling groups internationally often requires a longer and more complex adjustment period for the children. Sometimes, the children are foundlings from orphanages and little or no background history is available. For these reasons, adoptive families should approach international special needs adoption with great caution and only after talking with experienced adoptive families and agencies who understand this type of adoption.

Even with its added risks, international special needs adoption holds the promise of great emotional rewards for the families involved. In some cultures, a birth defect or handicap, or even just being born female, can keep children from ever gaining acceptance in society. Handicaps that are considered correctable in the United States can doom a child to outsider status in another culture. Out-of-country adoption may be the child's only hope for a normal life, and in some cases, for any life at all.

Advantages. There are many children waiting and fewer restrictions upon adoptive parents, although some countries have marriage and even weight restrictions for adopting parents. Many programs specifically look for parents over age 40 and welcome single adopters. Once the assignment of a child is made, the adoption usually comes to a successful conclusion, since children are almost always free for adoption at the time of referral.

Disadvantages. Background and health information are sometimes inadequate or nonexistent; some children, having been abandoned, will never have background information; birth parents are sometimes coerced into giving up children and some programs have placed stolen children (this is rare, but has been reported); the children are more likely to have lived in institutions such as orphanages or even on the streets prior to being adopted. Parents must often travel to the child's country of origin for extended stays, which is costly and presents a hardship to some adoptive families. Undisclosed or hidden costs of travel or "donations" can increase the final amount adoptive parents pay in total fees.

The Children. Infants to age 15, with or without special needs, usually not Caucasian, except in Eastern Europe. Some sibling groups.

Approximate Waiting Time. 9-24 months after completing the homestudy and dossier. After assignment of a child, the wait to bring the child home can be 4-12 months, sometimes involving a stay of weeks or months in the child's country of birth. Once the assignment of a child is made, the adoption usually comes to a successful conclusion, since children are almost always free for adoption at the time of referral.

The Costs. $8,000 to over $25,000 on average. Haitian adoption remains the lowest-cost type of international adoption available, in some cases, less than $5,000.

Identified or Open Adoption

Identified and open adoptions are those in which expectant and prospective adoptive parents identify (find) each other and then obtain the services of an independent adoption facilitator or adoption agency in arranging and finalizing an adoption. Such adoptions usually involve healthy infants, but some involve older children as well.

Identified adoptions begin with "openness," which refers to face-to-face contact between the birth and adoptive families of the child. Open contact may be frequent or infrequent, through letters or telephone calls or through personal visits, and may or may not involve exchanging complete identifying information. The authors define open adoption as adoption in which identifying information is shared.

When foster parents adopt, the resulting special needs adoption often contains some element of openness, and more and more adoptive parents are opening their formerly closed adoptions of infants and toddlers with special needs. Independent special needs open adoptions involve the same risk of denied benefits to the child as do closed adoptions, and for that reason the authors recommend that all special needs or at-risk adoptions occur with the assistance of a licensed adoption agency.

The benefits of open adoption are found in the relationships that result, the answers that are available to the adoptee, and the absence of myths and fears about the birth families. Although research on open adoption has indicated high levels of success among triad members, the problems that can occur in open adoptions are that adoptive parents may agree to a degree of openness that they are not comfortable with because a placement is imminent; birth parents may discontinue contact due to post-placement grief or other adoption issues; or birth parents may become intrusive or too needy for the adoptive parents' comfort. Finally, some research on open adoption has resulted in findings that ongoing contact increases the grief of birth parents. Prospective adoptive parents and expectant parents considering open adoptions should become informed about the potential pitfalls. More resources on open adoption can be found in the Appendix to this book.

Advantages. Birth and adoptive parents experience more self-determination and have more choice than in any other type of adoption. The birth family history is usually passed intact to the adoptee, the original birth certificate can be obtained and retained for the adoptee; the birth family need not wonder for a lifetime how the child is doing. In many open adoptions, contact is ongoing, allowing adoptees to have their questions answered as they recur. Research has indicated that birth and adoptive parents in ongoing-contact adoptions have a high level of satisfaction.

Disadvantages. Just as in older child adoptions, on occasion a poor "match" may occur, and birth parents may find themselves abandoned by the adoptive parents who promised ongoing contact, only to their minds once the adoption was finalized. Adoptive parents may experience a failed placement when a birth parent reclaims the child, as most such adoptions involve legal risk. As well, a rare adoptive couple may discover that the birth parents either want more contact than they had first anticipated, or want less contact than the adoptive parents and adoptee would like. Many people misunderstand the principles of identified or open adoption and its benefits to those involved, and thus may be negative about the arrangement.

The Children. Almost always infants, but occasionally older children.

Approximate Waiting Time. Varies.

The Costs. Depend on whether adoption is agency or independent, usually $3,500 to over $20,000.

Special Needs Adoption

Under federal guidelines, a child is designated as one having special needs when it has been determined that the child cannot or should not be returned home to his biological parents, and when the child has a condition or background that makes the child difficult to place without adoption assistance. *Adoption Assistance Payments* (AAP) are federal- and state-funded payments made to adoptive parents to help them meet the needs of children with special needs.

Agencies usually are more flexible about the adoption requirements for people who are willing to adopt children with special needs. The person who may be a successful special needs adopter can handle change and stress and accept a child with a history that may involve multiple moves, abuse, and relationships with the birth family. Special needs adoptive parents should have good emotional survival skills, encourage open communication, be able to cope with rejection and anger without taking the child's behavior personally, be ready to advocate for the child within all sorts of bureaucracies, and have a sense of humor.

Public agencies usually handle the adoption of waiting children or special needs children, but many private agencies do so as well. According to the Child Welfare League of America (CWLA), the five states annually placing the most children with special needs are New York, California, Michigan, Ohio, and Illinois. Those placing the fewest children are Wyoming, Hawaii, Alaska, Nevada, and West Virginia.

According to the CWLA *Child Welfare Stat Book 1993*, 47 percent of American children awaiting adoption are Caucasian, 42.2 percent are African American, 6.6 percent are Latino, and 2.5 percent were of other races and ethnic groups. Most are over age five. The remainder of this book focuses explicitly on the adoption of children with special needs, the advantages and disadvantages of special needs adoption, the costs, waiting time, and children who need this service.

A BRIEF HISTORY OF SPECIAL NEEDS ADOPTION

The first non-Native American to adopt in this country was also one of the first non-Native visitors, Christopher Columbus. He kidnapped and then later adopted a 12-year-old Native American boy who became his interpreter and traveled to Europe with him. Columbus's adoption was also the continent's first transracial and first older child adoption.

Before Columbus, special needs adoption was unknown in the land we now call America because in most tribes orphaned children did not wait for parents. Children were viewed by the majority of native tribes as a priceless resource. When a child was orphaned, a relative or other tribal member stepped forward to adopt the child on the spot. Adoption was regarded as a way to solve problems for children. The European philosophy, which immigrated with the first colonists, viewed adoption as a means of solving adult problems. When people needed extra workers in the family or an heir, adoption was one solution.

For the next four centuries, transracial adoptions between indigenous peoples and European Americans usually began as reciprocal kidnappings. But what happened to white children adopted by Indians was different from what happened to Indian children adopted by Caucasians. Raids by Indians on settlements in the West and settler raids on Indian villages sometimes resulted in mass slaughter. At other times, the children were spared and taken back with the raiding party. Indian children were adopted not by families, but by colonial society. The most humane course was thought to be arranging for a proper education. Accordingly, the Indian children were sent to distant boarding schools. The Caucasian child was adopted into the tribe and into an individual family where he or she became Indian in all ways but blood. Some of these children and their offspring even became chiefs.

In the mid 1800s, foster care was only an occasional experiment. Most orphans were living in almshouses and in mental institutions. Charles Loring Brace, the founder of the New York Children's Aid Society, began the orphan train movement in response to this problem. Orphans in large numbers were sent by train to mostly rural communities to be instantly adopted by rural families who met the trains. The orphan trains went from town to town until every last child had departed.

Brace believed it was better for children to be adopted and taught how to earn a living on farms than to grow up in asylums alongside the adult mentally ill. By 1859, 24,000 children had been placed in adoptive and foster homes via orphan trains. When the movement ended in 1929, the total was more than 150,000. Tragically, the adoptive and foster families were not investigated prior to these train platform placements. Some of the children were overworked and ill treated by their new families.

The nineteenth century also saw the passage of laws in Massachusetts and Michigan designed to protect all children, including orphans. Society's attitude toward children changed as children came to be viewed as having value in society. By 1955, American adoption philosophy began to consider the "best interests of the child" (Cole & Donley, 1990). This ideal was similar to the Native American adoption philosophy and modern attitudes toward children. The old English philosophy that saw adoption as a practical way for adults to solve a problem would hopefully be replaced.

The 1960s saw the development of the permanency planning movement as foster and adoptive parents demanded that waiting children be given increased opportunities to find permanency. As the number of adoptable healthy Caucasian infants decreased, the number of minority race and handicapped children needing adoptive families increased. Such children were considered unadoptable at the time, although some private agencies began placing biracial infants with success. As well, the success of international adoptions, such as those facilitated by Harry and Bertha Holt, captured the public's attention as well as those of would-be adoptive parents who were willing to love a child, any child. In 1967 in Ann Arbor, Michigan, a group of frustrated would-be special needs adoptive parents joined Joyce and Peter Forsythe in founding the Council on Adoptable Children (COAC). With its motto "concerned about the children who wait," COAC began to challenge the child welfare bureaucracy in Michigan through an educational newsletter about the needs of waiting children, monthly public meetings at the local library, and press coverage from the *Detroit News.* The newspaper also agreed to begin a "Wednesday's Child" article featuring a waiting child in a weekly column, following a Toronto paper's example.

Also in 1967, COAC sponsored its first national conference at the University of Michigan School of Social Work titled, "Frontiers in Adoption: Finding Homes for the Hard to Place." COAC co-founder Joyce Forsythe edited a conference-based book, published by the Michigan Department of Social

Services, by the same title. The "system" and special needs adoptive parents were, for the first time on such a large scale, collaborating.

Even so, it was clear that the child welfare system was only responding sluggishly to the best advocacy efforts of adoptive and foster parents. "A model agency was needed," wrote Joyce Forsythe, "one that would demonstrate for the others how to place even the hardest of the hard-to-place children. The new agency would fill a need by placing, on a referral basis, only the children the other agencies could not place" (Forsythe, n.d.). Under the administration of adoptive father Richard Schneider and through Warren Spaulding's donation of his farm and its 120 acres to the effort, Spaulding for Children was founded. Under the direction of its first full-time director, Kathryn Donley, Spaulding for Children, working with local newspapers to produce "Wednesday's Child" columns of waiting children, was soon able to place every waiting child for which it received a referral.

In spite of this success, state and private agencies were reluctant to refer their waiting children to Spaulding for Children, and many remained caught in legal limbo. A way was needed to move children from the foster care and court systems into permanency planning and adoption. With the help of the Junior League of Detroit, Joyce Forsythe convinced Judge James Lincoln of the Wayne County Juvenile Court to support a citizen's foster care review committee pilot project. As children began to move through the system, Judge Lincoln, also president of the National Council of Juvenile Court Judges, enthusiastically promoted similar efforts in five additional courts in various states through the Child in Placement Committee of the National Council of Judges. Not long afterward, under the direction of Peter Forsythe, the Edna McConnell Clark Foundation provided a grant to the National Council of Juvenile Court Judges to replicate the Michigan program in several states. The program eventually evolved into the Court-Appointed Special Advocate (CASA) program, which today has more than 25,000 trained volunteers assisting judges and advocating for children in every state.

Adoptive parents and professionals in other states and countries learned of the success of the original Spaulding for Children and COAC and founded their own groups and agencies. Soon there were groups or agencies in New York, Pennsylvania, New Jersey, Ohio, Maine, and even in England and Israel. Eventually over 600 adoptive parent groups developed with the purpose of advocating for the adoption of waiting children with special needs.

Realizing that coordinated efforts would be more effective nationally, parent advocates proposed the North American Council of Adoptable Children (NACAC) in 1972 at the Third North American Conference on Adoptable Children. The following year (1974), at the Fourth North American Conference, a resolution endorsing NACAC was passed and the first board organized. The organization was founded in part through a grant from the Edna McConnell Clark Foundation.

The idea of collaboration between public and private adoption agencies and adoptive parents was the result of changes in a system that had historically seen its role as one that would approve of adoptive applicants and thus control adoption, to a view of the system and the applicants as collaborators, one that gave agencies the role of educators and parents that of pupils. Children came to be seen as those who were the most needy, and professionals began to advocate for the right of children to have parents, rather than the right of parents to have children. One such professional was Kenneth Watson, then of the Chicago Child Care Society. In his 1971 keynote address at the First Colorado Conference on Adoption, Watson said that "we must come to grips with the fact . . . that it is not the right of any family to adopt. Rather it is the right of every child who waits to have an adopted family . . . Once we begin to perceive the adoptive family as not having to be like the biological family, we are free to do all sorts of wonderful things" (Dunn, 1980, p. 4).

In 1978 special needs adoption advocates brought about a revolutionary new federal law called the Adoption Opportunities Act (Public Law 95-266). This act sought to remove obstacles to adoption, provide for a means to match waiting children to families, and to establish regional Adoption Resource Centers. For the first time, the U.S. Congress sent a clear message that waiting children were valuable resources in this society. Two years later, in 1980, Congress enacted Public Law 96-272, the Adoption Assistance and Child Welfare Act of 1980. PL 96-272 provided a national uniform response to policy, practice, and financial issues raised by the needs of children in out-of-home care. The 1980 law provided, among other things, financial support to families adopting children with special needs. More recent laws, passed in the 1990s, provided income tax credits to those who adopt special needs children and removed barriers to transracial adoption.

In 1996 we remain unsure exactly how many American children are waiting to be adopted. Estimates range from 60,000 to over 100,000. Whatever the number, it is too high as long as just one child needs a permanent family.

WHY CHILDREN ENTER THE CHILD WELFARE SYSTEM

Today in the United States nearly half a million children live in foster care. According to the American Public Welfare Association, the number of children in foster care has increased 53 percent since 1987, to a high of 429,000 in 1992 (Reich, 1995). The number of such children available for adoption may be as few as 60,000 or as many as 95,000. No one can be sure how many children in America are legally free for adoption and waiting for adoptive parents, for while we keep statistics about how much wheat is exported, or tuna imported, we have yet to implement a tracking system for America's most dependent population, its children.

Of the children who are currently available for adoption and living in foster care, group homes, or residential treatment centers in this country, the majority can be defined as having one or more special needs. Such children have also been defined by statute as deprived children for one or more reasons. Usually the legal definition of a deprived child includes the child who is for any reason destitute, abandoned, or homeless; who has not had proper parental care or guardianship; whose home is unfit due to parental neglect, cruelty, or depravity; or who is in need of special care or treatment due to a physical or mental condition and whose parents or guardian is unable or fails to provide it; or to the child whose parents do not observe compulsory school attendance laws; or whose parent or legal guardian shows good cause to be relieved of the child's custody.

Children become available for adoption after entering the child welfare system through the courts. The circumstances in a child's life that usually bring her into the court system include neglect, physical abuse, sexual abuse, abandonment, or having parents who are unwilling or unable to care for her.

Neglect is the failure to exercise the same care a usually prudent person would under similar circumstances. Neglect occurs when a parent fails to provide the basic necessities of life for the child, such as food, shelter, clothing, education, and medical treatment. When a parent fails to protect a child from physical or sexual abuse, it is also considered neglectful.

Physical abuse is the mistreatment of a child by those responsible for the child's welfare. Courts remand children into state custody when the mistreatment poses a serious threat to the health, welfare, or safety of the child.

Sexual abuse is intimate physical contact with a child by those responsible for that child's welfare. When the person(s) responsible for the child's welfare fails to protect the child from sexual abuse by another person, the courts often intervene in order to protect the child.

Abandonment is when a parent or custodian leaves the child without adequate supervision, care, support, or parental contact for extended or excessive amounts of time. As well, parents may express an intention to sever the parent-child relationship.

Unwilling or unable parents cannot parent the child due to the mental retardation, mental illness, or physical disability of either the parent or the child.

WAITING CHILDREN

State adoption agencies place more special needs children for adoption nationwide each year than do private agencies. The number of children placed has increased every year in the United States. The two types of state adoption systems are county-centralized and state-centralized. In state-centralized adoption systems, policies and procedures are mandated by the state's Department of Human Services adoption unit, usually centrally located in each state. In such systems, counties follow the same basic rules and there are no city or county options offering alternative means of operation. State-centralized systems are generally more adoptive parent-friendly because the system operates the same no matter where in the state adoptive parents go, and because adoption subsidies and other services remain constant county to county.

Roughly a third of all special needs adoptions in the United States are fost-adopt placements, in which the adoptive parents have first served as the child's foster parents, and this trend is gaining strength. Years ago, many states had strict policies against placing children for adoption in their own foster homes, but today the exact opposite is true. There is no sound reason why children who are happy and doing well in their foster homes should be moved if and when they need to be adopted. Most states work with foster families so that they can adopt their foster children whenever this is a possibility. In many states, state laws give foster parents preference for adoption if their foster children become adoption eligible.

WAITING PARENTS: WHO CAN ADOPT?

When it comes to special needs adoption, agencies are flexible about who can adopt. The agency's basic question is, "Is this prospective adoptive parent capable of being a good parent?" If the answer to the question is yes, and if the homestudy bears that out, those factors that make each of us unique need not be an obstacle. For example, singles, people in their 50s, pregnant women, gays and lesbians, vegetarians, home schoolers, people with disabilities, and the self-employed have all adopted special needs kids. People with all kinds of political or religious beliefs, including Roman Catholic priests and nuns, have become special needs adoptive parents. Even a criminal record need not stop an adoption provided the original offense was nonviolent and that the adoptive parent has been stable and consistently law-abiding since the conviction.

THE ADOPTION PROCESS

Agency Adoption

The adoption process actually begins, of course, long before the application is initiated, since most adopters spend months or years researching adoption and grappling with the decision of whether or not to adopt. Following the initial application, the prospective parent is either screened in or out of the process via eligibility requirements that vary from agency to agency. Applicants who pass this stage enter the "formal application" process, which involves submitting paperwork such as copies of marriage licenses, birth certificates, financial records, health records, and other personal information to the agency. At this time applicants are also asked to indicate what type of child they hope to adopt and may be asked to attend adoption education or parenting classes.

During the formal application process, the couple or individual is evaluated through a homestudy process that is accomplished in writing and in person, through interviews with a social worker, and recommendations by personal references. Even one poor recommendation can permanently derail the application process. The applicants are then approved or disapproved. The process is meant to be rigorous for the protection of children.

Once the homestudy has been completed with a favorable final recommendation and the couple or individual is approved, they are placed on a waiting list of approved families and await matching with a child. Special needs adoption is not done on a first-come, first-served basis. Children must be carefully matched to prospective parents.

After a wait, the parents receive the referral of a child and begin visits (one or more depending on the age of the child), culminating in a formal placement. Either soon after placement or after about six months of post-placement agency or professional supervision, the parents file a petition to adopt with the court. The court usually orders an investigation of the family, which has already been accomplished via the homestudy process. The agency files its report with the court, and the matter is set for a hearing to determine if the child is legally available to be adopted and if the proposed family is suitable. The court almost always answers both questions in the affirmative if the adoption has been properly undertaken. If the court is satisfied, it temporarily places the child with the family via *interlocutory decree,* followed by a six-month observation period overseen by the court-ordered investigator. This process varies depending on the jurisdiction. In some areas, there will be only one six-month wait and the interlocutory decree will be waived; in others it can take a full year to legally consummate an adoption.

Eventually, if all goes well, the adopting parents petition the court to finalize the adoption. The court reviews the agency's final report and holds a hearing. If the court is satisfied with the results of the investigation and the adoption is recommended, it finalizes the adoption. After finalization, an adoptive family is legally indistinguishable from any other type of family. That is, the adoption cannot be annulled, except by the court, and then only for extremely serious reasons.

Independent Adoption

The independent adoption process in many states differs radically from the agency process. In many cases, parents receive the placement of a child before any homestudy or approval process has been undertaken. Instead, the child is placed with the family, the petition to adopt is filed with the court, and the court orders an investigation. An independent social worker or other investigator then provides a written investigation to the court, which, if satisfied, renders a final decree of adoption at a subsequent hearing. The six-month wait experienced by agency adopters is often waived, as are the pre-placement preparation, screening, approval process, and lengthy homestudy process.

THE HOMESTUDY

Once prospective adoptive parents have applied to adopt a child, whether through a licensed adoption agency or through an independent adoption facilitator, a written report regarding the applicants' lifestyle, and many facets of their private lives is required. Known as the adoption study, or *homestudy*, this process, the report and its contents and the amount of time it will take to complete differ from state to state. Prospective adoptive parents can receive homestudy guidelines from their state by contacting the state adoption unit. The homestudy process usually takes three to six months, but can take longer through state agencies or less time through non-licensed facilitators. The homestudy process also often involves adoptive parent preparation classes or other training in addition to the written report. In general, the following information is usually included in the adoption homestudy:

- Personal and family background. Family configuration and childhood experiences of each adoptive parent; feelings about their parents and childhood; significant experiences for each adoptive parent; sibling and family relationships, past and present.
- Marriage and family relationships. Feelings about one's marriage, oneself, and one's spouse or partner (if not single); one's ability to handle stress; significant experiences within the marriage; history of prior marriage(s) and reason(s) for divorce.
- Desire to adopt. Motivation for adoption; attitude of extended family toward adoption; feelings toward the birth parents of the adopted child; attitudes about open and closed adoption, search and reunion; feelings about and plans for helping the adoptee understand adoption.
- Expectations of the adopted child. Education plans, temperament, how parents will handle adoption issues, child training and discipline.
- Feelings about infertility (if applicable).
- Parenting and integration of child into home. Description of any parenting experience had by the prospective parents; parenting style and philosophy of discipline; adjustment of birth or other children to previously adopted children.
- Family environment. Parents' lifestyle, including social, cultural, and religious orientations; availability of health care, philosophy of education, area educational resources, neighborhood, community, and a complete room-by-room description of the family's house and yard.
- Physical health and history. Documentation that the ages and health of the adoptive parents are such that they can meet the needs of a child.
- Education, employment, and finances. Verification of the education of both adoptive parents, adequate insurance, and any other resources, and the plan for the child if both parents work. Some states require a credit history as part of the homestudy.
- References and background clearances. Includes criminal background check, checks for sexual offender, child abuse, and domestic violence records, and at least three written references from people other than relatives.
- Summary and recommendations. Verification that the home is a healthy, safe environment in which to raise a child; desires of adoptive parents and

recommendations of social worker regarding the age, sex, characteristics and special needs of children best served by the family.
- Court report disclosing complete costs of adoption (not required in all states).

FREQUENTLY ASKED QUESTIONS (FAQ)

On the Internet, discussion and information sites called newsgroups have FAQs, or computerized files listing all of the "Frequently Asked Questions" that people have about that topic. Borrowing from this concept, here is a special needs adoption FAQ, and some brief answers. See corresponding topics throughout the book for more detail.

Are There Any Babies Available for Adoption?

Yes, there are adoptable infants with special needs. They are usually of mixed and minority race. Many have challenges associated with pre-natal drug exposure. Some of them are at risk of developing disabilities later, or have been exposed to HIV, the virus that causes AIDS.

Unlike adopting healthy or low-risk babies, adopting infants with special needs usually requires a shorter wait, modest or no cost, and includes financial assistance programs for both the adoption, and for the cost of raising the child. Healthy U.S.-born Caucasian toddlers, pre-schoolers and small preschool aged sibling groups of two members are just as rare as healthy Caucasian infants and are usually not considered to have special needs.

Can I Adopt Transracially?

Yes. Ideally, children are placed with same-race parents, but until recruitment of minority families improves, transracial adoption will remain an option for those children who would not otherwise have found permanency.

Transracial adoption is not illegal anywhere in the United States. In fact, it is illegal to use race as the only factor in matching, or to delay a child's adoption on the basis of race alone. When reasonable efforts to obtain a same race family have failed, transracial placement may be considered. Prospective adoptive parents who know a child of another race who has been waiting for a family should ask the child's social worker when transracial adoption can be considered.

Can I Adopt An American Indian Child?

The federal Indian Child Welfare Act (ICWA) requires adoption agencies to try to place children with American Indian blood within their extended family and tribes first, within other tribes next, and then with non-Indian families who would raise the child in a culturally aware environment. Tribes may elect to be involved in adoptions involving their children, or they may choose to allow the adoption agency a free hand. Either way, the tribes must be given the opportunity to have involvement.

Waiting Native American babies are rare. Most of the Native American children in photolisting books who are able to be adopted transracially are older, have siblings who must be placed with them, or have significant disabilities.

When a waiting Native American child has special needs, the tribe an adopting parent belongs to and the amount of Indian blood he or she has is less important than in situations where young and healthy children need families. If a person has even one Indian ancestor, he or she should try to obtain documentation of that fact, and then contact the appropriate tribe for more information about waiting children.

Will the Birth Parents Change Their Minds?

Many adoptive parents are concerned about placement reversals in light of all the publicity some overturned independent adoptions have received. However, it is *very* rare that special needs adoptions entail significant legal risk. Unlike healthy children adopted as infants, children with special needs have usually been in the child welfare system for months or years, and their birth parents' rights are already terminated or will soon be terminated. Custody battles, when they do occur, are resolved before the child's availability becomes known and the child is photolisted. When parental rights have not been terminated, the child is placed in what is known as a "legal risk placement," and the adopting parents fully informed of their rights and risks in the situation.

There is sometimes ongoing birth parent–adoptive parent contact in special needs adoption, especially when a child is adopted by his foster parents, is older when he is adopted, or is adopted as part of a sibling group that has not been placed together into the same adoptive family. Sometimes, ongoing birth family–adoptive family contact is contraindicated because the adopted children were removed from their birth parents due to abuse or neglect, and ongoing contact would not be in the child's best interests. When birth family contact is mandated or sought in special needs adoption, it usually occurs when foster parents have adopted the child, and involves birth family relatives other than the birth parents, such as grandparents, siblings, aunts, or uncles. In their research, Rosenthal and Groze found ongoing contact with birth relatives to be "at least moderately positive" because "these contacts helped children to view the birth family—its strengths and its weaknesses—more realistically" (Rosenthal & Groze, 1993, p. 195). More about open special needs adoption can be found in Chapter 13.

What Will An Adoption Cost?

The cost varies from place to place but the good news is that with careful planning, special needs adoption *can* be a low-cost or no-cost process. Most expenses involved in most of the authors' domestic special needs adoptions were reimbursed.

State or public adoption agencies do not usually charge for any special needs adoption service. Fees at private adoption agencies for adoption services vary widely from no charge at all to several thousand dollars, or more.

When a domestic special needs adoption takes place in a state offering Purchase of Services (POS), the state with custody of the child may pay some or all of the private adoption expenses for the adoptive parent or parents. This is how a private agency can afford to operate without charging the family a homestudy or placement fee. Adoptive parents should be sure and ask a private agency about Purchase of Service adoptions.

In the United States, up to $2,000 of a family's one-time *special needs* adoption expenses is refundable for children who meet the requirements under the federal law. States may allow up to $2,000 per child, or less, but not more. The expenses are reimbursed after the adoption has been completed. Adoptive parents should keep receipts for all expenses from the homestudy to the cost of photolisting book subscriptions. They should be sure their agency participates in this refund program, and then be sure to request the necessary forms after placement has occurred but before the adoption is legally finalized. State and federal programs are also available to help parents with the cost of raising adopted children with special needs. Such assistance is discussed in Chapter 8 about Finances.

How Long Will An Adoption Take?

The time involved differs from place to place and adoption to adoption. The authors have both had adoptions that took only 40 days from application to matching. Anne experienced the equivalent of a one day adoption when she and her husband legally adopted their 18-year-old former foster daughter. Rita's adoptions averaged three months each after she understood the process. The first adoption application for Rita, though, did not bear fruit for several years. Anne's first adoption took over 18 months. The important thing to remember is that special needs adoption is not a passive process. A person who sits by the phone and waits can sit there for a very long time. There are concrete things a person can do to hasten the process.

Why Does the Adoption Process Take So Long?

Another way of asking this question is, "If so many kids are waiting, why is adoption so difficult?" The answer is simple and two-fold: Agencies must screen people who want to adopt children. This takes time and requires paperwork. The homestudy is designed to protect the child from adults who would abuse children. A second reason is that we don't have enough social workers, and the ones we do have tend to be overworked.

Everyone agrees that adoption generally takes too long and can be immensely frustrating and complex. But there are ways to successfully work within the system. This book is designed to help streamline the adoption process and minimize frustration. There are many ways to make the process an easier one.

What Is a Subsidy?

An adoption subsidy, more accurately called an *Adoption Assistance Payment* (AAP), is a monthly check that is paid to adoptive parents until their adopted child with special needs is grown. The AAP is intended to help parents with the expenses of raising the child. The idea behind AAP is that no child should be denied permanency because of money, and no family should have to sacrifice their standard of living or face bankruptcy to adopt a waiting child with expensive special needs.

The national average basic AAP rate is $328 per child. Subsidies have made special needs adoption affordable for tens of thousands of Americans who otherwise could not have adopted a waiting child. Since subsidized adoptions are less costly than long-term foster care, AAP has saved the American taxpayers a great deal of money, too.

CHAPTER 2

Choosing the Type of Child You Will Adopt

> *Natural child:* Any child who is not artificial.
> *Real Parent:* Any parent who is not imaginary.
> *Your own child:* Any child who is yours to love.
> *An adopted child* is a natural child with real parents, who is loved.
> —Rita Laws

When special needs adoption is a passive process for the prospective parent, it is also a very risky process. Special needs adoption begs for active involvement from the parents-to-be because social workers can never know parents as well as they know themselves. Adoption should never be the sit-by-the-phone-and-wait process stereotyped in old movies. It is up to the prospective adoptive parent to choose the type of adoption best suited to home, family, personality, goals, and financial situation.

There are many decisions to be made and concerns to be dealt with when prospective adoptive parents decide to build or add to the family through special needs adoption. Is special needs adoption the right avenue? Can I handle this? How do I get started? This chapter attempts to help future adoptive parents find the answers to these questions—their own answers.

MAKING THE FIRST DECISIONS

Adoptive Parents Need as Much Information about Adoption as They Can Get

Instead of thinking in terms of "right" and "wrong" or "best" and "worst," the adoptive parent should think in terms of being a fact-finder, or an adoption sleuth. One of the best sources of information about special needs adoption in the United States is the North American Adoption on Adoptable Children. Adoptive Families of America is an organization that helps all adoptive parents, particularly those of internationally-adopted children. Both organizations are listed in the Appendix to this book.

Adoptive Parents Should Read about Adoption

There is no substitute for doing one's "homework." A list of recommended books and periodicals can be found at the end of this book in the Appendix to this book. Every prospective adoptive parent should at least try to read some adoption-related books. There is a great deal of information out there, which will seem overwhelming at first. Those who have gone through infertility treatments, are already old hands at sifting through information and making decisions. Such strengths will serve the prospective adoptive parent well in adoption. As someone who has possibly had more control over the becoming-a-parent process, the fertile adopter may find the adoption maze more overwhelming at first. No matter what a person's experience, adoption education and awareness will pay off.

Adoptive Parents Should Attend a Support Group

There are adoptive parent support groups in every state in the union. The North American Council on Adoptable Children (NACAC) and Adoptive Families of America offer a nationwide list of such groups. One of the best ways to get a feel for adoption is to attend an adoptive parent support group. Newcomers will almost always find a group of people eager and able to help and compassionate about the entire adoption process. They will also receive the benefit of seeing that many happy families have been built through adoption and many children helped.

Adoptive Parents Should Recognize the Adoptee's Other Parents

Adoption positives are easy to see: Children who need families receive them, and families who want children find them. At the outset of the adoptive parents' adoption journey, it is more difficult to think about birth mothers and birth fathers or what they and adoptees face. But all adoptive parents should know that adoption is built on losses for all three sides of the "adoption triad"—birth parents, adoptees, and adoptive parents. Birth parents have lost children, adoptees have lost their biological parents, and adoptive parents have lost either the ability to give birth, or have forfeited the choice to give birth. Despite the sometimes voluntary nature of these losses, they are losses nonetheless.

Confronting such issues is also part of the adoptive parent preparation in many adoption programs. Every adoptive parent should confront the issues of loss in adoption, keeping in mind that loss does not equal failure. The losses and hardships of adoption do not mean that adoption is bad or wrong. Every adoptee experiences his or her status differently, but, eventually, for the parents' sake and that of the adopted child, adoptive parents will need to confront these issues so that they can help their child with them.

The first few months of considering adoption are not, however, always the best time to confront these issues. Initially, adoptive parents might do well to explore the adoptive parent issues before venturing into the world of others affected by adoption and trying to digest some of the experiences of birth parents or adult adoptees.

COMMON FEARS

There are certain fears that appear to be almost universal among adoptive parents, which result in questions such as, "How can I help my spouse who is uncertain?" "Can I handle this?" "What about my relatives?" "Will I bond to my child?" It helps to remember that many of these questions can be answered quite easily by seeking out support groups, experienced adoptive families, and by looking up research about special needs adoption. Reading this book is also a good first step.

CAN I HANDLE THIS?

When Rita and her husband filled out their first adoption application in 1980, they had not sought out the wisdom of others nor read anything about adoption. They were given a sheet of paper listing 50 or 60 different common special needs and asked to check "yes, no," or "maybe" next to each. This form told the social worker, "Yes, we will consider, but not necessarily accept, children with this special need," or "No, we will not even consider them," or "Maybe, tell us more." Rita and her husband checked "no" to most of these special needs and later learned that being uninformed had negative consequences. It made them appear to be far more rigid than they were. They should have looked up these conditions in a medical encyclopedia, and checked "yes" or "maybe" to most of them, since so many special needs are minor, correctable, or not nearly as frightening as they sound. Their many "no" answers severely limited the number of children they would be told about. Rita remembers two especially scary-sounding words: Encopresis and enuresis. Whatever they meant, she was sure she would be unable to handle them. Years later, she would adopt several children with these special needs which were, in each case, temporary conditions. These words can indicate a permanent inability to control bowel and bladder functions, or they can mean correctable problems, or temporary toileting "accidents" and bedwetting. Rita and her husband should have checked "maybe," and considered each child's case of encopresis and enuresis on an individual basis.

When considering what they can or cannot deal with as parents, prospective adopters should ask themselves a few questions:

With Which Special Needs Do I Have Personal Experience?

If someone has asthma in the family, a mildly retarded childhood friend, or a neighbor with a missing limb, these familiar special needs may not seem like special needs at all. Parents should begin by considering the special needs with which they have some experience. The social worker should be made aware of (and the homestudy should list) all such special needs experience.

What Are My Strengths as a Parent?

Parents should take a look at what they can do instead of what they can't. For example, the person who is unusually patient, nurturing, tough, and intuitive would have his skills maximized in a sibling group adoption. The parent with experience working with teenagers might consider an older child adoption. The "baby" person who is persistent and can advocate for a child might be ideal to parent a baby who is going through drug withdrawal and who is at high risk of developing learning problems later.

What Are My Needs as a Parent?

Different children fulfill different needs of parents. One couple adopted two mentally retarded sisters after raising a gifted son and daughter. Their older children had developed into the scholars they had dreamed of raising. Their younger children gave them something else, namely, a chance to view the world through eyes of innocence. They feel they received a great deal from both types of parenting experiences.

Which Special Needs Will Keep Us from Having the Kind of Family Life We Want to Have?

If dealing with a particular special need will severely restrict someone's lifestyle, this is a sound reason to put this type of special need in the "no" category. However, this should be investigated before making a decision. Talking to other families who have adopted children in wheelchairs, for example, will likely yield the fact that there is little a child in a wheelchair cannot do in an active family. Anne's family lives in a two-story house, camps, swims, and has an active lifestyle, even though one of her children uses a wheelchair.

Among Those Special Needs in the "No" Column, What Do I Really Know about Each?

This is where a good medical encyclopedia, available at any bookstore or library, is invaluable. Prospective parents should look up those special needs that sound frightening and learn about them. Parents must do their "homework." When Anne saw the photolisting of a child with spina bifida, she knew nothing about the condition but refused to be scared by it. She read about it in books, talked to families who were raising kids with spina bifida, and sought out and spoke with adults who have this birth defect. Then Anne and her husband were able to make an informed decision. A few months later, their new daughter was home. Had they decided not to adopt her, it would have been a decision based on fact, not fantasy or fear.

THE UNSURE SPOUSE

She wants to adopt, but he does not. He wants to adopt a second time, but she does not. She wants a sibling group, and he does not. One partner insists on a girl, but the other wants a boy. What's a couple to do?

The short answer is: Be careful. It is extremely risky to drag a spouse into an adoption. Adoption, especially special needs adoption, should be entered into unanimously, voluntarily, joyfully, and well informed. If one partner is coerced, there will be resentment if something goes awry with the placement, as in, "Remember, this was not my idea!" or, "I told you so!"

Wives are much more likely to initiate a discussion about adoption, at least the first time, but the reverse situation happens, too. Following are some noncoercive ways to generate discussion about adoption and to help a reluctant or uninterested spouse come to an informed decision. Some of these ideas are also helpful when dealing with relatives or friends who don't like your idea of adopting a child with special needs.

- Give your partner a good book to read with crucial passages bookmarked or highlighted. Set up a time to discuss them.
- Wait a few months and raise the idea of adoption again.
- Borrow a photolisting book from an adoption agency and leave it for your partner to view at his or her leisure. One woman's husband was completely against the idea of adoption at first, especially since they were fertile. When he saw the *individual* children's faces in the photolistings, he stopped thinking of adoption in general and began thinking of specific waiting children. He pointed to one child's photo and description and said, "We could parent her!"
- Ask your spouse about meeting just once with an adoptive parent support group. There's nothing like talking to experienced adoptive parents face to face (and looking at their family photos) who have already dealt with the same fears being grappled with by prospective adopters.
- Attend an adoption picnic where prospective adoptive parents meet and get to know waiting children in a relaxed party or picnic-type atmosphere. Such

gatherings are known for high "matching" rates, and for helping future parents decide if special needs adoption is for them or not.

- Get your spouse on-line with one of the many computer forums for adoptive parents on the Internet and on on-line services. He or she will find people in all stages of the process, including people wrestling with the same doubts and questions that he or she has.

INFANT SPECIAL NEEDS ADOPTION

In all states there are infants and toddlers with special needs who are free for adoption and who need adoptive parents. Generally, states with better post-adoption support programs have few young children waiting. Conversely, states without adequate programs and with below-average benefits for children with special needs have more young children waiting. In states where foster parents are encouraged and helped to adopt the infants and young children for whom they have cared from an early age, there are fewer little ones needing the service of adoption.

Waiting infants and pre-schoolers with special needs are usually of mixed and minority race although percentages vary from place to place. Healthy babies and pre-schoolers and small sibling groups of two healthy babies or pre-schoolers of all races are adopted quickly and are not considered special needs children. The very young children waiting for adoption or listed in photolisting books will probably have developmental delays, handicaps, or challenges associated with pre-natal drug exposure. Additionally, almost all of them will have one or more risk factors such as low birth weight, exposure to drugs, alcohol, or nicotine pre-natally, lack of pre-natal care and proper nutrition for the mother, traumatic birth, genetic predispositions, and others. Some of them have been exposed to HIV, the virus that causes AIDS. These are called risk factors because they put the babies' health at risk, although no one can say for sure which babies will be disabled and which ones will be relatively unaffected in the long term. Even among those babies testing positive for HIV at birth, most will eventually seroconvert and test negative.

Foster parents are most often the placement of choice when infants and toddlers become available for adoption due to the attachment that exists between the child and his or her foster parents. Depending on how much a state encourages and supports fost-adoption, applying to the state's fost-adopt program might well be the best way to adopt an infant with special needs.

Another effective but little known strategy is to send one's homestudy to adoption attorneys and traditional privately licensed agencies in the state and specify an interest in adopting a child with special needs. Attorneys and agencies that normally place only healthy newborns sometimes find themselves trying to find a family for a baby that was expected to be healthy but was born with special needs. Parents who take this route should include information on the challenges they feel they can handle, being specific (i.e., moderate physical disabilities, mild mental disabilities, high risk factors, etc.). Often there is a dearth of parents available to adopt children with certain challenges, and the family might well be a resource for both licensed agencies and adoption attorneys who need to place a child with special needs.

An adoptive parent should not, however, consider adopting a child with special needs or who is at risk of developing disabilities when a licensed adoption agency is not involved or cannot ultimately become involved. Adoption assistance payments and the accompanying medical assistance are not available to children who are adopted through private entities (such as attorneys or nonlicensed agencies). Nonlicensed facilitators should be willing to recommend a licensed adoption agency that can help complete the adoption procedure. An adoptive family can be ruined financially by adopting a child privately who is not eligible for adoption assistance payments due to this restriction.

BONDING AND ATTACHMENT

Bonding is the process whereby parents and children form a close personal relationship. "Will I bond to my child?" may be the most universally-asked question of all. Of course, it is asked by all parents, not just adoptive parents. Bonding breaks and difficulties can occur with adoptive, biological, step, and foster parents.

Scientists define "bonding" in terms that are beyond the ken of the average person. For the purposes of this book, we use to "bonding" to refer to the way parents and children fall in love, and stay in love, thus becoming family.

Bonding, like a child's resiliency, is something that defies prediction. It is different with each parent and between each parent and child within a family. In one adoption, bonding may seem instantaneous, and in the next, may take months, or even years.

In adoption, as with birth, bonding may begin before parent and child ever meet. "Photo-bonding" is a phenomenon that occurs when future parents fall in love with a waiting child's photo, description, or photolisting. Losing a child to whom one is photo-bonded is similar to a physical miscarriage in that it can be a devastating, grievous, and misunderstood loss. Rita and her husband were in the process of adopting a beautiful infant born with part of his brain missing when he died on the operating table. They had never seen this baby except in a photo, but his death was painful anyway.

Attachment, and the related processes of claiming and entitlement, are not the same thing as bonding and are discussed later.

RISK FACTORS AND RESILIENCY

What about risk factors? This a term future special needs adopters hear frequently. Risk factors are conditions that put infants and children at risk of developing problems later on. A baby exposed to cocaine in the womb, for example, is at risk of having learning problems, coordination difficulties, and problems associated with premature and low-weight birth. Does this mean that all cocaine-exposed babies will have problems? No. Can anyone predict which babies will have problems and which will not? No, but research has identified which babies are more likely to suffer permanent or long-term problems.

Much depends on the age and health of the babies and how many children have been born to the same mother previously. Young, healthy women giving birth to a first baby are more likely to give birth to mostly healthy babies because they are young and their bodies have not yet been physically and nutritionally ravaged by long-term drug use. They are more likely to have had at least some pre-natal care and to have enjoyed better nutrition while pregnant. Since younger women may not yet be fully addicted, their drug usage may not have been as chronic. And for reasons researchers do not understand, female babies are a little less likely to be adversely affected by the drugs than male babies.

And yet it should never be forgotten that these are generalizations. Exceptions occur in both directions; low-risk babies who develop serious problems, and high-risk babies who don't, because no one can predict how resilient any particular baby is. *Resiliency* is the ability of a human being to recover from or adjust easily to misfortune. Some babies are naturally more physically or mentally resilient than others. A child we'll call Ryan is an excellent example of this phenomenon.

Ryan, a first-born boy, was exposed to a cornucopia of illegal drugs, nicotine, and alcohol while his birth mother carried him in her womb. No one knows who his birth father is. The birth mother lived with and was supplied directly by a drug dealer during her pregnancy. She didn't realize that she was expecting until far into the pregnancy and had no pre-natal care. Ryan was a small baby at birth who suffered from drug withdrawal and lost weight for more than a month. A couple adopted Ryan at age five weeks. The adoptive mother breast-fed him and his weight increased steadily. But he screamed almost constantly. He had to be held and cuddled day and night for several years. As an infant, he couldn't ride in automobiles unless it was an emergency. Automobile movement sent him into hysterics. By any standard, this was a high-risk baby, and none of the experts could predict if Ryan would have major physical and mental disabilities.

Ryan proved to be extremely resilient, both physically and mentally. He blossomed into an extremely handsome, independent child with a delightful personality and a killer sense of humor. After a slow start in school, he took off like a rocket and made straight As. By the end of elementary school, he was admitted into the gifted and talented science classes. He quickly showed an incredible talent for all types of athletics. He is a gifted baseball player whose concentration is so fierce, he has earned the nickname "Mr. Hustle" and can play any position well.

In several ways, from a temporary speech delay to a serious but correctable eye disorder, Ryan was affected by pre-natal drug exposure, but his determination to excel in all things led him to find ways of coping with and integrating each condition into a full, active life. He is resilient.

OLDER CHILD ADOPTION: A CHANGING DEFINITION

More waiting children belong to the older child category than to any other in special needs adoption. The definition of an "older child" varies state by state and even agency by agency. In general, however, a child who is between the ages of six and eighteen years at the time of adoption is considered an older child. Some agencies consider all school-age children to be older children.

It often surprises people new to adoption to learn that the age boundary in the definition of special needs adoption in a particular geographic area is determined, in part, by "supply and demand." If many younger children are waiting, the age boundary is reduced by the state. In this way, the children can be placed into permanent homes more quickly using the programs and resources available only to children with special needs. If few young children are waiting in any given geographic area, the age limit is raised until it reaches that age at which a number of children are available and waiting to be adopted.

Race and gender are two factors that may determine the age boundaries of the definition of the older child. If a particular state or county has a large number of children in a certain gender or race category, the age boundary may be broadened temporarily to accommodate those children and help them find permanency. For example, in one Southern state with a high percentage of African-American children, fewer Hispanic kids, and a smaller number of Caucasian children waiting to be adopted, "older child" is defined as African-American children over the age of two years, other minorities over the age of five years, and Caucasian children over the age of eight years.

The social reasons are complex, but the statistics tell us that not only are fewer girls placed for adoption to begin with, girls are also in higher demand by first-time adopters than boys. This means that in most places in the United States, there may be anywhere from slightly more boys waiting than girls, to as high as twice as many boys as girls. Where males far outnumber females, male children might meet the special needs definition at younger ages than girls. This adjustment hastens the placement of boys since younger children are in higher demand than older children.

SIBLING GROUP ADOPTION

The adoption of a group of two or more siblings, called a small sibling group, is considered a special needs adoption when one or more of the children also meets another qualifying category for "special needs," such as age or disability or risk factors. When three or more siblings, called a large sibling group, are adopted at one time, the adoption is considered a special needs adoption, whether other special needs are present or not. That is, with three or more siblings present the sibling group size alone qualifies the placement as special needs.

Siblings groups as large as nine members have found permanency within a single adoptive family. When placing large sibling groups of more than five members, agencies will often place the children into the adoptive home two or three at a time a few weeks apart. In this way, the adoptive family can adjust more slowly. As with older child adoption, the challenges are great, and so are the rewards.

Sibling group special needs adoptions are subsidized without penalty due to the number of children placed. In other words, if the average subsidy rate for one child is $300 per month, then the rate for a sibling group of five children would be $1,500 per month. This is important because large families not only have added clothing, food, medical, and education costs, they also incur unanticipated expenses such as increased furniture, housing, and transportation costs.

Chapter 8 offers more information about how sibling group adoption can be made affordable for the average family, but the general rule is this: The larger the sibling group, the more financially flexible the agency can be, because it is no easy matter to place a large number of siblings together.

Rita once worked with a couple that had several grown children and were interested in adopting a sibling group of five from another state, two of whom were severely physically disabled. These parents had big hearts, but a small home and bankbook. The placing state took extraordinary measures to accommodate the family so that the siblings would not have to be split up.

Besides the usual monthly subsidy (times five), the family was offered an additional specialized rate due to the size of the sibling group, raising the subsidy amount by 25 percent. This money was used to add bathrooms and bedrooms to their home. Because two of the children used wheelchairs, the state allocated special one-time "home preparation" funds to build wheelchair ramps onto the front and back of the house. Because one of the children was mentally disabled and prone to wandering, the state paid to have a fence erected around the property. The state even helped the family buy a large used van at a discount. By spending a few extra dollars in an unusual situation, the state was able to make the placement work. Not only did the children remain together, the taxpayers actually saved money in the long run because even fully subsidized adoption is less expensive than foster care.

A UNIQUE EXPERIENCE

Older child and sibling group adoption are different from infant adoption. The bonding process is usually slower, and the child's personality is fully developed and evident immediately. Rather than hoping for immediate and close attachment, adoptive parents should work toward building friendship and trust with the child, although trust takes longer to cultivate. Older children are almost always survivors of abuse and neglect, so they bring psychological "baggage" with them. Older child adoption is more challenging but many would say it is highly rewarding, too.

In the United States, most adoptions of older children are subsidized so that adoptive parents can access the assistance necessary to help them raise the adopted child. Not only does financial assistance make this type of adoption feasible for many families, it may help the adoptive parents in a difficult placement feel less like "victims." As one exasperated mom put it, "So far, our daughter's adoption has challenged our marriage, our home's stability, and our daily existence. But at least it is not devastating our budget. Her therapy costs are all paid by Medical Assistance."

It's true that older child adoption is more likely to fail than the adoptions of infant and pre-school-aged children with special needs. Unfortunately, it is also true that no one can predict with certainty which older child placements will succeed.

Is older child adoption worth the risk? Most adoptive parents of older children would answer "yes." James Rosenthal and Victor Groze's research with special needs adoptive families showed that parents who adopted siblings tended to express more negative experiences, and parents who adopted children older than age six tended to say older child adoption had a more mixed or negative impact on the family (Rosenthal & Groze, 1992). Almost 36 percent of parents who adopted children ages 6-11 had mixed or negative experiences, while almost 29 percent of parents who adopted children ages 12-18 had mixed or negative experiences, as compared with only about 18 percent of adopters of children age birth to 5 years who expressed mixed or negative experiences. This research showed that the majority of adoptive parents of school-age children still said that the adoption had a positive or very positive impact on the family (64 percent of those who adopted children ages 6-11 years and 71 percent of those who adopted children ages 12-18).

Parents who participated in Rosenthal and Groze's research said that siblings adopted together tended to block "the process of emotional separation from the birth family and [prevent] bonding with the adoptive family," and that siblings sometimes set up a "dynamic of 'us' (siblings) versus 'them' (adoptive parents)" (Rosenthal & Groze, 1992, p. 197).

The authors have had mixed experiences in adopting sibling groups and older children. Rita and her husband adopted three school-aged children, a sibling group with a long history of abuse and neglect. The placement of the youngest child ended in disruption due to his dangerous acting-out. Of the other two, one child's emotional and behavioral problems eventually necessitated permanent out-of-home care in a locked facility. The third child had the most difficult middle childhood of all, but with determination and professional help, blossomed into a successful goal-oriented young adult. The first two experiences represent the toughest years in the family members' lives, while the latter experience serves as a never-ending source of joy and pride.

Looking back, Rita can see that the sibling group placement was inappropriate for her family at a time when she was mothering five other children younger than the youngest sibling group member. The "old" children provided ready-made targets against which the new children could vent their rage and grief. Had Rita and her husband been parenting no other children in the home when the new children arrived, the placement would have been less stressful for all concerned. Sadly, when older child and sibling group adoption fails, it is often because the matching was not sound to begin with. As we'll see in later chapters, successful older child adoptions begin with a good match between child and family.

Anne and her husband adopted a sibling group of two brothers that resulted in the "twinning" of children they already had at home. An undisclosed history of sexual abuse and sexual and other acting-out led to a placement that was doomed from the start. When the adoption failed after three years of interventions and therapy, rather than being the "forever" parents to these little boys she and her husband had hoped to be, Anne and her husband became another set of parents in a growing line who had failed to meet the needs of these boys. Failure of the placing state to fully disclose the boys' histories in spite of direct, written questions from these experienced parents, and the poor resulting match spelled disaster for the children and the adoptive family. Everyone, including children in the adoptive family who were abused by their new siblings, suffered. The only entity that came out of the failed adoption unscathed was the placing state.

This devastating experience taught Anne and her husband how to approach older child adoption with more caution and wisdom. They learned that not all social workers or states follow a policy of full disclosure of information to adoptive parents. After making contact with other parents of traumatized children, the Babbs learned that failure to disclose information and outright dishonesty are practiced by far too many agencies placing older children. Social workers and supervisors pressured to place children may withhold information through fear that the adoptive parents would refuse the child's placement if they received full disclosure. Such behavior is actionable and has resulted in a tort of "wrongful adoption," discussed in Chapter 12.

If full disclosure of these children's backgrounds, diagnoses, and behaviors been made, would our families still have attempted these particular placements? The answer is no, because placing severely emotionally disturbed children in families like ours with other young children is far too risky. However, the children could have been placed in other families as the youngest or only children.

Rita went on to adopt two other older children successfully. Anne and her husband went on to adopt an abuse survivor who had experienced several failed placements, and an adolescent who had lived with abuse for 15 years before becoming one of America's "street kids." Both adoptions have been successful because the child and the family experienced a good "fit" and because the adoptive parents had a full understanding of the childrens' histories.

MOTIVATION: CRAZY OR SAINTLY

When older child and sibling group adoptions are so challenging, why would anyone want to adopt these waiting children? Are such adoptive parents crazy? Are they saints?

Older child adopters may grin and admit to a little bit of craziness, but they are as sane as anyone else. The saint label is not only inaccurate, it endangers waiting children because it makes special needs adoption sound like a super-human deed to be undertaken only by super-human people.

Older child adopters have the same motivations as most other parents: a desire to parent and a love for children. In addition, they are aware of the tens of thousands of children waiting for a family and want to do what they can to reduce this shameful statistic.

Sometimes older child adopters are childless and fertile, but feel strongly that on an overcrowded planet, adoption is a better choice for people who want to parent. Some older child adopters are infertile and prefer the guarantee of an older child adoption over the uncertainty of fertility treatments and healthy infant adoption.

And then there are fertile older child adopters who, having enjoyed the typical biological parenting experience, want to apply their experience and open their home to the children who need permanency most.

Many adoption experts recommend that parents avoid an older child or sibling group adoption if their motivation is:

- to provide a similar-age sibling for a biological child,
- if they want a child to follow in their footsteps,
- if they are infertile and looking for the sort of a parent-child bond that usually only develops in an infant-parent relationship.

Many adoption experts recommend that parents avoid or be cautious about an older child or sibling group adoption if their situation includes:

- other younger or same-age children already in the home, or a current pregnancy,
- anything less than a truly solid marriage,
- an expectation of love, trust, and gratitude from the new child or children,
- no parenting experience or no support system of experienced parents who can offer help.

FULL DISCLOSURE A MUST

Love is not all a person needs to make an older child adoption work. A special needs adoption, especially an older child or sibling group adoption, has the best chance of succeeding when adoptive parents are given as full a picture as possible of the medical, behavioral, and emotional background of the child. Full disclosure can be a little scary because children are not taken from their biological families without very good reason, but to be forewarned is to be forearmed. There is more about this in later chapters.

Adoptive parents need to know what kind of relationships a child has had, because these relationships are predictors of how able a child will be to have a relationship with adoptive parents. The fewer moves and the longer the attachments a child has had early in life, the better the chances that the child will attach to adoptive parents. With increasing moves and breaks in attachment, the chances of a strong child-parent attachment decrease.

Adoptive parents should also know that older children who have spent years with their birth families will probably have developed strong attachment to their birth parents, even when such parents have been abusive. Because of such attachments, many adoptive parents of older children have maintained some level of ongoing contact between the adoptee and "safe" members of his or her birth (or foster) family. In their research, Rosenthal and Groze found that only 10 to 21 percent of adoptive families whose children maintained contact with a birth family member (including birth parents, siblings, grandparents or extended family members) said the contact did more harm than good to the child. The majority characterized the contact as positive and moderately positive (Rosenthal & Groze, 1992).

Adoptive parents should expect that most older children who have spent any length of time in the foster care system have probably been sexually or physically abused, either in their families of origin or while in foster care, even if the child's record does not reflect abuse. This is not meant to imply that foster parents are likely to abuse children. Indeed, foster and adoptive parents are statistically less likely to abuse children physically or sexually than are biological parents. However, being in the foster care system also means spending time in temporary shelters and around other children, some of whom are abuse victims turned abusers. Even children as young as six or seven years old can become sexual predators.

Married adoptive parents should expect that their marriage will be challenged, even seriously challenged. Older adopted children have a way of pitting one parent against the other, usually making the mother the target of their attacks. Many professionals in adoption recommend that the family begin family therapy with an *adoption-experienced* counselor early in the placement process. Some counselors not experienced with adoption issues may try to hold the adoptive parents accountable for problems that originated with the birth family.

Some of the problems that adoptive parents of older children encounter after placement are school problems, lying, the child running away or chronically missing curfew, foul language, stealing, eating problems, bed-wetting, problems originating from former foster homes and institutions, and problems from the birth family. Attachment-disordered children may play with matches, set fires, be disruptive in the classroom, abuse themselves, abuse other people (hitting, kicking, biting, shoving), mistreat animals, or destroy expensive items such as clothing, television sets, and stereos. Children who have been sexually abused may wet the bed, wet themselves, masturbate openly, become sexually active early, become a sexual predator, or molest younger children of the same or the opposite sex.

Prospective adoptive parents of *all* children with special needs should know that some children adopted as infants or toddlers and who have risk factors such as pre-natal drug or alcohol exposure, a family history of mental illness, breaks in bonding, severe neglect, or abuse may in turn engage in any of these behaviors or develop them over time. Adoptive parents should also know that sometimes such behaviors do not improve with time, but may even grow worse in intensity and frequency.

With all these negatives, why do we continue to advocate for the adoption of waiting, older children? Because such children, in the majority, need and want families and, in the majority, will be as well served by adoption as the adoptive family is served by their placement. Most older children and sibling groups who go into adoption do well and their families express positive feelings about having adopted. Parents must simply be aware of the pitfalls of older child adoption so that they can increase the odds of a successful placement.

THE KEYS TO SUCCESSFUL OLDER CHILD ADOPTION

- Other children in the adoptive family should be included in the adoption process after the final decision to adopt has been made.
- Parents should always insist on full disclosure of the prospective adoptee's educational, medical, psychological, social, and behavioral history.
- Parents should take the time before placement to research all of the available programs to help them financially, emotionally, and physically, such as subsidies, support groups, respite care, medical assistance, and SSI.
- Prospective parents should meet and get to know the child before they adopt and have the child visit in the home.
- Children should be told about the fact of adoption once the decision has been made, as well as about why they cannot remain with their foster parents.
- The child should be given the chance to make a transition between one family and the next in order to say his or her "good-byes."
- When adopting a toddler or preschool-aged child, the adoptive parents should spend time with the current foster parents so that the child receives the powerful message that it is okay to trust in the new adoptive parents.
- Parents should expect that all children, regardless of their age at placement, will experience grief upon separation from parents or caregivers to whom they are attached.
- Parents should be prepared to seek out support and help for the duration of their parenting career.

SELF-EVALUATION: CHOOSING AN OPTION

Many a parent has been swept away emotionally after seeing a "Wednesday's Child" program on television featuring children who need an adoptive family, or after seeing a child's photograph and biography featured in the local newspaper or in a photolisting book. "Love at first sight," however, is a poor determinant of whether parents will actually succeed at raising a particular child with particular needs. Adoptive parents should evaluate themselves in light of what is known about a particular type of adoption before deciding to proceed with the adoption of a particular child.

Prospective adoptive parents can more realistically evaluate themselves as parents of a child with particular challenges by meeting other children with similar challenges and talking with their parents. One of the best questions to ask parents of children with similar challenges is, "What do you wish you had known or that someone had told you about raising a child with this disability?" Asking questions and encouraging realistic and forthright answers will help prospective adoptive parents evaluate themselves and their capacity for raising a particular child or children.

STRETCHING AND FLEXIBILITY

Flexibility and *stretching* are terms adoptive parents should understand. *Flexibility* refers to the attitude of prospective adopters toward special needs. All other factors being equal, the rule of special needs adoption is that the more flexible the prospective parent, the quicker the adoption. An inflexible parent who will consider only young, same-race children, preferably female with mild disabilities or risk factors will probably wait a long time to adopt domestically. Inflexible adopters are happier spending the money required to go overseas to adopt a healthy baby or to adopt the rare waiting healthy infant born in the United States.

Stretching is the act of offering parents a child whose special needs are beyond the boundaries described by the prospective parents. Examples of stretching are a sibling group of four children offered to a couple who wanted no more than three, or a child with moderate mental retardation offered to a parent who had specified mild mental retardation. Placements in which the parents have been asked to stretch too much may be in danger of snapping and ending in disruption. People differ in what they can handle. However, stretching is a viable way to place children with special needs provided that the parent or parents do not feel any pressure to stretch more than they want to or are able. Many of us can do more than we think we can.

Stretching can also be an effective strategy when it is self-induced. People can be more flexible when they have located the child than when the child is located for them. The family that normally would not consider adopting a child with certain challenges may change their minds upon getting to know a child through foster care, community volunteerism, or prolonged visits.

A FLEXIBILITY TEST

Parents considering special needs adoption can take this flexibility test by answering either "yes" or "no."

1. Would you consider adopting a boy?	___yes___no
2. Would you consider children of a race other than your own?	___yes___no
3. Would you consider children of all races and mixed-race children?	___yes___no
4. Would you consider a small sibling group of two children over age six years?	___yes___no
5. Would you consider a large sibling group of three or more children?	___yes___no
6. Would you consider children aged 3 to 6 years?	___yes___no
7. Would you consider children up to age 12 years?	___yes___no
8. Would you consider children up to age 18 years?	___yes___no
9. Would you consider children with moderate or severe mental disabilities?	___yes___no
10. Would you consider children with moderate or severe emotional or behavioral disabilities?	___yes___no
11. Would you consider children with moderate or severe physical disabilities?	___yes___no
Total YES answers:	__________

5 or more yes answers. The person with five or more "yes" answers is flexible and probably has a good understanding of this statement, "It is not the special needs that are adopted, but the child." Such parents can have a reasonable expectation of adopting a waiting child in only months and will seldom wait more than a year or so to adopt.

3-5 yes answers. Those who have three to five "yes" answers are somewhat flexible. Such parents will find that they will compete with many other families to adopt, making the adoption process itself longer and more frustrating. Such parents, with time and experience, often become parents who are more flexible and who adopt more than once.

Less than 3 yes answers. Those having fewer than three "yes" answers may not be ready for special needs adoption at this time. Such individuals should re-think their level of flexibility and remember that many special needs adoptive parents, even those with very large families, started the adoption process with some inflexible attitudes.

Sometimes prospective adoptive parents are inflexible because they lack understanding or have fears. Reading books about special needs adoption, meeting waiting children, and attending an adoption support group and meeting special needs adoptive parents all are actions that can help parents become more flexible. Some adoptive parents we know first became interested in special needs adoption through their volunteer work with community service groups for the physically or mentally challenged.

WHEN SPECIAL NEEDS ADOPTION CEASES TO BE AN OPTION

For those people who ultimately decide that special needs adoption is not for them, a "traditional" placement of a non-special needs child may be in order. Such children include:

- the healthy, same-race infant, toddler, or pre-school-aged small sibling group of two;
- the healthy infant or toddler of another race;
- the healthy infant or toddler of another culture (transcultural adoption);
- the healthy infant or toddler of another culture and race (transracial and transcultural adoption).

CHAPTER 3

Finding a Child

> Religion that God our Father accepts as pure and faultless is this: to look after orphans and widows in their distress and to keep oneself from being polluted by the world.
>
> —*The Holy Bible,* James 1:27 (NIV)

Where do prospective parents find adoptable children with special needs? They find them in waiting child magazine columns, on television, and at open-to-the-public staffings held at the local state adoption agency office. They may hear about them first from a social worker. Sometimes, they meet the children in their everyday lives, as Rita met a waiting child who was one of her fifth-grade students. The most common way of finding children with special needs who are available for adoption is through a system called photolisting.

ADOPTION PHOTOLISTING

One of the most creative and effective methods ever devised to recruit families for our nation's waiting children is called the *photolisting book.* Consisting of a simple binder containing hole-punched paper for easy removal, this matching tool has proven to be highly successful in the 25 years since its inception. Each page has the photo and description of a different child or sibling group waiting to be adopted or sometimes even of a family waiting for a child. Photolistings are meant to be used by families and adoption workers to match children with families willing to adopt. Many different states maintain photolisting books, and there are regional, national, and international books also. Some photolisting books have even gone "on-line" and can be seen from the privacy and comfort of one's own home through a personal computer, modem, and connection to the World Wide Web. Parents can subscribe to one or more of these books or services directly or access them through their local Department of Human Services office or support group.

THE HISTORY OF PHOTOLISTING

According to CAP (Children Awaiting Parents) Director Peggy Soule, who has researched the history of photolistings and has also played an important part in that history, photolistings date back to the early 1970s. The Massachusetts Adoption and Resource Exchange, or MARE, had listed waiting children in its exchange since the 1950s, but did not add a photo with a brief biography and circulate the "photo-listing" to social workers until 1970. The Adoption Listing Service, ALS, of Illinois, first sent photolistings to adoption agencies in 1971. CAP, of Rochester, New York, followed suit the next year and was the first to supply photolistings to prospective parents. This created a revolution within the new special needs adoption movement. For the first time, prospective parents were directly involved in locating and applying for their own children.

HOW TO READ A WAITING CHILD DESCRIPTION

In general, a photolisting will contain the following information in addition to a photo:

- The child's first name, month and year of birth, state of residence, photolisting ID number, and date the photolisting was added to the book;
- some of the child's likes and dislikes;
- the child's social and medical history in brief;
- what type of home the child currently lives in and what type of adoptive home is desired (i.e., single parent, married couple, other children in the home, no other children, etc.);
- a phone number where parents can reach the exchange or the child's contact person.

UNDERSTANDING THE PHOTOLISTING

Photolistings look deceptively simple at first glance, but as anyone who has experience with them will tell you, there is an art to understanding and using them. The reason that photolistings are often misunderstood lies in the fact that a great deal of information is being concentrated in a small space. Certain phrases are used as short-cuts, but these widely used terms will seem foreign to people who are new to photolistings. These phrases may be meant to be taken literally, or they may represent certain common conditions that are seen over and over again in special needs children. Parents cannot know for sure until they call on the child and ask for clarification and further information. Here are some possible translations of common terms:

Description	*Possible Translation*
All boy; very active; impulsive; needs lots of attention; acts out.	Attention Deficit Hyperactivity Disorder (ADHD)
Needs structure and supervision; bossy and manipulative; has had several losses and is grieving; has had many moves.	Emotional or behavioral problems; Reactive Attachment Disorder of Childhood; Conduct Disorder.
Victim of neglect.	Malnourishment, Attachment Disorder.
Delayed speech, is immature.	Emotional problems, developmental delays.
Has difficulty in school, has been held back in school.	Learning disabilities, emotional problems.
Moody or sad.	Depression, dysthymia.
Developmentally delayed.	Mild to moderate mental retardation.
Toileting accidents, still being toilet trained.	Enuresis or encopresis, emotional problems.
Drug or alcohol exposure in the womb.	Fetal Alcohol or Drug Effect or Syndrome.

HOW TO SUBSCRIBE TO A PHOTOLISTING BOOK

Prospective adoptive parents who want to use photolistings in their search for a waiting child must first obtain a homestudy. Social workers will not discuss individual children or sibling groups with anyone who does not have a completed, or nearly completed adoption study.

Parents should begin by subscribing to the book in their own state, usually available through the local Department of Human Services or its equivalent. In order to provide continuity for the child and to save money, children are placed in-state whenever possible so every parent has a natural advantage in his or her own state. There are also several regional books and the national photolisting book called CAP (Children Awaiting Parents). *CAP Book* children can always be placed across state lines.

If the parent's state of residence does not have a photolisting book, application to adopt through the state can be made and then parental attendance at the regular staffings held at the state office on individual children available for adoption may be allowed. Parents may also subscribe to a nearby state's book, a regional, or national photolisting book. For example, since Oklahoma does not presently have a photolisting book, Oklahomans or their local adoption support groups may subscribe to the Texas book (Texas Adoption Resource Exchange, TARE) or the Rocky Mountain Adoption Exchange book that lists waiting children in the region.

For a list of photolisting books, parents should check the local library or book store for an adoption directory or resource guide, a telephone-sized reference containing the addresses of agencies, photolisting books, exchanges and support groups nationwide. Several titles are currently published. See the Appendix for a current list.

TIPS FOR USING PHOTOLISTINGS

- Subscribe to a photolisting book. As soon as the home study is finished, parents should consider getting a personal subscription to several photolisting books because children in the new update pages can be matched and removed very quickly, especially younger children. A parent should be able to call on new listings the day they arrive in the mailbox.
- Be efficient. Many parents save time and grief by sending out homestudies on several children at one time. As soon as the parents accept an assignment of a child or sibling group, they call on the others to ask to be removed from consideration.
- Invest in a good medical encyclopedia. Parents should research all medical terminology as thoroughly as they can. They should not hesitate to ask the social worker questions about the medical diagnoses, the severity of the conditions, and the treatments that will be necessary.
- Keep the photolisting book up to date by adding the new pages that arrive each month and removing those that are on the "placed" list.
- If most of the children in the new pages are already placed when you call, the book being used is not up to date. Consider subscribing to a different or an additional book.
- Avail yourself of other services offered by the photolisting book, such as listing waiting families, help connecting with social workers, and the free newsletters used to keep subscribers informed of special needs adoption news.

MAKING THE SYSTEM WORK

Self-directed special needs adoption is the term we use to describe an active type of adoption that has nothing to do with the stereotypical adoptive parent waiting impatiently by the phone to hear about a new child. Self-directed special needs adoption is not passive; prospective parents do the searching and matching themselves. The advantages to this are several:

- shorter waiting times for waiting children and adoptive parents;
- a better match, in some cases, because the parents sought and found the child themselves;

- voluntary or self-stretching (widening the scope of special needs) as opposed to forced stretching.

When parents do their own searching and matching, they decide how much and where to stretch. The social worker does not decide for them what types of children they can parent.

Not all self-directed matches are approved. For example, if a parent's homestudy approves him or her for "no more than two children," and the parent then finds a sibling group of four, the parent's social worker can stop the match before it is made. This is done to prevent a potentially risky adoption from happening. Happily, most self-directed matches are approved.

TIPS FOR SELF-DIRECTED SPECIAL NEEDS ADOPTERS

- Remember that many adoptions grow out of fost-adopt placements, so check into this route. You will only be asked to foster children who will be likely to become available for adoption.
- Get a copy of your completed homestudy. Once you are sure of its accuracy, make a pile of copies. These are unofficial copies because they come from the prospective parent and not from an agency. Clip a color photo of your family to each copy. If the agency has a policy against offering adopters official copies of their homestudy, they can ask for a copy marked "unofficial" or send a one-page typed family summary with color photo to the social worker. If the social worker is interested in the adoptive family, the family's social worker can always send an official homestudy later on.
- Make good use of your homestudy. Parents should fax or overnight mail a copy of their homestudy immediately after the social worker requests it. It should be clearly addressed to the correct social worker and include a cover letter explaining why the parents would be a good choice for a particular child.
- Subscribe to some good photolisting books or use the subscriptions maintained by a local adoptive parent support group or agency. Keep subscription receipts because up to $2,000 of special needs adoption expenses can be reimbursed by the placing state.
- Follow up by phone or mail. Mail sometimes goes astray and parents should check after several days to see if the social worker received the homestudy. If so, check later to see if the social worker needs more information or photos.
- Remember that most children who are adopted come from the new update pages that will arrive each month and most of the families chosen for those children were among the first to send in their homestudy. Timing is critical. Call on a listing the same day you see it.
- Think and talk about the child's needs, not your own. When you call about a particular child's listing, you should tell the worker why you are perfect for the child, not why the child is perfect for you. Social workers want to help children first; they are not there to serve adults. If the social worker requests an unofficial copy of your study, overnight mail or fax it the same day.
- If you are not allowed to have a copy of your homestudy, type up a summary with a family history and description, complete with photos. Offer the information a social worker would like to have about you, your home, your life, and your

community. Include the information that will allow the social worker to order an official copy of your homestudy (i.e., the name, address, and fax number of your social worker or agency).

- If you are not chosen, ask the social worker about other children like the one you originally asked about who will be photolisted soon. You may be able to get a match before the child's listing is even printed and distributed. Many matches are made this way.
- Repeat the above steps again and again, with as many children as you like. Rita usually applied on four to six different children initially, and then she and her husband accepted the first child or children offered, declining other children offered later. Flexible parents will eventually be chosen as the best family for one child or a sibling group.

AFTER THE MATCH IS MADE

Once a particular family has been chosen for a child, that family's social worker will be contacted about sending an official copy of the homestudy. At that point, the prospective parent will receive much more information about the child, and if they still want to continue with the adoption, a visit will be arranged. More on the early placement process can be found in Chapter 5.

ANATOMY OF A PHOTOLISTING SEARCH: GABE IS ADOPTED

One mother writes: "The new CAP Book pages had just arrived in my mailbox, and his was on top. His smile was bigger than his whole adorable face. Two year old Gabe from Maryland, the description said, has trouble gaining weight, and is very active. He came into foster care after being repeatedly abandoned by his birth mother. After calling the CAP Book to obtain more information, I was eventually connected to Gabe's social worker. He asked me to tell him about my husband, our other kids, and our lives, and then he told us more about Gabe. His trouble gaining weight was called 'Failure to Thrive' and he also had ADHD. After sending in our homestudy and corresponding for several weeks, we started researching some of the challenges facing Gabe while waiting for a decision about his placement.

"We looked at his medical diagnoses: FTT, or Failure to Thrive, ADHD, or Attention Deficit Hyperactivity Disorder, and, since he had a history of abandonment, we looked up AD, Attachment Disorder. We talked to people who had adopted kids with these challenges.

"In a few weeks, we received the news that we had been chosen as Gabe's new family from among the homestudies that had been sent in. Now we began our homework in earnest. We spoke with the people who knew him best, especially his loving foster mother who is now a part of our family, too. We requested a psychological evaluation to look into the possibility of Attachment Disorder. At first the state was unsure and seemed unwilling to have Gabe evaluated, saying he was too young to have an AD evaluation. As a result of our persistent encouragement, the state relented and agreed to have Gabe evaluated.

Gabe's evaluation showed an insecure attachment, meaning that he would need a 24-hour parent, and lots of attention in order to emotionally attach to his new family. With some intensive TLC and 'kangaroo-style parenting,' the doctors said, Gabe might not develop the devastating emotional disorder called AD.

"We exchanged calls, letters, and a visit, and Gabe was home at last. As the stay-at-home parent, I spent days and nights with Gabe for several months until the symptoms of insecure attachment faded. Slowly he gave us eye contact, exhibited normal parent-child separation anxiety, showed conscience development, and began to trust us to meet his needs. Spoon feeding him six to eight times a day added needed weight, and medication helped with the ADHD. Our family doctor prescribed medication for mild asthma, and after several months declared him free of FTT symptoms. Gabe blossomed.

"Today, Gabe takes for granted that he has a forever family, as every child should. At seven years of age, he loves school, his smile remains irresistible, and he is emotionally healthy. His weight gain is slow but sufficient. His Attention Deficit Hyperactivity Disorder (ADHD) is treated with minimum doses of medication and maximum ongoing doses of patience." Photolisting can claim another victory.

EXAMPLES OF PHOTOLISTING INTERPRETATION

The best way to understand how to interpret a photolisting may be to read an actual "interpretation" by someone with experience. The following photolisting interpretations are provided as examples of what may be included in a photolisting, and what might be understood by "reading between the lines." The names of the children have been changed. These interpretations are very blunt, but bluntness can be a virtue. Too many children are victimized each year by bad matches because agency workers were not blunt or honest enough, and because the parents did not know which questions to ask. No one volunteered essential information; sometimes incorrect information was volunteered. Adoptive parents might have fallen in love with the cute face in the photograph without fully understanding that the child pictured has been traumatized and had his or her life disrupted prior to becoming available for adoption.

Agency workers all too often allow prospective adoptive parents to enter an adoptive placement with unreasonably high expectations. Sometimes adoption professionals have purposely misled adoptive parents and withheld critical information. This victimization now has a name, "wrongful adoption," and the number of wrongful adoption cases pending in our courts is on the rise. Unfortunately, although adoptive parents can bring a wrongful adoption case to court, the rights of adoptees and their birth families to do so when defrauded or wronged by adoption agencies has not been established.

Interpretation of Two Random Photolistings with Comments and Recommendations

Thomas, from a State Adoption Services book, is an *"active young man."* This could mean he has ADHD, Attention Deficit Hyperactivity Disorder. Interested parents should ask about that. He *"generally does well in class."* When, specifically, does he not do well, what does he do and why?

He has *"poor impulse control and can anger quickly."* Impulsivity, hyperactivity and a short attention span are three major symptoms of ADHD. Anger is a hallmark of Attachment Disorder, or AD. Since ADHD and AD together are tragically common in older waiting boys, Thomas may have both of these conditions. The combination of them makes for one of the most difficult kinds of placements of all, especially when the child becomes a teenager.

He needs a *"structured, stable environment"* and a *"nurturing family."* Children with ADHD and those with AD need a great deal of structure and stability and very patient parents. Do not bring this child into a home with young children. Make sure you can give him nearly 24-hour attention. Insist on a detailed psychological evaluation for this child and a guarantee of help in writing in the subsidy contract from the state, should he need later to be placed in residential treatment or in a mental hospital for out-of-control behavior.

Teresa and Linda, a sibling group from a State Adoption Services book, almost certainly have Attachment Disorder, or AD. This is very common in children who have suffered *"abuse and neglect,"* as these girls have.

The photolisting says *"they are progressing very well and are responding well to therapy"*—most likely therapy for the behavioral and emotional problems caused by AD or a related emotional problem. This progress is evident in the fact that they have been in the same foster home for an encouraging three years. The long term of this placement indicates stability or improvement.

Teresa, who is learning *"how to trust and recognize boundaries"* probably has more serious behaviors than her older sister, Linda, who *"responds well to rules and has a respect for authority."*

Calling for *"experienced families"* is a red flag. These girls will require a great deal of patience to raise. They should be the youngest kids in their new families. They may try to pit one parent against the other so a single parent or a couple with an unusually strong marriage is a plus. Since non-Black families are being considered, these African-American girls almost surely have waited a long time, and offer many challenges to the adults who care for them.

A *"legal risk placement"* means that there is a chance, probably a very small one, that the girls' parents' rights will not be terminated. However, it is extremely rare that a legal risk placement does not work out. If there was a strong legal risk, the girls would not have been photolisted. Prospective parents should prepare for the girls to grieve the loss of their long-term foster family. This means behavioral regression and extra acting-out. Take it slow and informally adopt the foster parents as grandparents or as an aunt and uncle, and maintain foster and birth family ties wherever possible and appropriate to minimize their grief and loss. Residential treatment during and after puberty is a possibility, and help for this option should be written into the subsidy contract.

CHAPTER 4

Preparing for Parenthood

> The pressures of being a parent are equal to any pressure on earth. To be a conscious parent, and really look to that little being's mental and physical health, is a responsibility which most of us, including me, avoid most of the time because it's too hard.
>
> —John Lennon

In the past, many new adoptive parents were told that they should (and could) simply take the adopted child home and love him or her, and everything would go much as it would have had the child not been adopted, but rather born to them. Today we know that the fact of adoption brings both joys and challenges to the adoptive family. Children coming into adoption with special needs have issues to deal with that are unique to adoption. The information in this chapter is designed to give the reader an overview of what experience and research have brought to the adoption process over the last generation.

THE WAITING GAME

By the time the average prospective adoptive parent has made the first phone call to an adoption agency, months and even years have already been spent in thought, discussion, research, and sometimes treatment for infertility. The first phone call comes at the end of an arduous and often heartbreaking experience of decision making. Hopeful adoptive parents want anything but another arduous and heartbreaking experience to follow, yet that is what the adoption process most often becomes. Adoptive parents must learn to wait, and wait some more, and wait even longer. There is no easy cure for the impatience, longing, anxiety, and despair that sometimes characterize the wait for a child's placement. Yet adoptive parents still must wait. Fortunately, there are things that can (and should) be done during the wait.

Learn about Adoption

It cannot be emphasized enough that learning about all facets of adoption from all sides of the adoption triad is the best preparation any adoptive parent can have. Adoptive parents often make the mistake of reading books or periodicals tailored only to adoptive parents of their own ilk. While helpful to first-time adopters, this tactic is not helpful in the long run for the adoptee or the mature adoptive parent. Why? Because adoptive parents and adopted children grow up. Babies become toddlers and then pre-schoolers, school-age children, adolescents, and adults. Since 60 to 90 percent of adoptees want to know their birth parents, the majority of adoptive parents will one day be confronted with the fact of being only one of two parents in the adoptee's life. Most adoption experts and experienced adopters agree that it is far better for adoptive parents to learn early in their parenting lives about the different perspectives in adoption, including that of the adoptee and the birth parent, than it is to try to pretend that other perspectives do not exist or have no impact on the adoptive family.

Learn about Parenting

Although adoptive parenting is in many ways different from nonadoptive parenting, in many more ways adoptive parents experience joys and challenges that are the same for all parents. The Gesell Institute of Human Development's series of books offers some of the best available information on the behavior and development of children. Pediatric parenting guides by pediatricians such as Dr. Spock or Penelope Leach should also be in every adoptive home. And no adopter's library would be complete without Dr. Foster Cline and Jim Fay's books, *High Risk: Children without a Conscience, Parenting with Love and Logic,* and *Parenting Teens with Love and Logic.* These books in particular are highly recommended for families who adopt older children or those with special needs.

Volunteer to Work with Needy Children

Public and private adoption agencies alike have many demands made on their time and rarely have enough volunteers. One way waiting parents can cope with the impatience they sometimes feel is through volunteerism that helps waiting children. Prospective adoptive parents may volunteer through an adoptive parent support group, child advocacy group, become a Court-Appointed Special Advocate (CASA), or offer to do emergency or long-term foster care. Working with needy children or giving respite care to children with special needs will not only ease the impatience associated with waiting to adopt, it will also instruct prospective adoptive parents about the realities they will face once they become parents. Adopters who anticipate adding older, troubled children to their family would be better prepared as parents if they first volunteered at a local youth shelter or treatment center for troubled children.

ADOPTIVE NURSING

To this day in some undeveloped countries, foster babies are breast-fed. Some American mothers adopting infants from other countries have found, to their surprise, that their new baby acted as if he or she had never sucked on a bottle. In some Asian, African, and South American countries, women lactate their whole lives, often helping to nurse their grandchildren, too.

Even though breast-feeding adopted babies is an ages-old custom in almost all cultures and countries, many Americans are shocked to hear it exists, much less that it is becoming more commonplace each year. Yet adoptive nursing is advantageous for the infant and the adoptive mother. The mother need never have been pregnant to produce breast milk.

Thousands of adoptive moms in the United States have nursed their babies in the last 30 years, thanks in large part to guidance from an Illinois organization of volunteer moms called La Leche League International (LLLI).

How It Works

Adoptive nursing takes advantage of a simple lactation principle that is true for all mammals: The more the baby nurses, the more milk the mother produces. Therefore, if a woman stimulates her body to create milk by simulating the sucking of an infant, her body will automatically respond by making first a clear fluid called colostrum, and then milk. This early stimulation is brought about by the use of breast pumps, which are used every few hours for several weeks.

The Advantages

Obviously formula-fed babies can and do thrive, but breast-feeding (or even using purchased breast milk in a bottle) offers the adopted baby certain undeniable advantages. La Leche League points out that breast milk is not only very inexpensive compared to formula, but it is far more nutritious and digestible than any infant formula. There's no bottle warming and washing, and the totally breast-fed baby's stools do not smell foul.

Since studies indicate that the human fatty acids in breast milk actually help the brain finish developing in ways that formula cannot, and since many special needs infants are born at risk of developing learning problems, it could be argued that special needs babies need breast milk even more than other infants. Breast milk makes stronger bones and muscles than formula, and can prevent allergies and digestive problems in babies. Since there is immunological protection in mom's milk, baby gets protection from many diseases while being breast-fed.

And then there are the unique emotional advantages of adoptive nursing. Nursing, unlike using bottles, forces mothers and babies to spend time together, and to spend quality time. It is difficult to do other things while nursing, so the act of putting baby to breast actually encourages eye-to-eye contact and bonding. Nursing can help an anxious adoptive mother feel closer to her baby sooner and helps the baby, who is trying to get to know a new mother, feel secure and relaxed.

Re-lactation and Induced Lactation

The two types of adoptive nursing are called re-lactation and induced lactation. They differ in that re-lactation usually produces higher quantities of milk faster than induced lactation. Re-lactation is the fastest and easiest route. Women who have recently lactated and are re-lactating, or bringing their milk supply back, usually find that the process is a simple one. The body quickly "remembers" how to make milk again. In many cases, the mother who weaned her last child will continue to make minute amounts of milk for months or even years to come, thus making relactation a quick task.

Induced lactation is when a woman who has never been pregnant or lactated before stimulates milk production for the first time. A woman who has been pregnant, even for only a few weeks, will generally need less time to induce lactation than a woman who has never been pregnant at all, since hormones produced during pregnancy prepare the breasts for lactation. Of course, there are always exceptions.

Getting Started

Before nursing an adopted baby, every adoptive mother should be sure of the HIV status of both herself and the baby. There is some evidence that the HIV virus (the virus that causes AIDS) can go from mom to baby or from baby to mom during nursing, so it is best to be cautious. Babies known to be HIV positive can still enjoy the tremendous benefits of breast-milk in a bottle.

Regular sucking stimulation creates hormonal changes in a woman, which lead to milk production. The more stimulation, especially regular stimulation, the more milk. In modern times, women use hand-operated or electric breast pumps to simulate the sucking of a baby and bring in their milk before a placement occurs. The milk produced by such pumping can be stored in plastic bags and frozen. It makes a nutritious supplement for baby later on.

When the adoption has already occurred, some women use gadgets that supply the nursing baby with formula supplied to the nursing baby through a thin tube taped to the breast. The baby is encouraged to continue nursing even when a breast is not full of milk, which also stimulates the breast to create more milk. Adoptive mothers who use supplemental nursing devices say that they feel the experience brings them closer to the baby while stimulating milk production at the same time. Supplemental feeding devices and other nursing aids can be purchased through an LLLI chapter or through breast pump manufacturers. The Appendix includes the contact information for La Leche League and a major breast pump manufacturer, Medela.

Before starting a lactation induction, every new mother should consult her doctor first to be sure that her breasts are healthy and free from conditions that would make adoptive breastfeeding inadvisable. If the doctor is not knowledgeable or supportive of adoptive nuring, prospective mothers should ask the local La Leche League for referrals to physicians who are supportive of the practice. It is crucial for adopting moms to get the correct information about the process and the use of breast pumps. Mothers also need help learning how to know when to supplement breast feeding, and how much to supplement. The experts at La Leche League International have many different brochures and booklets about adoptive nursing available for purchase. Interested women should call their local La Leche League chapter (listed in the white pages), or contact La Leche League headquarters.

Measuring Success

When it comes to adoptive breast feeding, success cannot be measured in terms of milk volume, but in the final results. The results of induced lactation will vary widely from woman to woman. Some women will make milk rather easily, and others will never produce more than a trickle of milk. Of the hundreds of women Rita worked with personally as a La Leche League leader, only a few have expressed regret over the attempt to nurse an adopted baby. Those who viewed the attempt as a waste of time were disappointed in the amount of milk they were able to produce, or were nursing primarily because their husbands were encouraging them to do so for the baby's sake. A woman has to want to make the attempt if it is to be successful, and she must not think in terms of milk quantity, but in terms of the overall quality of the experience.

One mother credits breastfeeding with minimizing the effects of pre-natal drug exposure suffered by her adopted son, Terry. Terry came to her at age five weeks, still experiencing drug withdrawal, losing weight, and so constipated he needed medication to move his bowels. After consulting her doctor, the new mom stopped the medication and put Terry to the breast. He nursed constantly, which increased her milk supply and caused an immediate increase in Terry's weight. The constipation was gone within 24 hours and never returned. The drug withdrawal became easier to bear, and Terry slept much better than he ever had before. Within a few weeks, he went from sickly and thin to baby-chubby and healthy, off all medication. Terry weaned himself between his first and second birthday. Today, he is in gifted and talented classes at school and is an accomplished athlete as well.

SPECIAL NEEDS ADOPTION SUPPORT

You've found an agency that knows how to place children with special needs. You are prepared to become parents. Now what?

In the movies, we might see prospective adoptive parents do no more to prepare than sit by the phone waiting patiently for it to ring. This does not work in special needs adoption. Special needs adoption is not a passive activity. It requires action, self-determination, and dedicated preparation. The more prospective adoptive parents prepare, the more smoothly the adoption—and its aftermath—will unfold. Preparation means finding comprehensive adoption support.

Adoption support has been defined as the provision of any item or service that helps adoptive families to form, to function effectively, and to stay together. Adoption support is critically important to the success of special needs adoption. Several studies have shown that adoption support services have been waning, sporadic, inadequate, and difficult to locate, access, and keep (Barth & Berry, 1988; Cohen & Westhues, 1990; Groze et al., n.d.).

The Elements of Support

What do special needs adoptive families need? The elements of special needs adoption support are several. Here are some of the aspects of special need adoption support that are important to adoptive families:

- Buddy Families. Buddy families are experienced adoptive families who aid and support prospective adoptive parents.
- "Warmlines" and "Hotlines," telephone support and information.
- Prescribed Reading. Agencies may prepare children and parents by prescribed reading, using materials specific to special needs adoption.
- General Information regarding adoption, the adoption process, and adoption issues—such as that included in this book.
- Information and disclosure of all the child's medical, educational, psychological, and social histories to the adopting parents.
- Proper matching of child to parents. The elements of a successful match have been well documented by research and should be considered carefully. For example, highly educated adoptive mothers have not been a good match, statistically, for older children with severe emotional problems (Barth & Berry, 1988).
- Parent support groups, conferences, and social support at the local, regional, and national levels.
- Respite care is specialized baby sitting provided for special needs children.

- On-line adoption communities such as the adoption bulletin boards, live chats, and email mailing lists on commercial services such as Prodigy, CompuServe, and America OnLine or through internet service providers.
- Periodicals such as those listed in the Resources section.
- Triad Support groups. By attending a triad support group, adoptive parents will learn about how adoption has affected the lives of the other two-thirds of the adoption triad—adult adoptees and birth parents.
- Ongoing support, information, and financial assistance as the adoptee grows.

UNDERSTANDING ADVOCACY

Why Adopting and Advocating Are Two Halves of a Whole

You can certainly be an adoptive parent without being a child advocate, but it is almost impossible to be a special needs adoptive parent without advocating for your kids at some point with the social services, medical, government, and educational communities. Special needs adoption is unique. Children begin with the disadvantage of being "different." The adopting parents also start with a disadvantage, the challenge of having to work with a bureaucratic system that, while well intentioned, is about as easy to navigate as wild river rapids. Adopting and advocating are the two halves of the whole we call special needs adoption. To support one, parents must learn the art of the other.

The Art of Advocating for Special Needs Kids

In *The 7 Habits of Highly Effective People*, Stephen R. Covey discusses the importance of turning battles into win-win situations. This is crucial to know when advocating for the best interests of children. The people who parents deal with while advocating all have one thing in common: Each *believes* he or she knows what's best. Parents should help their adversaries save face by painting each situation in a win-win light.

For example, a woman called Rita recently asking for help in completing a sibling group placement that had been stalled for 10 months and was about to be shelved permanently. One of the children, a severely disabled toddler, had been in the adoptive home for four months and was now in danger of being sent back to her foster home since her four siblings could not join her. The snag in the placement revolved around three dueling county adoption units, each of which was accusing the other of acting without authority in the placement, and each refusing to complete the adoption. The desperate parents had tried everything to get their kids home, but to no avail. They were days away from losing their toddler, and was helplessly watching as five brothers and sisters returned to foster care.

Rita made two suggestions. First, to call the local North American Council on Adoptable Children (NACAC), National Adoption Advocacy Training and Referral Information Network (NAATRIN), and Adopt a Special Kid (AASK) representatives in that state, Adoptive Families of America (AFA), and the local adoption support group leaders, and seek their help. They would also be able to identify the person or persons at top levels in the state adoption units who have both the power and the willingness to break the logjam that was keeping the kids out of permanency.

If no such person existed or could be located, the one thing left to do was to contact the media for publicity. This meant drafting a letter or fax for the local television stations, talk radio, and newspapers, asking for help in bringing the kids home. It was also suggested that copies be sent to the office of the spouse of the state governor. Many times, we have seen governors' spouses take a personal interest in solving problems that affect kids.

In drafting the fax, it was imperative to banish personal animosity, anger, and frustration. Advocating is something done for kids, period. It is not about calling ourselves victims, seeking satisfaction, justice, or getting people fired. The brief fax was to state the problem in a succinct way and add a plea to help these kids find their way home to their forever family before it was too late. Writing the fax helped to define the problem and the possible solutions in the mother's mind. After writing it, she decided to make one more phone call before initiating a media blitz. She called the First Lady of her state.

Within minutes, she was speaking to a very concerned chief of staff for the First Lady who took notes and promised to get right on it. Less than an hour later, the mom's phone rang. It was the head of adoptions in one of the battling counties. This supervisor had just spoken to the chief of staff and was now ready to assure the family that the adoption would proceed with all haste because these kids need to be adopted. Everyone showed concern for the kids. Everyone looked good. Everyone saved face. Everyone won, most of all the children.

But the advocate's job was not done yet. It was now important to make sure the promises were kept. The mother next wrote a thank-you letter to the First Lady and to her staff, thanking them, informing them of the progress made, and promising to get back in touch in one week if the children were not on their way home. She sent copies of this letter to all of the county officials involved with the case. No fingers of blame were pointed. The letter was 100 percent positive. The adoptions went through.

Had all else failed, the mother might have considered litigation. If a cause is just and right, and especially if it involves violation to children's rights, parents can always find an attorney willing to work at reduced or no fees.

Persistence, pluck (courage), and patience. This is what advocating is all about. Almost any situation can result in the best interests of the child being served if the advocate remembers to:

- create win-win situations,
- look for the shortest route to a solution (identify the key people who can help),
- keep the focus where it belongs: on the needs of the children alone,

- stay positive,
- be assertive, not attacking,
- avoid being put on the defensive,
- use anger strategically,
- never give up, even if that means filing a lawsuit,
- network with the thousands of volunteer advocates across the nation willing to help.

Keep Good Records

"This isn't an adoptive family," complained one special needs adoptive mother, "this is a bureaucracy!" Adoptive parents who intend to become their children's most effective advocates do sometimes have to develop habits that seem bureaucratic. The mother we knew was complaining about the amount of paperwork required in special needs adoptions, both pre- and post-placement and after the adoption is finalized. Though tedious, the adoptive parents we know who keep meticulous records of their contacts with social workers, educators, and others involved in their children's lives find that they are more effective when it comes to getting what their children need.

We recommend keeping a record of every time you contact someone about something your child needs: name, address, telephone number, and date and outcome of discussions. Follow up every important telephone contact with a friendly letter reiterating what was said. Anne keeps a large three-ring binder (or two, or three!) for each child in the family, divided by sections such as Medicaid, AAP, SSI, Education, and so on, an idea passed on to her by one of her children's former foster mothers. With a three-hole paper punch and minimal effort, she knows right where to go when she needs to document something.

Financial Advocacy

Subsidies are cash payments of federal and state funds that are made on a monthly basis to adoptive parents of special needs children. Adoptive parents need help accessing subsidies, keeping the subsidies until the child is grown, and in advocating and applying for age-related increases in the subsidy amount. All prospective adoptive parents should take responsibility for knowing their rights and the benefits available to the child adopted with special needs *before* entering into an adoption agreement. The Finances chapter discusses this issue in depth.

THE LIFE BOOK

The "Life Book" is a pictorial history for the adopted child, a way of linking his or her past with the present. The most recent statistics available indicate that only 44.5 percent of children in foster care have had only one temporary placement, with 27.2 percent experiencing three to five placements, and 6.5 percent experiencing six or more placements (CWLA, 1994). Over one-third of all children in foster care (39.5 percent) spend two to ten years in foster homes (CWLA, 1994). It is easy to see how a child's history can be lost in the blur of moves in and out of foster care, through the ever-changing roster of social workers, and from foster home to foster home. It seems there is no one to retell the facts and anecdotes that would allow the children to build a sense of personal history. There is, however, a tool available to help fill this gap. That tool is the Life Book.

The Life Book usually takes the form of a scrapbook or photo album and is filled with the child's personal information and any photographs available. The book usually tells the story of the child's life in chronological order, beginning with the birth history, any photographs of the birth parents or extended family, and continuing until the child's most recent placement. When photographs of people are unavailable and cannot be collected, photographs of places or the child's drawings are sometimes substituted. The Life Book helps to provide a sense of continuity to the child whose life memories may seem like disconnected fragments.

Although the ideal would be to begin the Life Book when the child first enters foster care, this is seldom achieved. The Life Book is often started while the child lives in a foster family or prior to an adoptive placement. The child's social worker often helps the child create the life book, although it may also be started with the help of a foster parent or therapist. Adoptive parents should undertake this task themselves if it has not already been done.

Children enjoy helping with the Life Book, and can cut and paste pictures and maps, or make drawings and record information. Some information will be available in the case file, but the child may have memories and details to add.

When the child moves into a new placement, whether to a foster or adoptive family, the Life Book provides a way for the child to share his or her past without the shame of kept secrets, or the threat that feelings will be constrained. The Life Book can tell the story that is so difficult for the child to tell.

Adoptive Family Life Book

Adoptive families, too, may be asked to prepare a Life Book about them and their community. When preparing an older child for an imminent placement, the placing social worker will ask the adoptive family to submit their Life Book to the agency so that the adoptive family's book can be used to prepare the child for a new home. The adoptive family Life Book is very much like the child's life book. It will depict the family home, family members, pets, photos of the neighborhood, church, school the child will attend, and so on. Sometimes adoptive families exchange videotapes with the social worker as well.

WHY DOES ADOPTION TAKE SO LONG?

Why is special needs adoption so difficult when so many children wait? Most special needs adopters have asked this question. The answer lies in understanding how the system works. Those who understand how the system works and change their behavior in order to cooperate with it are more successful at adopting waiting children than those who don't understand the system or who try to fight it.

Social workers are among the most overworked people in the country. The majority of adoption workers serving waiting children simply do not have the time to treat adoptive parents like consumers. In a sense, adoption workers are the consumers and adoptive parents are the product such workers seek for the children they serve. Adoptive parents must take an active role in finding the child, send the unofficial homestudies, follow up to make sure the study arrived, make an effort to get to know the child through the child's social worker, and then stay involved in every step of the process to expedite the placement. No matter what adoptive parents have been told during preparation and training for special needs adoptive parenting, they cannot sit by the phone and wait for it to ring, at least not if they hope to adopt in a timely manner. Prospective adoptive parents who become foster parents or who become self-directed in finding a waiting child have shorter waits than those who rely completely upon the efforts of adoption workers.

WHEN A PLACEMENT MISCARRIES

One frequently misunderstood fact about special needs adoption is that prospective adoptive parents seeking to adopt a specific child are often disappointed due to the failure of a potential placement. Many state agencies mandate the reception of a minimum number of adoptive parent applicants for each waiting child or sibling group, a practice that pits one prospective adoptive parent against another. The adoption agency advertises the availability of a waiting child and solicits the homestudies of several prospective adoptive parents. Once the required number of homestudies (typically three to five) has been received, or after a certain time period has elapsed, the agency "staffs the child," or calls together staff members who will decide the fate of the child. At the staffing, one adoptive parent or couple will be chosen for the child in question to the exclusion of the other applicants.

To adoptive parents who have already seen the child's photograph, read his or her history, and have asked to be considered as the child's parents, being passed over has the emotional effect of a miscarriage, especially when parents are applying for one child at a time. Since the search for adoptive parents takes time, hopeful adoptive parents may have weeks or even months during which they imagine becoming a specific child's parents. Sometimes a social worker may even prefer a specific couple and communicate as much to them, only to have her choice negated during a staffing. Again, the adoptive parents are left feeling a loss and wondering why they were passed over and another couple or individual chosen.

Prospective adoptive parents of children with special needs should realize that, in spite of the "no one wants to adopt these kids" myth, the reality is that there are often several families interested in adopting a specific child or sibling group, especially for pre-school-aged children. This is especially true when a child is photolisted through a national or regional exchange, which can net dozens, even hundreds, of applications for the same child. In addition, often birth relatives or the foster family are being considered or are given preference, but adoptive parent applicants are not given this information because the state requires a certain number of applicants in every case.

There are waiting lists of people seeking to adopt children with spina bifida, hearing impairment, Down's syndrome and other specific challenges. To be sure, teens, severely handicapped or severely emotionally disturbed children, and large sibling groups continue to be harder to place. Most often younger waiting children are generally sought by the majority of prospective special needs adoptive parents, making the potential of a "miscarried" placement or referral a real possibility.

The stages of grief are the same whether parents experience a failed adoption, a lost placement, or a hoped-for referral that never comes to pass. Adoptive parents, especially mothers, who tend to be more motivated to adopt and more involved in the application and advocacy process, feel sadness and even despair over the loss. Repeated homestudy rejections cause adoptive parents to revisit the feelings of inadequacy and loss of control they experienced during the process of discovering and attempting to treat infertility. Adoptive parents who have never experienced infertility may enter the special needs adoption process with an expectation of entitlement and feel frustrated with the powerlessness and repeated disappointment they experience. Shock, anger, bargaining, and despair are emotions that will be experienced by the disappointed adoptive parent. As well, many a prospective adoptive parent of the child with special needs will feel intense frustration resulting from the conflict between the constant reports of waiting children and their own repeated referral losses.

What can hopeful adoptive parents do when they find their hopes dashed? Parents can minimize their feelings of grief by accepting in advance that they are probably going to have to apply for and lose several children before they are offered a single placement. Adoptive parents should give themselves time and permission to grieve the losses they experience during the adoption process, even when their losses are not recognized or understood by others.

Many special needs adoption advocates say that becoming empowered, self-directed parent activists finally resolved their repeated disappointments and frustrations. By sending out their homestudies on many children simultaneously and personally following the application and referral process, adoptive parents can find themselves in the position of being offered more than one placement at a time.

PART II

BECOMING FAMILY

CHAPTER 5

Early Placement: What Parents Experience

"Hello? May I speak to Jamie's mom?"

—Social worker, to newly-chosen adoptive mom

CONGRATULATIONS! YOU'VE BEEN CHOSEN

Prospective adoptive parents preparing for a special needs placement know, intellectually, that eventually they will become adoptive parents. Even so, most adoptive parents describe as the thrill of their lives the telephone call notifying them that they have been chosen for a child they applied to adopt. The social worker for the child or children you applied to adopt will probably tell you the dates on which the child's case will be staffed and a decision made. Many an adoptive parent has spent hours hovering near the phone, waiting to hear if they will be chosen as the parents for a particular child. Prospective adoptive parents experience anxiety, doubt, fear, depression, hope, anticipation, excitement, dread, and joy as they wait for The Phone Call. When the telephone call comes, and the social worker on the other end of the line says, "Congratulations!" adoptive parents experience a thrill and joy as intense and abiding as that of any new parent.

After the celebration, it's time to get to work. Experienced special needs adopters have learned that their most important and difficult work begins only *after* they have been chosen for a child. The task for the adoptive parents and their adoption worker is to decide whether the parents will still choose the child, after complete disclosure of the child's history and special needs.

STOP, LOOK, AND LISTEN

Although an adoptive parent may have waited months or years to adopt, he or she should follow the advice many children receive as newcomers to the public school system: STOP, LOOK, and LISTEN. Parents should *stop,* remembering not to rush; *look* at all of the information that is given about the child; and *listen* to everyone who has had contact with the child.

The basic information that should be disclosed to adoptive parents includes:

- Contact with former caregivers. Adoptive parents should ask for the name, address, and telephone number of all of the child's former caregivers. The adoption worker may say that the state's adoption laws forbid sharing of identifying information regarding former caretakers, including birth and foster families. However, even if adoption laws mandate a sealed adoption record after an adoption, *no adoption has yet occurred.* Parents can also ask the social worker to have former caretakers contact them. Adoptive parents should advocate to receive contact with the child's birth and foster families. The agency may even agree to facilitate such contact. Even so, some adoptive parents have learned after the placement that the agency only allowed the adoptive family contact with some foster families, but not all. Insist on having contact with all the families with whom the child has lived for more than a few months. Parents should also insist upon having contact with day care providers and teachers.
- Evaluation for Attachment Disorder. If the child has been institutionalized during infancy or toddlerhood, has experienced abuse or neglect, or is more than 12-18 months old at the time of placement parents should ask that the placing agency have the child or children evaluated for Reactive Attachment Disorder (commonly called Attachment Disorder, or AD) before agreeing to a placement. Such an evaluation should be conducted by a professional who has been trained in the diagnosis and treatment of AD and, ideally, who has treated adopted children. Many special needs adoptions fail because children have unrecognized and untreated attachment problems or Attachment Disorder. The disorder is discussed in a subsequent chapter.
- Birth information. The pregnancy and birth records are often overlooked, but contain crucial information. They should include the child's name, place, and date of birth including the hospital, county, state, and country; the child's weight, length, and time of birth, Apgar scores, course, and length of hospital stay.
- Birth certificate. In most states in the United States, an adoptee's original birth certificate is sealed and an amended birth certificate issued listing the adoptive parents as having given birth to the adoptee. When adoptees grow up, they are usually not able to access their original birth certificate unless they can prove dire need. Since the birth certificate is not sealed until the adoption is finalized, pre-adoptive parents are usually able to receive a copy of the original birth certificate from the agency, health department, or former foster parent. This document is invaluable and should become a part of the parent's permanent file for the adoptee.
- Pregnancy. Health of mother during pregnancy, history of labor and delivery, and post-delivery condition. Pre-natal care records where available.

- Siblings. Other children in the birth family, including gender and ages, whether they reside with the birth family. If any siblings live apart from the birth family, why and where?
- AFDC and Medicaid. Was the birth family receiving public assistance or Medicaid or eligible to receive them? If so, was receipt of assistance during pregnancy or up until relinquishment of the child now available for the new placement?
- Extended family information. Siblings of birth parents (number, ages, health). Information about grandparents such as health history, social history, cause of death (if deceased).
- Psychological history. History of any psychiatric illnesses in birth parents or extended family; psychological evaluation of child at the time of surrender or prior to placement.
- Counseling. Nature of counseling provided to birth parents during pregnancy or prior to the surrender of a child.
- Legal representation for the birth family independent of the adoptive parents or agency.
- Guardian ad litem, Court-Appointed Special Advocate (CASA) names, addresses, and telephone numbers.
- Treatment provider names, addresses, telephone numbers (including social workers, school teachers, therapists, day care providers, and physicians). Ask that the agency provide you with a signed release of information form allowing all professionals to release records directly to you if the child is in the agency's custody.
- Hospitalization history of the child.
- Ethnic, cultural, religious, and racial identity and history of the birth family.
- Immunization and other health records (medications taken, allergies).
- Copy of state statutes and regulations governing disclosure in the state of residence.
- Interstate Compact Agreement and information for placing state (in case the adoptive family moves to another state in the future).
- Complete information on Adoption Assistance Payments (AAP) and Medicaid for special needs adopted children.
- In voluntary surrenders, a letter from one or both parents expressing why the decision to surrender the child was made, whenever possible.
- In involuntary surrenders, the specific causes and reasons why the court terminated parental rights.
- Photographs, whenever possible, of the child and the child's extended family, former foster families and homes, pets, etc.

ACCESS TO RECORDS

Although all of the waiting child's casework records are confidential, the records can be released to other professionals and to the adoptive parents once the proper releases have been signed. Medical records can be received from the physicians and psychiatrists who have treated or seen the child. The child's social and educational history can be received from the adoption agency or other appropriate agency. Prospective adoptive parents should request *in writing* the release of all the information the agency has that relates to the child in question. When requests have been made in writing, they can be documented.

Other Information to Request

Besides the information listed, parents should also ask for a copy of the chart notes made by the child's current and previous social workers. The chart notes are part of the child's case file. Included in the chart notes will be notes the caseworker made after visiting the child or while gathering the child's history. Although the adoption worker may tell you that such notes cannot be disclosed because they contain confidential information, ask the worker to obscure identifying information before sending you the notes. When you request medical information, also request the chart notes made by nurses, doctors, psychologists, and other professionals who saw or treated the child during a hospitalization. If a child has been in the system for any length of time, such records will be extensive. But they are essential and as the child's parent you will need to become the expert on this particular child. In a special needs adoption, there is no such thing as too much information.

Get Good Advice

Once parents are satisfied that they have all the information they need about the child, it is time to share some of that information with their own spiritual adviser, social worker, pediatrician, and another special needs adoptive parent known to be very experienced in adoption. The North American Council on Adoptable Children (NACAC), Adoptive Families of America (AFA), Adopt A Special Kid (AASK America), or their own agency can put parents in contact with such an adoptive parent. Parents should ask the people with whom they share the information to be frank about any concerns or questions they have after hearing the information. Special attention should be paid to the comments and suggestions of other special needs adoptive parents.

If the child has a medical or psychiatric diagnosis, parents should make the effort and take the time to talk with two or three other parents of children with the same disorder. They should ask these experienced parents to be very frank about what it is like to parent a child with that disability. It also helps to seek out adults with the same diagnosis and visit with them about how the disability has affected their lives.

A MATCH IS MADE

The phone call came, the new parents did their "special needs research," requested full disclosure, sought advice, called all their friends and family members to tell them the good news, and spent days walking on air. Now what?

At this point, most adoptive parents enter a phase of short-lived but very real terror. "What on earth do I think I'm doing?! I can't do this! I'm adopting a child I don't even know! What if I don't love this child? What if she doesn't like me? This could be an awful mistake. What have we done?" All these questions and doubts and many more are completely normal. New adoptive parents who feel such fears and doubts can remember that other adoptive parents have had them, too. Parents who have no fears or doubts at all, and begin to worry about *that,* are also not unusual. Some parents, especially those who are veteran special needs adopters, become confident through years of experience, and panic over not having any panic!

TELLING YOUR EXTENDED FAMILY

People who have waited for years to become parents and then decided to adopt a child often find that initially their families are excited and happy for them. However, when they begin to consider and talk about special needs adoption, they sometimes find that their extended families aren't as supportive as they'd hoped they would be. Since some special needs adopters adopt after having biological children, their loved ones may be especially puzzled about the choice of special needs adoption.

At times like this, adoptive parents need the support and encouragement of other special needs adoptive families. Such families have walked in their shoes. They, too, have faced ignorance, fears, apprehension, questioning, and perhaps prejudice in their families as they became special needs adoptive families.

People who encounter problems with extended family as they seek to adopt a child or children with special needs might consider asking family members to read a book about adoption, such as Patricia Irwin Johnston's *Supporting an Adoption* booklet, or Jill Krementz's *How It Feels to Be Adopted.* They can also invite family members to attend a support group meeting or social event with other special needs adoptive families.

Some new adoptive parents, in their excitement over receiving a new child, have said later that one of their biggest mistakes was confiding too much of the child's history to family members such as parents or in-laws. Older parents, raised in a culture that did not embrace adoption and in which even same-race infant adoption was viewed with suspicion, may not be supportive or understanding when their beloved adult child adopts a child with special needs. Veteran adopters recommend that sensitive information such as a history of sexual or physical abuse, alcoholism or mental illness or retardation in the birth family, or even information about adoption assistance payments and medical assistance be shared sparingly at first, if at all.

YOUR CIVIC AND FAITH COMMUNITIES

More than one church-goer has been surprised to find that their announcement of a pending special needs adoption met with something less than enthusiasm from their faith communities. Likewise, co-workers and neighbors may react, initially, by trying to talk the prospective parent out of the idea. When a transracial adoption is contemplated, a few neighbors have been known to put their houses up for sale.

To expect a few negative reactions is to be prepared to deal with them. It is helpful to understand that many Americans simply do not understand what special needs adoption is all about. They may not realize that matches are not made randomly, or that the process is painstaking, and that placements cannot be finalized for a minimum of six months after placement. With patience and time and education, most people come around and become supportive.

Sometimes, though, even friends, neighbors, and co-workers who are quite supportive of an adoption are at a loss when it comes to helping adoptive parents welcome a new child into the family. One adoptive mother became depressed when she noticed that her church regularly welcomed newborn infants into the church "family" with a baby shower, but failed to acknowledge her adoption of a two-year-old child with medical problems. When she and her husband adopted their second child with special needs, she found she had learned through advocating for her older child how to ask for support as well. She told members of the church staff and her women's Bible study class that she and her husband were expecting to adopt a five-year-old boy who would come to them with few clothes and no toys, and that she and her husband would be thrilled to be honored at an "adoption shower." Their faith community was more than happy to respond and subsequently planned other adoption showers for new adoptive parents in the church.

PRE-PLACEMENT VISITS

Once satisfied that they have the information about the child that will help them make an informed decision, and after careful consideration and not a little self-doubt, the prospective parent has decided to say "yes" to a proposed match. Adoptions of younger children require less pre-placement visitation than those of older children.

The First Meeting

Custom varies a great deal from place to place. Prospective parents may be required to make several visits, or there may be only one brief visit prior to placement. Generally, all costs associated with the visit are paid by the state agency that has custody of the child or children. In some cases, parents are given an expense account and are reimbursed later. Some experienced adopters keep a credit card clear of charges to use during adoption visits, knowing that the fees will be reimbursed even before interest began to accrue on the debt.

The first meeting between the parents and their new child will come after a great deal of groundwork has already been laid. The placing agency will probably ask the parents to send their Life Book if the child is old enough to benefit. The child's social worker may arrange to have the parents talk with the child's foster parents and even the child (if older) on the telephone prior to the first visit.

If the placement is to take place in-state, visits will probably be quickly arranged and the placement will occur within a few weeks after the first parent-child meeting. In many out-of-state placements, adoptive parents are asked to spend three to five days in the placing state and then return home with the child. In such a situation, more preparation of the child prior to the first visit will be essential to help the child make the move. If no one has suggested the use of videotapes or some preparatory telephone calls, the parents should suggest these. Everyone involved in the placement should also remember that the child has probably had little to say in the matter. The child will need time to adjust to the reality of another move and a new family.

With in-state adoption, a first visit will probably be arranged at the agency or at a public place such as a park, playground, or recreation area. The parents will probably meet the child's current foster parents at this time, especially if the child is an infant or toddler. If the child is somewhat older, the adoption worker may suggest that the parents meet the child for the first time without the foster parents present. If the child is old enough to state a preference, it's wise to ask him what he prefers.

During the first meeting, everyone will be excited and nervous. Children may be exceedingly active or exhibit withdrawn behavior. They may call their new parents "Mom" and "Dad" from the first meeting, or they may call them by their first names. The adoption worker will probably have prepared the parents and child ahead of time for what will take place. During the first meeting, many adoptive parents bring a small gift for the child or children that will break the ice and serve as a permanent and treasured memento of the meeting.

The first meeting can last a matter of hours and may end with the social worker taking the child home or with the foster parents coming to pick the child up. The social worker will probably give the new parents an opportunity to talk with her about the child, their first impressions, and their feelings. She will also talk with the child later about how the child felt about the meeting.

Subsequent Meetings

If everything went well, subsequent visits will be planned. During the next visit, parents may go to pick up the child at her foster home and have more opportunity to talk with the foster parents. This visit can last four to six hours, or a whole day. At the end of the visit, the parents will return the child to her foster family or meet the adoption worker, who will want to know how things went. The parents will also have the opportunity to discuss the visits privately, even if the placement is an out-of-state visit. In the case of an out-of-state visit, the second visit will probably take place on the second day of the trip, the third visit on the third day, and so on.

Providing things are moving along smoothly, the next visit with the child will probably be an overnight visit to the parents' home, if the home is within driving distance from the foster home. If the placement is an out-of-state visit, the child will spend the night with the new parents at a hotel. The third visit will probably last two days and one night. If the placement is in state, the child may come on Friday and go back to her foster home on Sunday. Depending on the age and circumstances of the child, one more visit may occur, the next one lasting a week. Some adoptive parents have arranged for vacation leave and had the child come visit for five more days prior to the final move.

No matter what is arranged, children who are older than toddlers need to have the opportunity prior to a final move to say good-bye to foster parents, siblings, birth family members, classmates, pets, and even places that are dear to them. Without the opportunity to say "good-bye," children find it difficult to say "hello" to new people and places in their life.

Infants and Toddlers

The placement of an infant, toddler, or non-verbal child (including a child whose first language is not English) requires some creativity. A time-honored technique in introducing the very young or disabled child to new adoptive parents is to have the adoptive parents visit the child in the child's home and to take over a feeding, bathtime, or bedtime ritual from the child's current parents. When the adoptive parent takes over a parenting task from the foster parent in the safe and familiar environment, the child experiences less threat and receives the foster parent's permission to be cared for by the new parent.

The adoption worker will probably also ask the foster parent to give the child verbal permission to love the new parents and go home with them. This will be difficult and emotional for the foster parent, but important for the child and new parents to hear.

When Rita and her husband adopted a two-year-old son named Jared, the moment of separation proved very painful to the devoted foster mother, Mary. In spite of her efforts not to, she began to cry. At this point, Jared began crying, too, and reaching for his foster mother from Rita's arms. Knowing this was not a good way to begin an adoption, Mary sat down on the sofa with Jared on her lap and calmed him down. Then she told him that it was okay to go with his new parents because they loved him as much as she did. She promised to remain in his life as his new grandma. Jared smiled immediately, jumped off of Mary's lap, and raced Rita to the car. The permission his foster mother gave him to let go of her and attach to a new family seemed to find a home in Jared's young heart, because his attachment to the family grew. Whenever he missed Mary, he was able to call her and reassure himself that she still cared for him.

PLACEMENT

In spite of all the preparation associated with the adoption process, the day the child comes home carries with it the sensation of instant parenthood. One minute the carefully prepared bed is empty, and the next a new child is being tucked in.

The Rules of the Roost

Most children will feel more comfortable if they can know what the rules of a household are as soon as they move in. The parents should sit down and think through which rules are absolute essentials and which are only preferences. They should make a list of essential rules and post them on the refrigerator or in another public area. Two excellent books that can help parents with child discipline are *Parenting with Love and Logic* and *Parenting Teens with Love and Logic*, both by Foster Cline and Jim Fay.

When Anne and her husband adopted older children, they included a list of their essential household rules in their family's Life Book. They took a photograph of the "time-out" chair they used for very young children, with one of their children sitting in the chair. The caption told the new children the purpose of the time-out chair, when time-out would be used, and what types of discipline would not be used in the household. They also included a list of "Rules for Parents" in the Life Book that included behavioral standards for the grown-ups in the household, rules such as "Parents will not hit children or each other," and "Parents will not scream, yell, or shout at children or each other in anger." That such rules existed in the family helped alert older adopted children that their new family would not follow the same sorts of rules that had been used in some of their other families, in which hitting and screaming had been part of family life.

Extended Family

The adoptive parents' extended family will want to meet the new child (or children) and get to know them. New adoptive parents will want to think through the introductions they will make between family members and the child. A matter-of-fact introduction usually works best. "This is my mother, Helen Smith. That makes her your new grandma. You can call her 'Grandma' or 'Grandma Helen'." "Mother, this is Amber, our new daughter, and your new granddaughter! Amber is eight years old and her favorite color is purple. Amber's favorite subject at school is art." Similar facts about the child's new extended family members can also be shared so that the child knows something about the family.

Some adoptive families find it helpful to have few visitors during the first week or two of placement so that the new family can get used to one another. Others throw an "arrival party." What a parent does depends on the age and temperament of the child, personal preferences, and the circumstances surrounding the placement. The first responsibility of the new adoptive parent is to do what is best for the child, not to act and think only in terms of personal needs or wishes. Parents should consider the losses and difficulties the child has faced and then ask themselves what they might find helpful in similar circumstances. Then they can act accordingly.

DEALING WITH INTRUSIVE QUESTIONS

Family members, friends, and even strangers will ask questions or make statements about adoption they would never make to a person who had children by birth. In *The Essential Adoption Handbook*, Colleen Alexander-Roberts (1993) points out that curiosity often overcomes the etiquette of many people, and she advises adoptive parents to prepare in advance to answer intrusive questions. Intrusive and rude questions are a fact of life, especially when the adoption is transracial, or when the child has noticeable disabilities. One new mother strolling through a grocery store with her Korean-born daughter was approached by a stranger who nodded at the child and asked, "What is it?" A Caucasian dad shopping in a department store with his African-American daughter was stopped and searched by a police officer on suspicion of kidnapping. A mom pushing her newly adopted son in a wheelchair was stopped by a neighbor and asked, "Why would anyone adopt a crippled child?" And a month doesn't go by that parents of large adoptive families don't hear questions in public like, "How many of them are really yours?" or "Which ones are natural?"

Since intrusive questions will be asked once in a while, parents should think through their answers ahead of time so that they will be prepared. The best answers start with using correct language. Children are biological, born to a couple, birth children, or adopted, not real or natural. Birth parents are just that, or can be called "original parents," not "real parents."

Neighbors and friends in the community, whether at church or at the local play group, will all notice the new child. Introducing an infant is straightforward no matter what the situation. Introducing an older child, or a child with obvious handicaps is another matter. Both parents and child will need to have what some experts have called the "cover story." Parents should decide what they will say to strangers by considering what the child feels comfortable with. What they say to strangers about adoption and specifically about their child may come back to haunt them. Divulging sensitive information should be done on a need-to-know basis.

When Rita's transracially adopted children were younger, she prepared answers to intrusive questions herself. As her children grew older, and when she adopted older children, she sought their input on the answers. Some of her children preferred that she give "educational" answers, or "friendly" responses, while others asked that she not give any information to questioners, saying, "I prefer to guard our privacy." By forming answers based on the preferences of the children who were present, each child approved of the handling of such questions.

TIES THAT BIND

Bonding, attachment, claiming, and entitlement are all psychological terms that relate to processes that occur in parenting situations in roughly the order listed above. Space does not permit in-depth descriptions of these important processes, but basic definitions are given here.

We call bonding the process whereby parents and infants "fall in love" with each other. Bonding begins in the womb as the baby learns to recognize his or her parents' voices, and continues after birth as parents and infant get to know each other. Bonding is facilitated through contact such as holding, massaging, cuddling, feeding, and playing. Bonding can also occur between adoptive parents and children but takes longer, especially when adopting older children.

Attachment grows from bonding, usually in the 12-18 months after birth for most infants. Attachment is a bond of trust that slowly develops between baby and parents as baby cries, making known his or her needs, and parents respond with food or loving care. If baby cries and no one responds, as in parental neglect, the cycle of attachment is broken and baby will not learn to trust that others will meet his or her needs. This sets the child up for Attachment Disorder or AD. Attachment disorders can improve with treatment as parents and children recreate the attachment cycle. There is more about this in later chapters.

Claiming is a process whereby a child claims his or her parents as his own, and the parent claims the child. After an adoption, it is a good idea to encourage claiming behaviors. For example, parent and child may wish to address and mail adoption announcements together, or to plan an adoption party. Introducing your child as "my son," or "my daughter," or the child proudly writing out his new last name are all part of claiming. Ceremonies and festivities surrounding the finalization of an adoption in court are perhaps the most significant claiming activities in adoption.

Entitlement is related to claiming in that it is the process whereby a parent feels entitled to be called Mom or Dad. Bathing the new baby is an entitlement activity, so are feeding, administering medication, or advocating for the child educationally. The more parents act like parents, the more entitled they feel to their new roles, and the more comfortable they are in them. Anne went through a five-day hospital stay with one of her children soon after adopting him. The round-the-clock care the child required gave her a ready sense of entitlement.

CHAPTER 6

Early Placement: What Children Experience

Children's talent to endure stems from their ignorance of alternatives.
—Maya Angelou

Imagine that it is the end of a normal workday. You've arrived home and opened the front door to the smell of onions and garlic simmering in olive oil, the beginnings of your husband's special spaghetti sauce. "Hi, honey! I'm home!" you call as you toss your keys onto the dining room table and begin to sort through the day's mail. Your husband mumbles a greeting in your direction as you flip through the pages of a new catalog. The sound of your children playing a video game in the next room filters into the kitchen.

You are heading upstairs to change clothes when the doorbell rings. As you reach the door to open it, your husband also enters the entry hall. He has a dish towel in his hand and an odd look on his face. You open the door to a tall woman you don't know, wearing a navy blue suit and a kindly smile. Your husband opens the door wide and invites her in as she apologizes for being late. They turn and look at you with an expectation that make you wonder why this woman has come to your house.

As the three of you sit down in the family room, the woman turns to you and says, "Honey, I'm Barbara Perry, a social worker from the Department of Human Services. I'm sorry," she continues, "But we're going to have to move you." She tells you that you'll be moving to a new family and that they are very excited about you coming to live with them. You look at your husband as her words register. "Honey?" you ask, but your husband only looks away.

"There's nothing we can do," he says, and you can see that he is near tears. "It's not your fault," he adds, then, "We'll go and get her things."

Your heart pounds as your spouse and children quickly pack your belongings in whatever suitcase, paper bags, or boxes can be spared. Your mind is reeling. How could this happen? You wonder what you did to bring this about. You sift through the past few days and weeks and wonder what made your family so angry with you that they would send you somewhere else to live. "It's not your fault," your husband said. So why is this happening?

Before you can make sense of anything, your family has gathered around you to hug you and say goodbye. Your husband and children have tears flowing down their cheeks. You begin to cry, too. The social worker takes you to her car and says to get in and fasten your seatbelt. You leave familiar neighborhoods and streets behind and are surrounded by unfamiliar landscapes as the sun sets.

After a long drive, you pull up in front of another house in another town. A new family, strangers to you, opens the front door as you stand shivering under the porch light. "Hi, honey, I'm your new husband!" says one tall fellow. Unfamiliar children crowd around you, saying, "And we're your new children!" A flurry of introductions has names flying about your head like birds disturbed from their evening roost. You are taken to a new bedroom, your belongings piled into a corner, then offered some food. But you're not hungry, even though you haven't eaten since lunch. The smells of the garlic and onion from your last home are still in your clothes.

Everyone seems happy to have you there. The children keep talking excitedly about how glad they are to finally have you "home." You notice that the husband looks at you with worry in his eyes. You think he might understand your sadness and help you get back to your real husband, but then he smiles and pats you on the back and says something about being your "forever husband." You hardly hear another word until Mrs. Perry leaves. You mechanically go through the motions of getting ready for bed.

As you lie in a new bed in this new house full of strangers, your eyes fill with tears. You cry quietly into your pillow, but nothing will make the pain and confusion you feel go away. You miss your own bed; the patterns of light thrown on these new walls by passing cars are frightening. After lying awake a few hours, full of grief and fear, you finally fall asleep.

The next day you are given pancakes for breakfast by your new husband, even though you usually only eat fruit. Your stomach feels funny, but you eat some of the pancakes anyway. You are then taken to a new job where you are expected to start all over again with a new boss and co-workers. You spend the day trying to explain how you got there, though you don't even know yourself. Twenty-four hours after you left your other family, the family you'd called your own for years, you are back at the new place, amid new family members.

The smells, sounds, and even the taste of the food at your new house are different. At night you lie in bed with your new spouse and try not to let anyone know that you miss your old family. Is your husband thinking of you? What are your children doing? Do they miss you? You think about the things you left behind. You miss your cat. Will you ever see your family again? Can you go back? How are you supposed to just forget them and start all over again? You feel scared, unbelieving, and oh, so sad. There is a sadness in you that is so big you can hardly stand it. Everyone else is happy, though.

Why can't you feel better about being adopted?

THE CHILD'S ADJUSTMENT TO ADOPTION

No matter how needful or positive adoptions are from the perspective of the adults who facilitate or are party to them, being adopted is a confusing, frightening, and traumatic experience for the adopted child. Since most children with special needs are past infancy at the time they are adopted, most experience the move from foster family or institution into the adoptive family as a trauma, no matter how well the professionals and adults involved handle the move. All but the most severely handicapped children are aware of having new parents and new surroundings. Those children able to process the experience have normal grief reactions, and those who have been abused or suffered breaks in attachment in the past may have severe stress and grief reactions to being placed in a new family. The child may grieve for days or for weeks and months, or even for years; but the child will grieve. Adoptive parents who are understandably celebratory upon the arrival of a new child must be aware that in the midst of their joyful family lives a child whose experience of being adopted may be far different from their own. Like the divorced parent who remarries, the adoptive parent must be mindful that a child with a very different perspective is also involved.

INITIAL REACTIONS

In their new children, adoptive parents may see adjustment reactions temper tantrums, diarrhea, withdrawal, bed wetting, head-banging, depression, over-eating, poor appetite, and hyper-vigilance, among other reactions.

Children are born with a unique temperament and enter the adoptive family with their own particular histories. Although there are some responses to adoption that could be called "common," not every child will experience them. As well, the same behaviors can mean different things in different children. The following sections highlight some common adjustment reactions of the adopted child.

THE PERFECT CHILD

It is not uncommon for newly arrived children to be quiet, passive, and compliant. Some appear to be "perfect," doing what they are told to do, showing shallow affection, answering when spoken to, and staying out of trouble. Such children often have had more than one set of parents or caretakers and have come to feel that if they could only be good and stop making mistakes, sooner or later they would find parents who would keep them. Other "perfect" children are simply frightened out of their wits, numb from shock, and operating on something akin to an emotional autopilot. Such children will, after a period of grieving, usually begin to display a more spontaneous, joyful approach to life. Sometimes the child has been the oldest among siblings who were severely neglected or abused, and took on a parental role even at the age of three, four or five years. Or perhaps a child has cared for a mentally or physically ill parent.

The perfect child who stays "stuck" in perfection will benefit from therapeutic parental intervention. Some adoptive parents of "perfect" children have found that making light of their own mistakes not only provides comic relief, but also eventually drives home to the child the fact that perfection is not a prerequisite of being loved in the adoptive family.

Still other parents have found help for their children through individual therapy when a child's need for perfection persists in spite of the best efforts of the adoptive parent to express acceptance and forgiveness. Many adult adoptees speak of being the "good adoptee" out of a fear of being abandoned by the adoptive parent. Adoptee Betty Jean Lifton's book, *Journey of the Adopted Self*, speaks eloquently to this.

THE FEARFUL CHILD

Some hurt children manifest their feelings of worthlessness and shame by being fearful and unsure of themselves. They are passive observers of life rather than active, autonomous participants. This is particularly true of children who have lived in orphanages or institutions. Such children may also exhibit a profound mistrust of adults, including kindly adoptive parents. Displaced children have met kind social workers, kind foster parents, kind sponsors or kind orphanage workers who nevertheless "abandoned" the child by failing to give the child permanence. At any time, the new adoptive parents, kind as they are, may whisk the child away to yet another home. Why should the child trust new adoptive parents, when so many other adults have failed her?

Routine and consistency help with children who are fearful and anxious about being abandoned, which may describe the majority of older adopted children. Although many may express an air of competence, we have never met an older adopted child who has not experienced abandonment fears. Since every child is different, the adoptive parent cannot know whether the child will come to believe in the permanency of the parent's love after one hundred "proofs" of commitment and reliability, or one thousand, or one million.

Upon placement, the new adopted child may exhibit security with only one or two adoptive family members. If one parent traveled to escort the child from a foreign country, the child may cling to that parent. Conversely, the child who has had several mothers may reject the adoptive mother in favor of the adoptive father or a sibling. One adoptive mother tells the story of her newly arrived two-year-old who shunned every advance she made and persisted in calling everyone and everything—including the furniture—"mommy." Except for the actual mommy, of course.

Other children not only prefer one or two family members, but also become clingy. One of Anne's children adopted in late infancy had such a fear of abandonment that every time Anne left the child's sight outside the home, even if just for a moment, the child would wail and frantically run around looking for Mom. This behavior persisted until the child was eight years old. Children who perceive a move from a foster or birth family into adoption as being "taken from the family" (rather than as a rejection or a planned placement) react with extreme anxiety upon being left with a babysitter or losing sight of the adoptive parent. If the foster parent or birth parent "disappeared" suddenly without warning, and the child has not had cognitive and emotional help understanding the move, she may continue to fear being taken away from her new adoptive parents for some time to come. Such anxiety can be irritating to the parent, but with time and reliability, both child and parents can anticipate eventual relief.

NEW KID/OLD KID

Parents who already have children and then adopt find that rivalry between the "old" children and the "new" child or children is common. Even placements that begin amid the clamor of children begging for a new sibling may turn sour as the reality of the new child's presence sinks in. Typically it is the child closest in age to the newly-arrived child who has the hardest time accepting the "new kid." Newly arrived children require time and energy and receive a great deal of attention from the adoptive parents and their relatives and friends. Children who have been in the family a while, particularly those whose position in the family is most threatened, usually react by being irritable, complaining about the new child, arguing, and even attacking the new child.

Adoptive parents should not only prepare their children for the new arrival, they should also discuss the negative and positive feelings the children will have about their new sibling. Parents should also be clear and firm with their other children about behaviors and attitudes that are acceptable, and those that are not.

Another common reaction of children to a newly arrived sibling, especially among adopted children, is fear resulting from seeing that children are given up for adoption by their parents. Although adopted children in the family have (we assume) been told about their adoptions and understand that they have original parents who do not raise them, seeing a child suddenly arrive in the family as a result of being relinquished by, or taken from, her original parents can still inspire fear and sadness in other adopted children.

Finally, the newly arrived child may also become competitive with her new siblings upon realizing that there are more resources and less competition in the adoptive family than there were in the institution or foster family in which the child formerly lived. Post-institutionalized older children, in particular, have survived by being aggressive and successfully competing for limited resources. The new child may demand food, attention, or possessions and react aggressively if denied them. When thwarted, the child may throw terrifying tantrums.

SLEEP DISTURBANCES

One of the most common reactions to moving into the adoptive home is sleep disturbance. Newly arrived children are often unable to sleep at night, may have night terrors or nightmares, or may even walk in their sleep. They may be unwilling to sleep in the bed given them, preferring the floor or a new sibling's bed instead. Siblings who enter the same family, in particular, often want to sleep together. Children who come from cultures in which families share one sleeping room or the same bed initially have a difficult time adjusting to western sleeping arrangements. Such children are best served by being allowed to sleep in the way most comfortable to them, whether that means sharing the parental bed or sleeping on a pallet on the floor. An excellent book on the family bed is William Sears's book, *Nighttime Parenting.* The family bed is not for children with a known history of sexual abuse, or who have lived long in an institution, where sexual acting-out can be assumed.

The child may sleep excessively, being hard to awaken in the morning and sleeping often during the day. Either reaction results from the child's feelings of fear and insecurity. A child who has been traumatized and moved repeatedly has a hard time trusting his environment enough to relax and invite sleep. Other children may sleep too much in order to escape the reality of their many losses. Eventually these sleep problems should subside. Children who continue to have problems sleeping, or sleep excessively, should be evaluated by a professional for post-traumatic stress disorder, depression, or other psychiatric or medical illnesses.

ELIMINATION

Enuresis, or "Wetting"

It is not at all unusual for children to regress in toileting upon arriving at their new home. Fear, hostility, and anxiety all may result in bed-wetting at night or toileting accidents during the daytime. Some toileting problems may occur as a result of the child's change in routine and diet, which can cause an upset stomach. After some weeks or even months have passed, if elimination continues to be a problem, parents should consult a physician in order to rule out physical causes.

Some children adopted from other countries experience digestion problems due to parasites, some of which are not apparent until months after a child has arrived. Children adopted from undeveloped countries should be tested for parasites every four to six weeks during the first six months after arrival. One new mother of a Vietnamese infant was horrified to discover a six-inch worm in her new son's stool about eight weeks after he had arrived. Once the worm had passed, her son's appetite and health increased.

When a child has problems with enuresis, parents should educate themselves by reading a book or pamphlet from an organization specializing in this problem. Bed-wetting does not have to be a problem if parents understand the causes and the treatments.

Encopresis, or "Soiling"

Soiling that is not caused by an illness or disability is called encopresis. Children who have encopresis also often have other problems, such as short attention span, poor coordination, and a low tolerance for frustration. Not surprisingly, a child without a history of encopresis might start soiling after a sudden and major trauma, including a move into an adoptive family. As with enuresis, more boys than girls have the problem, and all school-age children with bowel control problems should be evaluated by a physician to rule out physical causes.

Most children can control their bowels by the time they are four years of age. Problems controlling bowel movements can cause soiling, which leads to frustration and anger on the part of the child, parents, teachers and others important to the child. The social stigma of encopresis can be severe as the child is ridiculed by his peers and even shunned by adults. Such treatment will leave the child feeling bad about himself.

Encopresis can result from problems during toilet training, physical or mental disabilities that make it hard for the child to keep himself clean, physical illnesses, or family or emotional problems. Children with persistent encopresis should be seen first by a physician and, if the problem is not resolved after sufficient time for adjustment has passed, by a psychologist or other mental health professional.

EATING

Newly placed children react to food in the adoptive home in different ways, both emotionally and physically. Many children who came from deprived backgrounds are unaccustomed to having a surplus of food available. Such children may over-eat or hoard food, if not both. Children who have been punished through the withdrawal of food may eat too quickly; others may eat with poor, if any, manners.

Due to the increased stress of the new adoptive placement, it is important that the entire adoptive family eat a good, balanced diet. Parents should take the lead and apportion food to the child rather than letting the child fill her own plate at first. Many parents also allow between-meal snacking on certain foods, such as raw carrots and fresh fruits, which they keep in good supply.

Children who are fearful about not being given enough food may persist in stealing food and hiding it. In such cases, parents should emphasize that food not properly preserved will spoil and make the child ill. They can make fresh food available to the child, store a covered container of healthy snack food in the refrigerator, or make other arrangements that are safe for the child. Even so, eating problems may persist over many months or even years for the older adopted child. Some parents report that their children have a seemingly unsatiable desire for sweets, while others eat until they are sick. Others have found their newly adopted children eating food stolen from the kitchen floor or trash can. With time and the acquisition of trust, most such problems are resolved, but parents should be alert to health-endangering eating problems such as over-eating, bulimia, or anorexia nervosa.

BELONGINGS

While some children hoard food, others hoard belongings. Few children come into the child welfare system or are placed with special needs without first having been deprived materially and emotionally. Such deprivation may cause the child to hoard objects, or, conversely, to have no sense of ownership and to be careless about whatever objects are given to him. In most cases, children will need to be taught which belongings are theirs and which are those of another person, how these objects should be cared for, and where they should be stored. The routine of caring for and storing possessions in and of itself can give displaced children some of the security they need.

Some children move into adoption having lost beloved possessions as well as people. One adoptive father comforted his two new children in their grief over losing so much when he replaced the Barbie doll and cowboy boots they had lost in their foster home.

EMOTIONAL REACTIONS

While some children show a near absence of emotions upon placement, others have intense emotional reactions such as anger, temper tantrums, crying, or hyperactivity. Some children may act silly, be overly talkative, or seem to be on "center stage," begging for attention through theatrical behavior.

Others are shame-based and react with intense humiliation and sorrow after making a mistake or being reprimanded for misbehavior. Sometimes parents must treat the adoptee with "kid gloves," or appeal to the child for months or years to come as a trauma survivor.

Many an adoptive parent of an older child has found that two or three years into the adoption, the adoptee continues to exhibit shame, anger, and sorrow on levels that seem much the same as those they experienced soon after placement. One myth about adoptive families has been that after 6-12 months, the adopted child should be fully adjusted to the family, and any problems arising after the first year must arise from faulty adoptive parenting.

The adoptee will revisit the traumas of separation and loss, rejection and withdrawal, over and over again as she matures and comes to a new understanding of adoption and family life. The process of adoption is never static, and adoptive parents who expect an instant or even an eventual resolution of all adoption issues for the adoptee misunderstand adoption from the adoptee's perspective. While some adoptees do resolve their loss issues, others say they never do. While some enter adoption happy, others seem to never cast a backward glance or think of what might have been.

INADEQUACY

Closely associated with the feelings of shame many adoptees carry with them is one of not being "good enough." Feelings of inadequacy seem to increase with the number of homes a child has had. Even though adults repeatedly tell the child that each move was not the child's fault, the child comes to believe that he is bad because so many parents have rejected him.

Children who wait long in the system come to believe that they are not good enough to be adopted because they are so often passed over. This is particularly true of children who are repeatedly shown at "adoption parties" and who are old enough to understand that the eager adults talking to them nervously are would-be adoptive parents. Each time such a child leaves a party without being matched, and every month the photolisting is sent out to no avail, he receives another psychic wound that reinforces the "not good enough" label. Although photolistings, waiting child columns and broadcasts, and "adoption parties" have been used so successfully to place many waiting children, some child advocates say they are damaging to children for these reasons.

GRIEF

The losses of adoption are difficult to grieve because our culture has no rituals for grieving losses such as the loss of one's birth family and subsequent foster families, the loss of one's dream of birthing children, the loss of a child who is taken from a parent because of that parent's own behavior, or the loss of children who are voluntarily surrendered. Yet all of the losses we experience in adoption are real, and all are accompanied by varying degrees of grief. This is as true for the child of four as it is for the adult of 64 years.

Elisabeth Kübler-Ross identified six stages of grief: Shock, denial, anger, bargaining, sadness or despair, and resolution. In adoption, we often hear people speak of "resolving" their adoption issues. In reality, a resolution is actually more of an acceptance of whatever reality adoption has brought into a person's life. For the child, accepting that she has two families, and knowing and accepting the "why?" of this reality, is enough.

Adoptees should be encouraged to mourn their losses as often as they remember them. For most children, this will mean a re-cycling of grief through various developmental stages, even into adulthood. Adolescence, marriage, childbirth, and traumas such as divorce and death will probably cause an adoptee to revisit her original losses. Birthdays, holidays, and anniversaries of past losses are often accompanied by grief. One adoptive mother we know makes it a point to light a "birth family" candle on the mantelpiece for each adopted child's birthday. She explains to the child that, though the birthday is a happy time, it is also a sad time because on that day the child's birth parents are probably thinking of the child, and she of them. The candle is a candle of remembrance of what the child has gone through before that birthday, an honoring of the past, and a grieving for it as well.

TIES TO OTHER FAMILY MEMBERS

Sometimes a child enters the adoptive family apart from siblings who have either remained in foster care or an institution, with the birth family, or gone into a different adoptive family. The loss of a sibling is a major loss for the adoptee, who may have only had an older brother or sister upon whom he could rely when he lived with a birth parent. Or, the older sibling might have taken on a parental role in the birth family, only to lose that role by going into adoption without his younger sibling(s).

Adoptive parents whose children have been separated from birth family members should do all they can to facilitate ongoing contact with siblings, aunts, uncles, grandparents, and birth parents, when contact is not a danger to the child or the adoptive family. We have known some adoptive parents who took matters into their own hands and proclaimed a total cutoff as being in their new child's best interests, when in fact the only interests they were protecting were their own. New parents naturally want to have the child all to themselves and may consciously or unconsciously encourage the adoptee to leave the past, and all it contained, including family members, behind.

Forcing such cutoffs is usually a mistake, for no one easily leaves lifelong attachments behind. Adoptees grow up and eventually come to know the truth for themselves. Though adoptive parents who selfishly cut off sibling, birth family, or foster family contact from a child may buy some short-term comfort and control with such actions, one day the adoptee will grow up. Research shows that the majority of adoptees want to re-connect with birth family members and search out their histories as adults. Many adoptees also seek out former foster families, foster siblings, half-siblings, and relatives they remembered from before their adoptions. When adult adoptees seek, and learn, the truth of their severed connections, they usually feel renewed grief, and especially anger, over the circumstances that led to their losses. If adoptive parents treat sibling and other attachments in the adoptee's early life with disregard, one day the adoptee may learn the truth. Many such adoptees have told us over the years that they have distanced themselves from their adoptive parents because their adoptive parents withheld such contact from them, discouraged it, or even threatened to abandon the adoptee if he or she searched or re-connected with birth family members.

PART III

REALITIES

CHAPTER 7

Living with Special Needs

I think I can, I think I can, I think I can.

—The Little Engine That Could

Living with children who have disabilities is a mixed bag of challenge and unique rewards. There is no need to reinvent the wheel when so many adoptive parents have gone before and have so much to share. Every adoptive parent of children with disabilities should have a support group or system, preferably specific to a child's disability.

What is the most challenging disability of all? Chances are you did not say emotional and behavioral disabilities. Yet research shows that the adoptions that are most difficult and the most likely to fail are those of children who have emotional and behavioral problems, particularly sexual promiscuity, physical aggression, stealing, vandalizing, suicide threats or attempts, and wetting or soiling (Rosenthal & Groze, 1992). Many experienced parents agree, saying that it is their children's emotional and behavioral disabilities, not physical ones, that are the most challenging to live with.

This chapter takes a broad look at the categories of special needs and at what it means for families to live with these challenges.

Many children who have special needs have histories that place them in the "at-risk" category. These kids have pre-natal drug or alcohol exposure, a history of abuse or neglect, or a birth family history of mental illness or disability. How such experiences affect children and the families who adopt them is discussed in the following sections.

ABUSE SURVIVORS

Physical Abuse

The statistics on physical child abuse are alarming. Of the estimated hundreds of thousands of children battered each year by a parent or close relative, an estimated 1,200 will die each year (Gelles & Straus, 1987; CWLA, 1994). For those who survive, the emotional trauma remains long after the external bruises have healed. Often the severe emotional damage to abused children does not completely manifest until adolescence or later, when many abused children become abusing parents. In 1987, Gelles and Straus estimated that severe parent-child violence in the United States has remained at 11 to 14 percent for the last ten years, defining "severe" physical violence as parental kicking, punching, hitting, biting, hitting with an object, beating, threatening with or using a gun or a knife against a child (Gelles & Straus, 1987). Children who have been physically abused may display:

- A poor self-image;
- Inability to depend on, trust or love others;
- Aggressive and disruptive behavior;
- Passive and withdrawn behavior;
- Fear of entering into new relationships or activities;
- School failure;
- Serious drug and alcohol abuse;
- Illegal (anti-social) behavior.

Battering is not the only kind of child abuse. Many children are victims of neglect, sexual abuse, or psychological (emotional) abuse. In fact, many studies show that physically abusive parents are also psychologically abusive. The following sections describe different types of abuse, their effects on children, and what adoptive parents can expect when parenting young abuse survivors.

Emotional or Psychological Abuse

John Briere defined psychological abuse in terms of eight parent or caretaker behaviors (Briere, 1992).

1. *Rejecting:* The child is avoided or pushed away and made to feel unworthy and unacceptable.
2. *Degrading/devaluing:* The child is criticized, stigmatized, deprived of dignity, humiliated, made to feel inferior, etc.
3. *Terrorizing:* The child is verbally assaulted, frightened, threatened with physical or psychological harm.
4. *Isolating:* The child is deprived of social contacts outside the family, not allowed to have friends, kept in a limited area for long periods of time without social interaction.

5. *Corrupting:* The child is "mis-socialized," taught to behave in an antisocial manner, encouraged to develop socially unacceptable interests and appetites.
6. *Exploiting:* The child is taken advantage of, used to meet the needs of his or her caretakers.
7. *Denying essential stimulation, emotional responsiveness, or availability:* The child is deprived of loving, sensitive caregiving; his or her emotional and intellectual development is stifled, the child is generally ignored or neglected.
8. *Unreliable and inconsistent parenting:* Contradictory and ambivalent demands are made of the child, parental support or caregiving is inconsistent and unreliable, and familial stability is denied the child.

Psychological abuse is often tolerated or even condoned in our culture. It is underreported because it is underrecognized. Many adoptive parents of older children find that, as their relationship with the new child unfolds, they become privy to many of the child's memories of past mistreatment. One child we know was left alone for days on end, with all meals being shoved through the door without comment. The child was allowed to attend school, but no other human contacts were allowed. The child often ate, slept, and lived in isolation, with other family members warned not to speak to the "bad child." The parents who designed this form of child "discipline" were upper-middle-class Caucasian adoptive parents, the child the casualty of a poorly executed private adoption. Neither the public school teachers who taught the child nor the neighbors surrounding the family would ever have defined these parents as psychologically abusive, or considered the child a victim. Yet had this same behavior been practiced in the child's biological family or that of a working- or welfare-class family, it probably would have been defined as "abuse." Some adoptive families of such children have found that their children were abused not only in their original family, but in subsequent foster and even adoptive families as well.

Parenting the Physical or Psychological Abuse Survivor

Children who have been physically abused react differently to such abuse, depending on the type of abuse, its frequency, severity, and how long the child was victimized. Not all children will display all symptoms, and some children may exhibit no symptoms at all, having buried all reactions to the abuse.

In considering how best to parent a child who has survived physical abuse, even torture, parents would do well to learn about how adults who have been victimized by rape, war, or other acts of violence have responded. Research shows that children respond to trauma and loss in much the same way as adults. Whereas some adults like to think of children as having resilience peculiar to childhood, this thinking is largely the result of myth. While some children can be said to be resilient survivors of abuse, showing few long-term side-effects, many more suffer varying degrees of trauma. Because every child is different, it is impossible to predict how a particular child will react to abuse or what the long-term effects of the abuse will be.

Post-traumatic Stress

Many adults became familiar with the term "PTSD," or post-traumatic stress disorder, after World War II and the Vietnam war. Returning prisoners of war or war veterans displayed psychological symptoms resulting from the terrible traumas they experienced during war time. Children react to traumatic events with like symptoms:

- nightmares
- intrusive thoughts
- flashbacks (intrusive thoughts accompanied by sensory memories that make the flashback seem real)
- a numbness or apathy and lack of responsiveness to the here-and-now
- sleep disturbance
- poor concentration
- increased startle response ("jumpiness")
- terror reaction to events that remind the survivor of the original trauma

Parents and therapists must insist on receiving a *complete history* of the child from the placing agency, including social worker chart notes that date back to the child's initial emergency intake into the child welfare system. Unless parents know the original circumstances of the child's abuse, they are unable to fully plan for successful parenting of the child.

Depression and Anxiety

Anxiety and depression accompany the survivor of childhood abuse much like Sorrow and Suffering accompanied Much-Afraid in Hannah Hurnall's Christian classic, *Hind's Feet on High Places.* Some research shows increased depression scores among adults who had histories of being emotionally abused as children. This comes as no surprise to adoptive parents of older children, many of whom come with a diagnosis of *dysthymia,* or mild depression. One dad described his daughter as "a kid who seems nearly always on the verge of tears, and who can't seem to get much enjoyment out of life." Adult children of alcoholics and children who have been sexually abused likewise show higher levels of depression.

Children who have been traumatized also experience an elevated sense of anxiety. Anxiety lingers in abused children long after the abuse has subsided. After living with an adult whose behavior is unpredictable and dangerous, the child learns to approach life and people cautiously and with no small degree of fear. He fears sudden attacks, pain, or maybe even death.

This residual depression and anxiety are sometimes accompanied by cognitive distortions that cause the child to continue to be hypervigilant, always watchful for danger or threat, and to have a need for control, since the child comes to believe that he can only protect himself through controlling his environment.. Some abuse survivors even interpret non-negative interactions as threatening. Adoptive parents must learn to walk, and talk, softly with such children.

Stinkin' Thinkin'

Twelve-step groups such as Alcoholics Anonymous and Al-Anon talk about "stinkin' thinkin'," inaccurate thinking that results from an addiction or living with an addict. Abuse survivors experience "stinkin' thinkin'," too. Psychologists call the negative and destructive thoughts that arise from such experiences *cognitive distortions.* Such thinking grows from a victim's reaction to actual abuse, as well as from the victim's interpretation of the abuse.

Those who abuse children often give the child a rationale for the abuse, such as telling the child she is bad or has misbehaved. The child comes to believe that she is, in fact, a "bad child," especially since many times abuse occurred in the context of no actual misbehavior on the part of the child. The child, in effect, becomes bad. John Briere calls this the "abuse dichotomy," the circular reasoning of abuse survivors that says, "I was (and continue to be) hurt because of my badness, and evidence of my badness is that I have been (and continue to be) hurt" (Briere, 1992, p. 28).

The messages given to the child by an abuser can find a lifelong home in the child's heart. Abusive parents often give the child a rationale for the abuse immediately before or during the abuse, such as, "You're getting what's coming to you," "You asked for it," or "You want more, don't you?" One of our children was taken to a telephone booth by his birth mother so that she could call the state agency to come and pick the child up. He overheard her telling a social worker, "Come and get him before I kill him. He's so bad, nobody can keep him." After disconnecting the phone call, she turned to her five-year-old child and said, "You know this is all your fault, don't you? You're a bad boy." The love, stability, and therapeutic interventions of his new adoptive family did nothing to decrease his violent acting out, sexual molestation of siblings, or fire-setting. His adoption failed, met with a shrug and a raised eyebrow on the part of the child, as if to say, "What can I do? I'm a Bad Boy."

Emotional Reactions

In addition to feeling chronic sadness, apathy, or anxiety, your adopted child may have other emotional reactions that linger long after he has left an abusive environment. He may be rigid and controlling, having learned that abuse is about the power of the strong over the weak. Some children tend to become aggressors through identifying with their abusers. Others, who learned to survive abuse by being passive receivers, have only passivity and helplessness among their coping skills when confronted with problems later in life.

Children who have been the victims of very severe and chronic abuse may also experience psychological problems such as dissociation (separating memories of abuse from one's consciousness) or, very rarely, multiple personality disorder. Such children may have no memory whatever of their abuse, even to the point of denying it ever happened.

Relationship Reactions

Perhaps the most troubling result of child abuse is the difficulty it causes for survivors in intimate relationships. Because the abuse originally occurred in the context of an intimate relationship, often the parent-child relationship, survivors may be conditioned to expect danger or pain in association with intimacy. Adoptive parents and, later, spouses of children who entered adoption because of abuse often experience more difficulty with the adoptee than anyone else. Besides constant fears of abandonment, the survivor may feel isolated and yet fear getting close in intimate relationships. Even infants who have been abused and neglected, or whose parents were simply emotionally unavailable, can exhibit ambivalence about close human relationships (Egeland, et al., 1983). Children who have been abused tend to either avoid closeness with others based on past experiences, or become willing to tolerate mistreatment or violence in close relationships, even seeing such violence as normal. Thus, the child who has been long mistreated will probably regard adoptive parents who do not use corporal punishment and never or rarely raise their voices as not only strange, but even as ineffectual parents.

Girls who have been abused, in particular, are in danger of later victimization by men either physically or sexually. Boys, on the other hand, may tend to be more accepting of violence or aggression in themselves than they ought to be.

Physical Reactions

The anxiety arising from ongoing abuse can lead to a variety of physical symptoms and ongoing problems. Sexual abuse survivors, in particular, have a higher rate of sexual dysfunction than those who have not been sexually abused. But survivors of physical and emotional abuse, too, have been found to experience problems such as stomach pain, sleep disturbances, headaches, nausea, asthma, eating problems (over- or undereating), muscle spasms, chronic muscle pain or tension, and high blood pressure.

Victims of childhood violence also may have problems that affect their health such as indiscriminate or early sexual activity, self-mutilation, substance abuse, over-eating or other food problems, and overt risk-taking. Having become accustomed to chronic anxiety, trauma, and distress in the abusive environment, the survivor may "engage in any of a number of external activities that anesthetize, soothe, interrupt, or forestall" painful feelings (Briere, 1992). Some parents say that their traumatized children seem to seek chaos or trauma simply because to them such drama has become "normal." Like codependent people used to living with an addict, they become "addicted to excitement in all their affairs." The challenge for the adoptive parent is to recondition the child to be able to tolerate some boredom or to seek excitement in functional ways, such as through sports, performing arts, or competition.

CHILD SEXUAL ABUSE

There is widespread disagreement among professionals and the public about how child sexual abuse is defined, and the legal definitions of child sexual abuse vary from state to state and culture to culture.

Researchers have identified child sexual abuse as involving behaviors such as sexual intercourse, oral and anal sex, and fondling of the breasts and genitals. Noncontact abuse refers to encounters with exhibitionists and solicitations to engage in sexual activity. Some children who have been sexually abused have been abused in these ways.

The Effects of Sexual Abuse

Many studies of children who have been sexually abused come from clinical populations—children who are being seen by a mental health professional. It is much more difficult to study children who have not been seen by a mental health professional, but some studies have indicated that there are children who survive child sexual abuse with few, or even no, bad effects. Such children are sometimes called *resilient children* or *resilient survivors.*

Emotional Effects

Among children being seen by counselors, several consequences of sexual abuse have been seen. Sexual abuse survivors express many feelings about having been sexually abused. *Guilt* is experienced by many, as are *anger* and *depression.*

Sexual abuse survivors also experience *anxiety.* Such anxiety is usually expressed through increased fearfulness, somatic complaints, changes in sleep patterns, and nightmares. The child may express or feel a sense of personal powerlessness, which arises from the child's inability to stop the repeated invasion of their bodies. Children who enter the child welfare or legal systems also experience increased powerlessness.

Sexual abuse victims also express a *sense of loss.* Loss is most keenly felt by children who have lost their families after being sexually abused. A child whose family supports the perpetrator and allows the child to go into foster care or adoption loses not only her family, but also her innocence, her sense of normalcy, and her trust in adults.

Sexual Effects

Child sexual abuse victims often express *heightened sexual activity,* both in childhood and later as adults. Some sexually abused children act in sexually provocative ways toward older males. Other children have what is known as "hypersexual behavior," which results from children whose erotic impulses have been prematurely awakened.

Several different researchers have found that adults who have been sexually abused as children report a history of many superficial and brief sexual encounters or sex with several different partners (Herman, 1981). Thus, the child who has been sexually abused is at higher risk for sexual problems in adolescence and adulthood. In addition, children who have been chronically sexually abused have learned that their genitals are valuable to the powerful adult. Prostitution is the logical outgrowth of such a value, and some studies have found a connection between sexual abuse in childhood and subsequent prostitution in adolescence or adulthood.

Behavioral Effects

Boys frequently react to sexual abuse by developing *aggressive behavior* in an attempt to reestablish their masculinity. They may pick fights, bully younger children, or display chronic disobedience and antisocial behavior. Boys who have not been sexually abused, but who are experiencing other stress, also have exhibited these behaviors, however.

Some researchers have noticed that children who have been sexually abused have higher *suicidal thoughts and actions.* Such children may also have more *para-suicidal behavior,* such as self-mutilation by cutting, burning, or scratching themselves. Any mention of suicide by a child should be taken seriously and immediate psychological help should be sought.

Physical Effects of Sexual Abuse

Children who have been sexually abused may afterward act in sexually provocative ways as a method of dealing with their anxieties over the abuse or with their prematurely-awakened erotic feelings. Thus, they may be more likely to be sexually abused again by an opportunistic individual or pedophile. Children who are experiencing ongoing sexual abuse tend to have physical symptoms such as stomach aches, headaches, urinary tract infections, and lack of appetite. Psychological symptoms include difficulty sleeping, nightmares, and minor mood swings. Socially, the child may experience a drop in grades at school, irregular school attendance, increased fighting or stealing at school or at home, and refusal to attend social activities. The child may also be withdrawn and display inappropriate sexual behavior. Several researchers have found that girls who have experienced sexual abuse often report chronic pelvic pain as adults.

A physical examination of a child who is the suspected victim of sexual abuse may not always establish that such abuse has, in fact, occurred. Research indicates that less than half of sexually abused girls had irregularities in the vaginal area and that the percentage of irregularities among non-abused girls who have vaginal infections or similar problems is similar to the percentage of those who had been sexually abused.

Parenting the Sexually Abused Child

Adoptive parents who consider or accept the placement of a child who has been sexually abused must prepare themselves to deal with more than the sexual abuse issues. Such children have often experienced several moves to different families or caretakers in their young lives. Many had chaotic and neglectful experiences while they lived with a birth parent or relative, and it was in such an environment that the sexual abuse occurred. Adoptive parents should realize that drug and alcohol abuse of a birth parent, relative, or partner of a birth parent may also have been involved. Thus, the foster or adopted child is dealing with sexual abuse trauma, one or more breaks in attachment, the loss of the birth parents and biological family, the results of emotional, psychological, physical, or medical neglect or abuse, and an adjustment to a new family. The child cannot and should not be expected to make such a move into placement easily or without visible symptoms.

Some children who have survived sexual or physical abuse make false abuse allegations against their new adoptive parents. The accusations may sound convincing because the child is describing actual abuse suffered prior to adoption. Children may make such accusations to seek revenge, to test new parents, as a manipulative ploy, or to sabotage the placement. See Chapter 12, "When Things Go Wrong," for information about how to handle false abuse allegations.

Some sexually abused children display sexualized behavior toward one or both new adoptive parents or to extended adoptive family members. Children may ask about the sexual habits of the adult, may take their clothes off, masturbate openly, or rub their bodies against a parent or fondle a parent. Such behavior may occur because some victims have learned that the behavior is an appropriate way to interact with adults. Other victims may be comparing the responses of the new parents and the abuser as a way of testing the sincerity of the adoptive parents and gauging the safety of the adoptive home.

Overt sexual behavior from a child is disconcerting to adoptive parents and is one of the most common reasons that adoptions of sexually abused children fail. An adoptive parent can make several responses to such sexualized behavior, and it is a good idea to plan a general response strategy ahead of time so that the parent can act with authority and in a purposeful manner. One tactic is to *establish clear guidelines about behavior in the family* and then remain predictable and consistent if the child breaks the rules. Parents who ignore the obvious behavior of the child to engage the parent through seductive behavior will lead the child to view the parent as unrealistic or phony. Parents should realize that overt sexual behaviors are inappropriate attempts by the child to relate to the parent, and can explain this to the child. Afterward, the parent can give the child suggestions about ways the child can relate appropriately to the parent.

The child who was sexually abused by a parent apart from physical abuse may associate the presence of sexual feelings with warmth and trust. In such a case, the parent can tell the child that she does not have to act in a sexual manner in all circumstances involving warmth and trust, and then offer alternatives.

Another tactic is for the parent to *say that inappropriate physical contact makes them feel uncomfortable and that they do not want to participate in such activity.* In this way, parents model the type of self-protective behavior that it is hoped the child will develop.

Children who have been abused may, over time, express positive feelings toward an abusive parent and begin to remember the good times and good qualities of the parent, which may be difficult for adoptive parents to accept. However, parents who discourage the child from expressing these loving feelings and good memories may teach the child that only certain feelings are acceptable. This perception may reduce the child's genuine expression of emotions in the adoptive family or in life outside the family. It is normal for children, including those who have been abused, to have fond feelings for their birth parents. Because the child's identity is intertwined with that of the biological family, the good qualities of biological family members are those that can be encouraged and emphasized in the child. Bad actions, on the other hand, should be identified as such, and people should be characterized as being lovable and having both good and bad qualities and of exhibiting both good and bad behaviors. The adoptive parent who characterizes a birth parent as "bad" teaches the child that a person can be only "bad," and is in danger of supporting the child's concept of himself as a "bad" child who was abused or given away because of his "badness."

School

Parents should anticipate that the sexually abused child may act out at with classmates or friends at school. They should consider sharing the child's history with the teacher or school counselor and devising a plan for handling any problems that may arise.

Helping a child to perform well at school is important to the child's self-esteem. Many children adopted at an older age have had checkered attendance histories. This, coupled with the trauma of abuse, moves in and out of the child welfare system, or into adoption, may have distracted the child from focusing mental and emotional energy into academics. Parents can help by giving the child tutoring or special academic help. Some parents have held the child back in school a year and others have opted to home school their child for a brief amount of time. There is more information about working with schools and educators in Chapter 9.

Damaged Goods

As mentioned earlier, many sexually abused children worry about why they were "chosen" to be abused. If they have been abused and subsequently relinquished for adoption, or taken from their birth parents, this concern will probably be heightened. These children may view the abuse as punishment for their misdeeds and believe themselves to be evil. Other children look at the abuse as a sadistic attack.

Adoptive parents can handle these fears in the child by emphasizing that many child molesters abuse several children and do not seem to pick victims because of their personal characteristics. Studies of pedophiles have showed that the average number of victims per pedophile is 62. Thus, the child was probably only one of many victims of a particular molester.

The child may also fear that he or she has been permanently damaged by the sexual abuse. A careful and thoughtful physical examination can help the child to understand what, if any, damage has occurred and what the consequences of such damage might be.

GOOD PARENT/BAD PARENT

The behavior of a sexually abused child may differ with men and women, and thus with fathers and mothers. Girls who have been abused may fear the new adoptive father or behave in sexually provocative ways if they have been abused by a male. They may often try to split the alliance of the mother and father by siding with one parent against the other. Girls may also act as if the mother is a rival with them for the father's attention. Or, boys may compete with the father for the mother's attention.

A child may be an "angel" with Dad and a "devil" with Mom. It is mothers, in fact, who tend to draw the most anger from the adopted child. Although this is not always the case, adoptive parents should be aware that each parent may have a very different experience with the child.

1132455

Parents can encourage growth in the right direction by refusing to allow the child to split the parental alliance. This can be done by agreeing beforehand that parents will make decisions jointly and will discuss such decisions apart from the child and present the child with a "united front." The child should not be allowed to ask Mom for something and, if denied, go to ask Dad and receive an approval. Parents will need to check with each other to discover whether the other parent has already made a decision.

Eventually it is hoped that parents will be able to discuss their ideas and decisions openly in front of the child so that the child can learn about healthy male-female relationships and shared responsibility and decision making.

FAS, FAE, FDE— PRE-NATAL DRUG EXPOSURE

The National Institute on Drug Abuse reports that over 750,000 women used alcohol during pregnancy between October 1992 and August 1993. Women who smoked and drank were more likely to also have used drugs (National Pregnancy & Health Survey, 1994). Many special needs adopted children have been exposed to drugs prenatally—alcohol, tobacco, marijuana, crack-cocaine. Such exposure results in birth defects in many cases.

There is no level of drinking during pregnancy that has been established as safe. Alcohol-associated disabilities generally occur with levels of alcohol consumption in the mother associated with drunkenness. Recent research suggests that very early gestational drinking before a mother even knows she is pregnant can produce brain damage that cannot be reversed with subsequent gestational abstinence (Clarren & Aldrich, n.d.).

Fetal Alcohol Syndrome (FAS) is recognized by the Federal Government as a unique developmental disability even when the IQ is normal. It is caused by alcohol exposure in utero. The following criteria must be evident for a diagnosis:

- History of pre-natal exposure to alcohol
- History of pre-natal and/or post-natal growth deficiencies
- Specific cluster of facial features
- Central Nervous System (CNS) damage, evidenced by possible mental retardation, behavior disorders, learning disabilities, and developmental delays

FAS is seldom identifiable at birth, and there are no lab or radiological tests to identify it. The child's early development may follow the normal curve. FAS children may be attractive and have no obvious handicaps while they are young.

The physical characteristics of children with FAS are most noticeable between ages two and 12 years. Such children are "short, scrawny, have similar facial features and permanent brain damage with lower levels of intelligence and learning problems coupled with difficulties in reasoning, memory and judgment which make them unpredictable and a potential threat to themselves and others" (Clarren & Aldrich, n.d.). FAS manifests itself in childhood as a mental or physical impairment, which is chronic, incurable, severe (58 percent have subaverage intellectual functioning), manifested in childhood, irreversible brain damage, substantially limiting in three or more of the following developmental areas:

- self-care (needs to be reminded to bathe, eat, dress warmly)
- receptive language (problems with comprehension)
- expressive language (superficial, difficulty with the abstract)
- learning (average adult reading is at fourth grade level, spelling at third grade level, math at second grade level)
- mobility (motor delays)
- self-direction (poor judgment and understanding of consequences)
- capacity for independent living (many are homeless or incarcerated)
- capacity for economic self-sufficiency (cannot keep a job or budget money)

Although more than half of all children with FAS do have below-average intelligence, about a third or more have average or above-average intelligence. As a result, FAS children are difficult to diagnose. The lack of cause-and-effect thinking and inability to plan ahead, especially when seen in adolescents and adults, are hallmarks of FAS.

Fetal Alcohol Effects (FAE) is a developmental disability caused by pre-natal alcohol exposure. FAE is sometimes referred to as the invisible disability because the facial features may appear normal. Consequently, organic brain damage is often unrecognized or misdiagnosed as a "conduct disorder," for example. Children or adolescents are often considered willful, stubborn, hyperactive, undisciplined, or even predatory when in reality they were permanently disabled by pre-natal alcohol exposure.

Fetal Drug Effects (FDE) is a phrase used to describe children thought to be affected in some way by pre-natal exposure to one or more drugs. The scientific study of FDE is new and complex, since most women who use illegal drugs during pregnancy also use alcohol or a combination of drugs. We do not know the long-term effects, and the prevalence of FDE is impossible to estimate at this time. There appears to be a growing number of children attending school that are prenatally affected by alcohol and drugs (Burgess & Streissgruth, n.d.).

POST-INSTITUTIONALIZED CHILDREN

Post-institutionalized children often suffer developmental effects from being institutionalized. At high risk for Attachment Disorder, auditory processing deficits, language disorders, delayed development, and autistic disorders are children who spent the early weeks, months, or years of their lives in orphanages or other institutions. We have seen an increase in the number of children experiencing these problems as Eastern Europe and the former Soviet

Union republics have opened their doors to Americans and others seeking to adopt their orphans. Americans flocked to Romania to adopt orphaned children. To all outward appearances, many were healthy and young. Parents expected that with love and stability, these Romanian orphans would thrive in American families—and most did.

Some post-institutionalized children do not fare well, however. Many have problems with other children and struggle with impulse control. Because they have had to rely on themselves for so long, some have not developed the ability to recognize adults who can help them with their problems; they have trouble with problem solving in general. Other formerly institutionalized children go through life in a robotic manner, having lost their spontaneity and ability to think and act in creative ways. Still others cannot persist at problem solving, make poor transitions to new activities, and have little ability to defer gratification. All these effects of institutionalization result in behaviors that are difficult for parents and teachers, and hard on children too.

Characteristics of children who have been institutionalized for the first three or so years of life include (The Parent Network for the Post-Institutionalized Child, Spring 1995):

- Inadequate personality development
- Inability to give or receive affection
- Hostile aggressiveness
- Temper tantrums, often of exceptional violence
- Enuresis or encopresis
- Speech defects (ranging to near mutism)
- Attention-demanding behavior
- Shyness and sensitiveness
- Difficulties surrounding food (refusal, fussy, slow eater, refusing meat, voracity)
- Stubbornness and negativism
- Selfishness
- Finger sucking
- Excessive crying
- Over affectionate or repelling affection
- Hyperactivity
- Seclusiveness
- Submissiveness
- Difficulties in school adjustment
- Sleep disturbances
- Fearfulness

Many post-institutionalized children may also be diagnosed with:

- Sensory Integrative Dysfunction (SID) (see related section)
- Attachment Disorder (known in the DSM-IV as Reactive Attachment Disorder) (see related section).
- Central Auditory Processing Disorder (CAPD)
- Conduct Disorder

- Attention Deficit Disorder (with or without Hyperactivity) (see related section).

Adopters from affluent societies should also consider that children coming from Eastern European and former Soviet republics often did not live in environmentally safe communities. Some, particularly those from Russia, have been exposed to lead, pesticides, heavy metals, and radiation. In Russia, the Ukraine, Poland, and other former Soviet republics, alcohol abuse is high among men and women, and children may have FAS or FAE besides showing the effects of institutionalization.

Central Auditory Processing Disorder

Post-institutionalized children often exhibit Central Auditory Processing Disorder (CAPD), which refers to the limitations in the ongoing transmission, analysis, organization, transformation, elaboration, storage, retrieval, and use of information contained in audible signals (see Post-Institutionalized Children). It may involve the listener's conscious and unconscious ability to filter, sort, and combine information at appropriate perceptual and conceptual levels. Children may score well on standard picture vocabulary tests, but often have a difficult time responding correctly to multiple commands, sequencing, and answering questions. These issues may lead to a misdiagnosis of Conduct Disorder because children do not follow verbal commands. Difficulty in reading comprehension or math skills may be apparent.

Auditory processing difficulties can be caused by chronic ear infections and auditory deprivation. Children may be hypo- or hypersensitive to sound. A child may dislike intensely the sound of a hair dryer, vacuum cleaner, lawn mower, or other loud sounds to the point of covering her ears at certain sounds or sound levels. Sounds that may be ignored by the parent are often noticed by the child, such as a high-flying jet or a far-off train. In the school setting, such problems may cause lack of attention in the classroom, leading to the mis-diagnosis of ADHD.

Children with auditory processing problems have difficulty making sense of what they hear and struggle to retain what they are hearing or have just heard. They especially have trouble with "wh—" question words, adjectives, pronouns, and prepositions. Although most transculturally adopted children learning English go through a phase of repeating words without understanding what they are saying, children with auditory processing problems persist at this, a habit called *echolalia.*

Some new therapies have been developed for the treatment of CAPD, including Auditory Integration Therapy (AIT). AIT consists of auditory stimulation using specially selected music processed through a machine that modulates, randomly, different frequencies present in the music. More information about the disorder can be found in the Appendix. Children who have spent time in institutions, particularly in foreign countries, are those who most commonly show signs of CAPD.

Sensory Integrative Dysfunction

Sensory Integrative Dysfunction (SID) is a neurological disorder identified by Jean Ayres in the 1970s. The disorder results in inefficient organization of sensory input received by the nervous system. Children who have been deprived of touch, movement, sound, and other normal sensory input may exhibit SID. The syndrome appears most often in institutionalized children (those in hospitals or orphanages). The characteristics of SID include:

- Overly sensitive to touch, movement, sights, or sound
- Underreactive to sensory stimulation (such as pain) or seek out intense sensory experiences (body whirling)
- Activity level that is unusually high or low
- Coordination problems
- Delays in speech, language, motor skills, or academic achievement
- Poor organization of behavior
- Poor self concept

Dr. Sharon Cermak, professor of occupational therapy at Boston University, volunteered at Romanian orphanage Bucharest No. 1 and later published *Romanian Children Show Sensory Defensiveness.* The book can be immensely helpful to adoptive parents who adopt post-institutional children, including those who have been hospitalized at length during infancy due to illness or disability. Children with spina bifida, prenatal drug exposure, and autism, it should be noted, sometimes also show SID symptoms.

MENTAL ILLNESS IN A BIRTH PARENT

Mental illness in birth parents represents a risk for children in the family. These children have a higher risk for developing mental illnesses than other children. The risk is particularly strong when the parent's illness is manic depressive illness, schizophrenia, alcoholism or other drug abuse, or major depression. When both parents are mentally ill, the chance is even greater that the child might become mentally ill later.

Risk can be genetically transmitted from the parents but can also come from living in a chaotic, sometimes frightening environment created by the mentally ill parent. Mental disorders can keep parents from providing the love and guidance necessary for a child's healthy development. An inconsistent, unpredictable family environment contributes to psychiatric illness in children similar to the results produced by abuse.

When a parent is mentally ill, and especially when both parents have mental illness or a child is living in a single-parent household, the child may become responsible for the adult. We have known of very young children, some even of pre-school age, who have had to take on responsibilities far beyond their capabilities.

When circumstances like this require a child to grow up too quickly, the child uses immature coping skills in order to solve adult problems. They become street-smart and expert at hiding the chaos of their home lives until they grow up. Once in adulthood, it becomes painfully obvious that the child never really was trained to manage her life the way a healthy adult does. Instead, the child just did the best she could for the mentally ill parent. Such adopted children are "nine years old inside, but 19 years old outside," as one such child has said.

Children whose birth parents were mentally ill need to know that the illness was not their fault and that, in spite of the parent's behavior, he or she still loved the child. The adoptive family offers stability for such children sometimes for the first time in their lives. Children who are naturally resilient and self-confident, often those we say are "survivors," can do well in adoption when allowances are made for their over-competence and parentified selves.

MENTAL, EMOTIONAL, AND BEHAVIORAL DISABILITIES

The effects of long-term abuse, institutionalized living, or repeated breaks in attachment, take their toll on the emotional lives of children. Adults who believe that children are naturally resilient or will somehow outgrow the effects of what brought them into adoption should stop and consider how the traumas many of our children suffer would affect any healthy adult. Children have fewer coping skills and less maturity than do adults. Being separated from one's family and familiar surroundings is trauma enough; having suffered months or years of abuse or chaotic living adds insult to injury. The results for most survivors are mental, emotional, or behavioral disabilities.

Some prospective adopters naively think that emotional disabilities will be eventually healed through love and stability. Such parents opt to adopt children diagnosed with behavioral or emotional disorders rather than physically or medically challenged children because they think emotional disabilities will be outgrown or cured. Emotional disabilities can sometimes be hidden, while physical disabilities cannot. Some emotional disabilities, such as Attachment Disorder, are particularly beguiling because children so diagnosed are superficially charming, attractive, and affectionate, captivating whoever will present an audience to their center-stage behaviors.

Parents who believe that children with physical disabilities are tougher to raise than those with emotional or behavioral disabilities will probably find that adopting the emotionally disturbed child is a rude awakening, presenting far greater a challenge than they could have imagined and offering fewer immediate rewards. Indeed, research with special needs families shows that parents of children with Down's syndrome, serious medical conditions, or multiple handicaps express very positive outcomes much more often than parents of emotionally disturbed children, and that emotional and behavioral problems are most often a factor in failed adoptions (Rosenthal & Groze, 1992).

Nevertheless, we advocate the adoption of children with emotional and behavioral problems. Though each of us has experienced the failed adoption of emotionally disturbed children, we have each also gone on to successfully parent such children again. The difference is in knowing a child's whole, unadulterated history, knowing oneself, and being able to say "no" to the referral of a child whose problems will only exacerbate our own.

People who adopt waiting children with emotional disabilities need to know that their children are just as impaired as those who cannot walk or see or hear. A child whose limbs are paralyzed will not be cured through good parenting, though good parenting will help such a child live up to his full potential. Likewise, a child who is emotionally handicapped will not be "cured" through enough love and stability, though we would like to think so. Israel's patriarch, Jacob, wrestled mightily all night long with an angel. He came away with a blessing and a lifelong limp. Likewise, our children who come to us after mighty wrestlings can leave our families and enter adulthood with a blessing—and a lifelong emotional disability that will continue to need extra attention.

ATTACHMENT DISORDER

Attachment Disorder, known by clinicians as Reactive Attachment Disorder of Childhood, is a disorder that causes people to have difficulty forming loving, lasting, intimate relationships. The words "bonding" and "attachment" are often used interchangeably in special needs adoption, although among social scientists these words do not have the same meanings.

Attachment Disorder (AD) can vary in severity from mild to moderate to severe, but the diagnosis is usually reserved for people who show a severe inability to be truly affectionate or caring with others. AD children usually fail to develop a conscience and find it difficult, if not impossible, to trust.

Parents may see some, most, or even all of the following symptoms:

- superficially engaging, charming (phoniness)
- lack of or poor eye contact
- indiscriminately affectionate with strangers
- lacking ability to give and receive affection (not cuddly)
- lack of self-awareness
- extreme control problems, often manifest in covert or sneaky ways
- destructive to self and others (aggression)
- cruelty to animals
- chronic, crazy lying
- poor or no impulse controls
- learning lags and disorders
- lacking cause-and-effect thinking
- lack of conscience

- withdrawal
- over-competency
- abnormal eating patterns
- poor peer relationships
- preoccupied with fire, blood, gore, and violence
- persistent nonsense questions and incessant chattering
- inappropriately demanding and clingy
- abnormal speech patterns
- chronic control issues with others
- trouble recognizing own feelings or those of others
- lacks spontaneity; difficulty having fun

There are many possible causes of Attachment Disorder, but the following circumstances or events place a child at risk for the disorder:

- Physical, emotional, or sexual abuse
- Neglect
- Frequent moves or placements (foster care, failed adoptions)
- Inconsistent or inadequate day care
- Chronic maternal depression or post-partum depression during an infant's first year
- Hospitalization of the child, causing separation from the parent
- Unrelieved physical pain
- Parents who are attachment disordered, leading to abuse and neglect
- Inappropriate parental responses not leading to a secure or predictable relationship.
- Genetic factors
- Pervasive developmental disorders
- Caregivers whose attachment needs aren't met, leading to overload and lack of awareness of a child's needs

Prospective and new adoptive parents sometimes think that their risk of adopting an attachment-disordered child is decreased when they adopt a child under two or three years old. Unfortunately, this is not the case. Every child who has experienced abuse or neglect, even the youngest, is at risk for Attachment Disorder. As many parents adopting Eastern European orphanage infants discovered, the youth of a child alone cannot prevent Attachment Disorder from developing. In fact, the first year of life is critical in developing a secure attachment, and no child entering adoption from our child welfare system, an orphanage, or other institutional care can be considered immune to attachment problems. Although every child adopted after the first year of life will not have attachment problems, all adopted children have experienced a break in attachment. Some such breaks may occur even in the womb, when a child is carried in what some have called a *hostile womb,* or by mothers who are ambivalent or unhappy about being pregnant. Children may thus be securely attached, inadequately attached, insecurely or ambivalently attached, or unattached.

Parenting the Attachment-Disordered Child. Parenting children with attachment difficulties is a job that requires a great deal of patience, understanding, courage, solid support systems, and personal fortitude. Children with attachment difficulties rarely and only superficially return love. Therapists, teachers, child protective services, and even spouses often do not understand the challenge and deception an unattached child displays toward an adoptive or foster parent in charge of primary care. Oftentimes the child will project the greatest amount of pathology towards the mother-figure in attempt make the world believe that if the mother was not so harsh and controlling, the child would be as lovable as she professes to be.

Parents who are adopting a traumatized child or any child with a history of neglect, abuse, multiple caregivers, or institutional living should have the child evaluated for attachment disorder by a professional experienced in assessing attachment. Children going into adoption are best assessed *before* the adoptive placement, since the child will have no attachment to the adoptive parent, but may have an attachment to the previous caregiver. More information about attachment disorder and finding help for attachment-disordered children can be found in the Appendix of this book.

Attachment Therapy. The therapist's first introduction to attachment disorder is usually through the parent. The professional meets a parent who is angry, resentful, and full of blame toward a child who is charming, full of energy, affectionate, and apparently confused by the anger the parent expresses. The unsuspecting therapist often reacts by thinking, or even saying, "If Mother would stop being so controlling, maybe this poor child wouldn't have so many problems!" The therapist, naively believing that "all this kid needs is love," creates an alliance with the child against the parents, possibly even preventing the family from getting the help they so desperately needed.

The basic purpose of attachment therapy is to help the child resolve a dysfunctional attachment. The goal is to help the child bond to the parents and to resolve the child's fear of loving and being loved. Children with Attachment Disorder or insecure attachments may already have been diagnosed with Oppositional Defiant Disorder or Conduct Disorder. Many have a secondary diagnosis of Attention Deficit Hyperactivity Disorder. The child's symptoms could also be understood as a Post-Traumatic Stress Disorder or depression stemming from a delayed grief reaction in response to one or more significant losses early in childhood.

Traditional therapy is often not successful with attachment disordered children because the child is unable to form a positive therapeutic relationship or trust with the therapist. Confrontational or "rage reduction" therapies that involve holding techniques or high challenge or confrontation (such as Outward Bound or other wilderness experiences) have been more successful in treating attachment disordered children but are also controversial. Parents adopting children with breaks in bonding or other risk factors in their backgrounds must arm themselves beforehand with information and training specific to parenting children with emotional and behavioral problems. Two excellent books about helping AD children are Keck and Kupecky's *Adopting the Hurt Child* and Martha Welch's *Holding Time.* See Chapter 8, "Finances," for information about a financial safety net for AD children.

ADHD: Children Who Can't Pay Attention

Children who are diagnosed with Attention Deficit Disorder (with or without Hyperactivity) have a pattern of behavior that combines impulsivity, inattention, and sometimes hyperactivity that begins before age seven. AD(H)D affects children at home and at school, but often is not formally diagnosed until a child begins school. Children who have spent any time in the child welfare system may be diagnosed more often, since the nature of the system and its changes of routine and caretakers usually increase the usual symptoms of ADHD.

Inattentive children are characterized by:

- leaving tasks unfinished
- being easily distracted
- have problems sticking with a play activity
- problems concentrating on school work or other tasks

Impulsive children often act in these ways:

- act before thinking
- have less temper control
- rapidly move from one activity to another
- have problems organizing work
- need a great deal of supervision
- are often disruptive in class
- have problems taking turns or waiting for their turn

Hyperactive children often act in these ways:

- have problems sitting still
- are always "on the go"
- have difficulty staying seated
- are harder on clothing and belongings

Some children have ADD without hyperactivity, but still have the characteristics of impulsivity and inattention. Others have hyperactivity as well. Children are diagnosed with ADD or ADHD by a medical professional, either a doctor or a psychiatrist, through testing, interviews with parents and teachers, and the use of child behavior checklists. After a child is diagnosed, treatment involves medical and nonmedical interventions. Nonmedical intervention can involve behavior management, more structure in the home and school, a special diet, and sometimes special education in the school setting.

Medical intervention involves using medication to control some of the child's symptoms. Medications such as methylphenidate (Ritalin or Cylert) or d-amphetamine (Desedrine) are typically used. Drugs that have a central nervous system stimulant effect in adults have just the opposite effect in children, and are often used to curb symptoms of distractibility, impulsivity, and hyperactivity. Sometimes anti-depressants such as imipramine (Tofranil) and beta-adrenergic blockers such as propranolol (Inderal) are used with good results. When drug therapy is used, it is managed by a physician and involves periodic blood tests and monitoring of the child's weight, height, and behavior. Research clearly documents that medication can be helpful, and that medication prescribed for ADHD works best as part of a comprehensive plan of treatment including ongoing evaluation and, often, medical psychotherapy for the child, help for the family, and consultation with teachers.

Without proper treatment, children diagnosed with ADD may fall behind in schoolwork, and friendships may suffer because of poor cooperation in playing and other social activities. Self-esteem suffers because the child experiences more failure than success and is criticized by teachers and family who do not recognize a health problem.

ADHD has been associated with pre-natal or peri-natal trauma, maturational delay, fetal alcohol syndrome or lead poisoning, and even food allergies. Some physicians and parents believe that excessive sugar or allergies to food additives, milk, or wheat can increase symptoms of inattention and hyperactivity, but research has failed to entirely support this theory. Research has indicated a genetic component and possible metabolic abnormality in the brain causing ADHD. As well, there is increased hyperactivity in children whose original families had alcoholism or antisocial behaviors (Cadoret, 1990).

There is a high rate of co-existence of other psychiatric disorders with ADHD, particularly oppositional and conduct disorders. Approximately 25 percent of children diagnosed with ADHD also have a learning disability. Studies also show that children with ADD are more likely to fail a grade in school, drop out of school, underachieve, and have social and emotional adjustment problems. Identification and treatment of the problem can reduce the risk for these problems, but ADHD itself is a disorder that continues into adulthood.

Because children waiting to be adopted are much more likely to have AD(H)D than children in the general population, prospective adoptive parents should be informed about ADD and its impact on family living. Anne and Rita each have sons diagnosed with ADHD and have learned, as have many other adoptive parents, that these sons are hard on clothing and belongings, more prone to fights and arguments at school, and have a tougher time disciplining themselves to complete school work. They require more structure at home and at school.

Some suggestions for parents of children who have ADD are:

- Supervise the child closely, especially the young child.
- Be consistent in rules and discipline.
- Speak quietly and slowly.
- Insist on eye contact to maintain attention.
- Keep your emotions "cool."
- Brace yourself for expected turmoil.
- Avoid a universally negative approach characterized by "don't" and "stop."
- Separate disliked behavior from the child (say, "This is bad behavior," not "You are a bad child.")
- Have a clear routine for the child including times for play, work, naps, meals, and bed, interwoven with physical activity that will release excess energy.
- Demonstrate new or difficult tasks, or tasks with several steps, and help the child practice.
- Give the child responsibility.
- Consider giving the child his own space.
- Become familiar with the child's pre-explosive warning signals.
- Restrict playmates to one or two at a time.
- Know the name and dose of medications, and possible side-effects.
- Openly discuss with the physician fears you have about use of medication.
- Lock up all medications.
- Always supervise the taking of medication.
- Share your successful techniques with the child's teacher or others (support group leaders, parents of children with ADHD, home schoolers if you home school).

Finding Help for Hurt Kids

Older children entering adoption can require a great deal of therapeutic support. Post-placement social worker visits may not provide as much support as the child needs, and many children coming out of the foster care system continue to need counseling for years.

Experienced adoptive parents, however, are often heard to complain that most professionals are inexperienced with adoption, perceiving adoption as a happy ending to a sad story, and expecting that the traumatized child will be assimilated into the family within 6 to 12 months, eventually living "happily ever after." Both Rita and Anne have had to work with professional counselors or psychologists who believed that adoption would actually erase their children's emotional scars left by breaks in bonding and attachment and past abuse. Such professionals discount the parents' assertion that a child's acting-out is the result of past traumas. Instead, many counselors inexperienced with older child adoption will tell parents that it is their current parenting style, rather than past traumas, that are the source of the child's problems. Other professionals believe that the results of abuse are lifelong and cannot be resolved by any means. Adoptive parents are usually looking for a therapist who understands abuse and separation from one's original family as traumas that can be healed through love and patience, but which will leave emotional "scars." Like accident survivors, our adopted children will go through life with some emotional scars that, though healed, show evidence that a trauma happened long ago.

How can parents find a therapist who is experienced with adoption or who is open to such concepts? As we wrote in an earlier chapter about advocacy, parents must begin by advocating for the child to receive services appropriate to the child. If a child needs ongoing therapy, then the parent must find the therapist best suited to the child's circumstances and personality. They must also find a therapist who will work with the parents, not against them. Attachment style parenting is often more controlling and intrusive to a child than normal parenting requires. Professionals may label adoptive parents trained in love-and-logic parenting as overbearing. Likewise, parents who train their formerly abused children, particularly those who have been sexually abused, in assertiveness skills might be called over-protective or too permissive, depending on the focus of their parent-child interventions.

Following are some guidelines parents can use when evaluating professionals who may give services to the newly-adopted child. Parents should engage a therapist:

- who has had experience working with adoptive families and adoptees whenever possible;
- with whom both parents and child feel comfortable;
- who has been trained in family systems theory;
- who is willing to see the entire family together from time to time;
- who has specialized training in areas in which the child has need (i.e., specialized training and experience in working with sexually abused children if the child is a sexual abuse survivor);
- who is willing to learn from the parents and to teach the parents;
- experienced and trained about separation trauma, the effects of abuse, and attachment;
- who can assist parents with here-and-now parenting issues as well as the child with situations that occurred in the past.

Types of Treatment Programs. Communities provide different types of treatment programs and services for children and adolescents with mental illnesses. A complete range of programs and services is called the continuum of care. Not every community has every type of program on the continuum.

When parents are concerned about their child's behavior or emotions they should start with an evaluation by a qualified mental health professional. At the conclusion of the evaluation, the professional will recommend a certain type of program from what is available in the community. Each type of program on the continuum offers several forms of treatment, such as individual psychotherapy, family therapy, group therapy and medications. The programs that may be used include:

- Office or outpatient clinic: Visits are usually under one hour. The number of visits per week depends on the youngster's needs.

- Intensive case management: Specially trained individuals coordinate or provide psychiatric, financial, legal and medical services to help the child or adolescent live successfully at home and in the community.
- Home-based treatment program: A team of specially trained staff go into a home and develop a treatment program to help the child and family.
- Day treatment program: This intensive treatment program provides psychiatric treatment with special education. The child usually attends five days per week.
- Partial hospitalization (day hospital): This provides all the treatment services of a psychiatric hospital, but the patients go home each evening. Emergency/crisis services: 24-hour-per-day services for emergencies (for example, hospital emergency room, mobile crisis team).
- Respite care: A child stays briefly away from home with specially trained individuals.
- Therapeutic group home or community residence: This therapeutic program usually includes 6 to 10 children or adolescents per home, and may be linked with a day treatment program or specialized educational program.
- Crisis residence: This setting provides short-term (usually fewer than 15 days) crisis intervention and treatment. Patients receive 24-hour-per-day supervision.
- Residential treatment facility: Seriously disturbed patients receive intensive and comprehensive psychiatric treatment in a campus-like setting on a longer-term basis.
- Hospital treatment: Patients receive comprehensive psychiatric treatment in a hospital. Treatment programs should be specifically designed for either children or adolescents. Length of treatment may be acute (a few days to 30 days) or intermediate (30 to 120 days).
- Attachment Center: Treatment centers and programs specific to Attachment Disorder are available throughout the country. See the Appendix for information.

In-Patient Psychiatric Treatment. Children who have emotional, psychiatric, or behavioral disabilities may have had or may need in-patient psychiatric treatment at some time. hen in-patient treatment is proposed for a child or teenager, the parents should ask the following questions:

- Why is psychiatric inpatient treatment being recommended for our child, and how will it help our child?
- What are the alternatives to hospital treatment, and how do they compare?
- What does the treatment program for inpatient treatment include, and how will our child be able to keep up with school work?
- What are the responsibilities of the people on the treatment team, and who are they?
- How long will our child be in the hospital, and how do we pay for these services?
- What will happen if we can no longer afford to keep our child in this hospital and inpatient treatment is still necessary?
- How will we as parents be involved in our child's hospitalization, including the decision for discharge and after-care treatment?
- Will we be allowed to attend staffings about our child?
- Is this hospital approved as a treatment facility for youngsters of our child's age, or will our child be on a specialized unit or in a program accredited for treatment for children and adolescents?
- How will the decision be made to discharge our child from the hospital?

- Once our child is discharged, what are the plans for continuing or follow-up treatment?
- Do you have any outcome studies available about results from the particular treatment program in which our child will participate?

Hospital treatment is a serious matter for parents, children, and adolescents. Parents should raise these questions before their child or adolescent is admitted to the hospital. Parents who are informed about the hospital's treatment plan and procedures can fully contribute to the effectiveness of their child's treatment.

Learning Disabilities

Adoptees are more likely than non-adoptees to have a learning disability or other condition (such as Attention Deficit Disorder/ADD) that makes learning a challenge. Adoption experts theorize that people who surrender children for adoption may be more prone to having genetically based learning problems or impulsivity. Or, adoptees may be predisposed to developing learning problems due to experiences in the womb, such as lack of prenatal care, drug or alcohol usage of the birth mother, high anxiety levels during pregnancy, or the effects of separation from the mother. Finally, early experiences in infancy and toddlerhood such as neglect and abuse may also predispose the adoptee to developing learning disabilities or attention deficit hyperactivity disorder (ADHD or ADD).

Whatever the cause of learning disabilities, adoptive parents will find that raising a child who has learning disabilities will make the process of learning more difficult for the child. Adoptive parents who have high expectations of the adopted child academically will do well to adjust their expectations according to the child's abilities.

Having learning problems in school can set the child up for a series of failures, which in turn can cause the learning disabled child to believe that he or she is "dumb," and to even believe that an adoption occurred because the child had problems.

Child and adolescent psychiatrists point out that learning disabilities are treatable, but if not detected and treated early, they can have a tragic "snowballing" effect. For instance, a child who does not learn addition in elementary school cannot understand algebra in high school. The child, trying very hard to learn, becomes more and more frustrated, and develops emotional problems such as low self-esteem in the face of repeated failure. Some learning disabled children misbehave in school because they would rather be seen as "bad" than "stupid."

Parents should be aware of the most frequent signals of learning disabilities, when a child:

- Performs differently from day to day.

- Has difficulty understanding and following instructions.
- Has trouble remembering what someone just told him or her.
- Forgets easily.
- Fails to master reading, writing, or math skills, and thus fails schoolwork.
- Has difficulty distinguishing right from left—for example, confusing 25 with 52, "b" with "d," or "on" with "no."
- Lacks coordination—in walking, sports, or small activities such as holding a pencil or tying a shoelace.
- Has poor coordination.
- Late gross or fine motor development.
- Has trouble naming familiar people or objects.
- Does not adjust well to change.
- Difficult to discipline.
- Easily loses or misplaces homework, schoolbooks or other items.
- Cannot understand the concept of time; is confused by "yesterday," "today," "tomorrow."

Such problems deserve an evaluation by an expert. A professional who commonly works with children will work with the school professionals and others to have the necessary comprehensive evaluation and educational testing done to clarify if a learning disability exists. After talking with the child and family, evaluating their situation, reviewing the educational testing, and consulting with the school, the professional will make recommendations on appropriate school placement, the need for special help such as special educational therapy or speech-language therapy, and steps parents can take to assist their child in maximizing his or her learning potential. Sometimes individual or family psychotherapy will be recommended, and sometimes medication will be prescribed for hyperactivity or distractibility. It is important to strengthen the child's self-confidence, so vital for healthy development, and also to help parents and other family members cope with the realities of living with learning disabilities.

MENTAL RETARDATION

Parents of children with mental retardation are among the happiest and most satisfied of all adoptive parents (Rosenthal & Groze, 1992). Although raising a child with mental retardation has its challenges, experienced adoptive parents say the joys far outweigh the sorrows because they are able to experience the world through the eyes of their perpetually innocent children.

The term "mental retardation" is often misunderstood and seen as derogatory. It is the diagnostic term used in the *DSM-IV*, and is the term we use in this book. Some think that retardation is diagnosed only on the basis of below-normal intelligence (IQ), and that retarded persons are unable to learn or to care for themselves. Actually, in order to be diagnosed as mentally retarded, the person has to have both significantly low IQ and considerable problems in adapting to everyday life. However, most children who are retarded can learn a great deal, and as adults can lead at least partially independent lives. Most important, they can enjoy their lives just as everyone else.

In the past, parents were usually advised to institutionalize a significantly retarded child. This is rarely done today. Now these children are expected to live in a family and take part in community life. The law guarantees them educational and other services at public expense, although public school programs for handicapped children are under attack.

Retardation may be complicated by physical and emotional problems. The child may also have difficulty with hearing, sight, or speech. All these problems can diminish the child's potential and provide additional challenges to parents.

It is very important that the child has a comprehensive evaluation to find out about his or her difficulties as well as strengths. Since few specialists have all the necessary skills, many professionals might be involved. General medical tests as well as tests in areas such as neurology (the nervous system), psychology, psychiatry, special education, hearing, speech and vision, and physical therapy are useful. The family doctor, pediatrician, or an educator can refer the child for the necessary tests and consultations, put together the results, and jointly with the family and the school develop a comprehensive treatment and education plan. Early intervention programs are available for the youngest children and have been found to be extremely beneficial to children with mental retardation. Thus, the earlier a child is diagnosed with mental retardation, the better for long-range planning.

The definition of mental retardation has three components:

1. Intellectual functioning is sub-average (IQ below 75);
2. The deficit results from an injury, disease, or abnormality that existed before age 18;
3. The individual is impaired in his or her ability to adapt to the environment as evidenced in at least two of the following areas: communication, self-care, home living, social or interpersonal skills, use of community resources, self-direction, functional academic skills, work, leisure, health, and safety.

The IQ score can be considered a percentage of normal intelligence. Thus an eight-year-old with an IQ of 75 would have a mental age of a normal six-year-old. Intelligence growth is not believed to extend beyond age 16, so this can be used as a baseline for calculating the mental age of a retarded adult. Thus a child with an IQ of 50 would be expected to have a mental age of about eight as an adult. The adult will obviously be different than the child because he has had much more experience, but may not have the ability to think abstractly or to adapt to change. Down's syndrome, spina bifida, and cerebral palsy are all associated with mental retardation, although not all children diagnosed with these conditions will have intelligence that falls in the retarded range. Table 7.1 shows the degrees of mental retardation and the possible attendant capabilities of the person with mental retardation.

Table 7.1
Degrees of Mental Retardation

Severity	Mild	Moderate	Severe
IQ RANGE	50-75	35-50	Less than 25
EDUCABILITY	yes	no	no
TRAINABILITY	yes	yes	no
INDEPENDENT LIVING	often	with some supervision	no
ROUTINE SELF-CARE	yes	yes	limited
VOCATIONAL CAPABILITY	often	in sheltered workshop	limited or none

Mental Retardation and Other Disabilities

Parents of children who have mental retardation and a physical disability naturally find that their parenting has more challenges. Whereas a child of average or above-average intelligence could problem-solve and compensate for his disabilities, the child who is retarded and physically disabled is often thwarted by his handicaps. In addition, cerebral palsy and spina bifida can be associated with learning disabilities and seizure disorders that cause further insults to the child's cognitive functioning. Parents interested in adopting a child with multiple handicaps that include mental retardation should take a long look at their energy level, health, and support systems beforehand.

PHYSICAL DISABILITIES

Children with physical disabilities comprise a substantial minority of children waiting to be adopted today. Their disabilities range from minor, temporary, and correctable to permanent and life threatening. Volumes have been written about the thousands of disabilities and disorders. The National Organization of Rare Disorders lists many rare conditions and is an excellent resource for individuals considering adopting a child with physical handicaps. We highly recommend that all adoptive parents buy a good medical encyclopedia and make use of many of the resources we suggest in the Appendix of this book to learn more about specific disabilities.

The most common physical disabilities seen among adopted children are vision, hearing, or other physical impairments, including orthopedic disabilities. Few legally blind or hearing-impaired children are listed in the national exchanges, however, because they are placed through exchanges or support systems specific to waiting children who have those disabilities. Physical disabilities more commonly seen among children listed through adoption exchanges are cerebral palsy, limb deformities or missing limbs, bone diseases, and poor coordination. Other handicapping conditions that may fall into this category are seizure disorders and burn scars, which may impair a child's mobility.

Orthopedic Impairments

Orthopedic impairments are those problems that make standing, walking, or running difficult or impossible for the child. These may include post-polio complications, spina bifida, cerebral palsy, missing or deformed limbs, and birth defects that make walking a challenge or even impossible.

Parents who raise children with significant orthopedic impairments say that having a child who uses a wheelchair or other mobility aids only slows the family down insofar as society enables barriers to continue. Although federal law requires that all public and government buildings be accessible to the handicapped, not all are in compliance yet. Parents adopting a child who has significant orthopedic problems may need to make structural changes to their home, buy a new vehicle that allows for installation of a wheelchair lift, or even move to accommodate the child's disability.

Anne, whose family includes a child with Spina Bifida, writes: "We have found the greatest barriers to exist, interestingly enough, on the university campus only miles from our home. Sports arenas and stadiums probably present the biggest barriers, followed by concert halls, movie theaters, restaurants, and churches. Because our church is not wheelchair accessible, two men must carry our nine-year-old daughter and her wheelchair up and down the stairs to Sunday School every Sunday. Because of her personality, she enjoys the ride; but it continues to trouble me that some of the most important buildings in my college community are not accessible to wheelchairs, or allow only minimal access. When we go to a basketball game or concert, we must stand in the back, while our daughter sits behind a concrete wall that totally blocks her view. When we go to the movies, because parking her wheelchair in the aisle presents a fire hazard and violates the fire code, we must sit in the very back of the theater in a row that is too short for our large family. It is an ongoing frustration that has become a part of our regular lives."

We know several families whose children use wheelchairs, walkers, or crutches, and have noticed that such children are often singled out publicly for special attention, either positive or negative. One friend has a son whose missing limbs regularly cause strangers to approach him and offer money. Another has a child who is often approached by elderly shoppers and given dollar bills. And, one cold January morning, a Department of Human Services social worker stood at Anne's front door because a neighbor had complained that her daughter was sitting in her wheelchair and waiting for the school bus "in plain sight, out in the cold." In the same neighborhood, this child's siblings and more than 30 other able-bodied children waited outside in the cold for the school bus; the only objection was about the "crippled child in a wheelchair."

Each of our friends with orthopedically impaired children has at some point been the butt of someone's complaint. Usually a passerby or someone who does not know the family or the child complains out of pity a sense of discomfort about an obviously disabled child who is being "allowed" to play outside with other children or participate in activities that some believe should be reserved for the able-bodied.

Adoptive parents of physically challenged children must remember that laws mandating the education of all handicapped children are of relatively recent origin. Many adults cannot remember attending school with even one person with a physical disability. Many people do not have friends or acquaintances who are disabled. Our culture, while claiming to be inclusive and welcoming of all people, has only recently showed through its laws and its mandated structural changes that we really intend to be inclusive of those with physical disabilities.

The adoptive parent of a physically handicapped child will need to be able to handle misunderstandings, prejudices, dismay, and even disgust from the narrow-minded, the entrenched, or the uninformed as they advocate for a child who has every human and legal right to be included.

Speech and Language Impairments

Children waiting in our child welfare system to be adopted, and children past infancy adopted from other countries often have speech and language delays. Sometimes such delays prove to be actual impairments. Speech and language impairments refer to difficulties communicating. A child may have a problem with articulation, fluency (such as "stuttering"), or aphasia—difficulty using words. Environment or hearing loss can cause language impairments, as can learning disabilities, mental retardation, cerebral palsy, and the effects of institutionalization. Children with cleft lip or palate might have speech problems, too.

Children who have speech and language impairments are noticeably behind their agemates in language. Sometimes such children understand much more than they express, and have a hard time communicating an idea or experience. Other children have articulation problems, such as substituting the "w" sound for the "r" sound, or "th" for "s." This is particularly true of children whose second language is English, which applies to all internationally adopted children past infancy.

The best help available for children with speech and language problems can be found through speech and language specialists employed in the public schools or in the private sector. Very young children with these problems should be tested by the schools and, if eligible, can receive early childhood intervention in a preschool setting in the public schools. School-age children can receive regular help at school through a speech pathologist, special tutoring, or even special classes if warranted. Parents of children with speech impairments should know that many such children may qualify for a personal computer and speech and language software through the state that placed the child for adoption. The funding for these computers usually comes from medical assistance programs. See Chapter 8, "Finances," for details.

SERIOUS MEDICAL CONDITIONS

Children with serious medical conditions such as spina bifida, cystic fibrosis, heart problems, or muscular dystrophy (among other conditions) occasionally are available for adoption in the United States. Usually children with serious medical conditions are raised within their families of origin. When such children do become adoptable, they may be placed through an exchange specific to children who have that condition. Thus, children with serious medical conditions comprise a minority of those available for adoption. Rosenthal and Groze found that parents of children adopted with serious medical conditions reported better outcomes for their children, as did parents of children with multiple handicaps, than did parents who adopted children with minor impairments such as learning disabilities or developmental delays or those whose adopted children had behavior and emotional problems (Rosenthal & Groze, 1992).

Parents interested in adopting a child with serious medical problems can learn more about the condition by contacting the national organizations devoted to such conditions or the National Organization for Rare Disorders, listed in the Appendix.

Living with Dying

Baby Joseph will not live long enough to go to the prom. In fact, he won't ever see first grade. He was born with severe birth defects of the heart and brain, and has only months, perhaps a year, to live. Greg has just adopted Joey and is enjoying every moment he has with his son. Greg has worked in a nursing home for many years, and has helped several people find peace in death. He wants to be there for Joey as he lives, and as he dies.

Why would anyone adopt a child who is sure to die? Because every child deserves to have a forever family, regardless of his lifespan. Because sometimes critically ill children live much longer than anyone had predicted. Because parenting is a privilege, even if it is for a short time. Because helping a child to die well is as priceless a gift as helping a child to live well.

Debra has adopted two critically ill children, both of whom have since passed away. She says it is a "special calling." While it is never easy, she feels privileged to have parented her angels, as she calls them, until they went back to heaven. She says she does not know if she has the strength to adopt another such child, but she teaches a class on parenting dying children at the hospital where she works. She trains others to do what she has done.

Whether parenting through a permanent foster care arrangement, or an adoption, parents should be sure their adoption contracts call for full reimbursement of extraordinary medical expenses not covered by medical assistance or insurance. They must all be sure that the contract allows for the funds that will be needed for burial. With the financial considerations taken care of, the parents' energy is freed up to care for and nurture the child for as long as they have together.

AIDS and HIV

AIDS (Acquired Immune Deficiency Syndrome) is a chronic illness caused by infection with HIV (human immunodeficiency virus). As many as 1.5 million Americans are believed to be infected with HIV. Some of them have AIDS, but most have no symptoms at all, and many do not know they are infected. There are medical treatments for HIV infection, but so far there is no cure and no preventive vaccine. More and more infants and children with HIV need adoptive families, and adoption exchanges and projects supporting their adoption originated in the 1990s.

AIDS testing for waiting children is becoming common but is not yet universal. Parents should inquire about whether the child has been tested for HIV, what the results were if the child was tested, and what the placing state's privacy laws allow. Some states disallow the release of information about HIV, so parents should be sure to ask and be willing to have the child tested themselves.

HIV is transmitted through exchange of certain bodily fluids such as blood, semen, vaginal secretions, and breast milk. To produce an infection, the virus must pass through the skin or mucous membranes into the body. The HIV virus dies quickly when it is outside the human body. It cannot be transmitted by day-to-day or even close social contacts not mentioned above. Family members of an HIV-infected individual do not catch the virus if they share drinking glasses with the patient. There is no known instance in which an HIV-infected child has passed the virus to another child in school.

HIV infection occurs in all age groups. Twenty to 40 percent of the babies born to HIV- infected mothers develop HIV infection themselves. Many of these children die within one or two years, but some live for years, although their development may be delayed and they can get many infections. Other infants born testing HIV positive convert to negative status some six to nine months later and do not develop HIV infection or AIDS. Thus, families who adopt HIV-positive infants should know that many such infants convert and grow up healthy, while others continue to carry the virus and eventually develop AIDS. Children in the latter group are living into their teens, and with the ongoing research and new treatments of HIV, we may find that HIV and AIDS come to be treated as chronic illnesses rather than a death sentence for the person so diagnosed.

AIDS and HIV, along with sexually transmitted diseases, should also be of concern to adoptive parents of adolescents who are sexually active. Parents whose children are sexually active should educate their kids about safe sex and monitor their behavior and companions as much as possible.

OLDER CHILDREN

Age alone can be considered a "special need" for children who are eight years old or older at the time of their adoptive placement, not because age alone constitutes a special need, but because older children almost always have behavioral or emotional problems. If a child is of minority race, a slightly lower age may qualify the child for services and entitlements as a special needs child. Older child adoption is more like an arranged marriage than anything else. Each person involved may want the family to work, but will probably also feel awkward, uncomfortable, and scared about the process.

We know after many years of research that older child adoptions can and do have good outcomes. In their research into the impact of special needs adoption, Rosenthal and Groze found that about 18 percent of families who adopted children under age five, 30 percent of those who adopted children ages 6 to 11 years, and 28 percent of those who adopted children ages 12 to 18 years reported mixed or negative results to the adoptive family (Rosenthal & Groze, 1992). The majority of adoptive parents said that the adoption had a positive or very positive result.

The process of an older child's placement was discussed in Chapter 5. Once the initial rush of excitement and newness of the placement wears off, parent and child are left to work through their tentative relationship as best they can, utilizing the support of agency professionals or a helping professional whenever possible. Some parents we have known entered their older child adoptions through attorneys who knew nothing about special needs adoption. We do not recommend do-it-yourself special needs adoption, supported only by one's determination or romantic view of what adoption is about. What we do recommend is self-directed special needs adoption through a licensed child-placing agency offering post-placement support. To undertake any other type of older child adoption is to court disaster by imperiling the emotional and financial well-being of the adoptee and the adoptive family.

Relationships to Former Families

In her book, *A Child's Journey Through Placement,* Vera Fahlberg (1991) underscores the importance of face-to-face visits with birth and foster families as a child moves into adoption. Whenever possible, we support giving children, especially older children, the opportunity to visit with significant caregivers before, during, and after the move into the adoptive family. Some adoptive parents, eager to claim their children and gain a sense of entitlement as parents, feel fear or anger toward the birth or foster parents to whom a child is attached. However, any time a child expresses a positive attachment to an adult, new adoptive parents should consider it a sign that the child can, and probably eventually will, attach to them. Many parents of older children "adopt" the foster parents, too, who become grandma, grandpa, aunt, or uncle. This is as wonderful for the foster parents as it is for the children.

Former caregivers who are unwilling to be supportive of the adoptive family will undermine the placement. Instead, adoptive parents can display photographs of the birth and foster families, give the child free access to her Life Book, and use videotapes of former families. Keeping other loved ones fresh in the child's mind helps decrease the fantasizing and distortion of facts that can occur if grieving is not facilitated.

Getting to Know You

Even in the best placements, in which every bit of history is relayed to adoptive parents and all records are divulged, there will be years of the child's past that are lost to the child and the adoptive parents when memories are not exercised, nurtured, and recorded. It may be months before a child is willing to share a memory or an experience. Adoptive parents should be attentive listeners and ask open-ended questions in order to elicit more information about the past, taking care to record memories for the child.

One of Anne's daughters entered the family at age eight, having had a different mother every two years of her life and a failed adoption besides. One day, as the casual conversation turned to clothing, Janet suddenly asked, "Mom, what happened to that fluffy purple dress that I wore to our friend's baptism?" Neither the baptism nor the purple dress rang a bell for Anne. "Honey, I don't remember a purple dress. Can you tell me more about what it looked like and when I might have seen it?" Janet went on to describe in detail a crushed velvet dress, dark purple, with layers of petticoats that made the dress stick out and look "fluffy." Janet had worn the dress, she said, "in my foster family back before I went to live with our grandma and grandpa."

Janet had been two years old at the time she wore the purple dress, which had been sent with Janet from family to family. Since Janet had long ago outgrown the dress, it had been relegated to the back of her closet. As an experienced adoptive parent, Anne knew not to throw away anything that had come to the family with her new daughter. The dress served as a tangible link to a warm and special memory in Janet's mind.

Shared memories link a child's past and present, give adoptive parents the opportunity to enter into the child's experience, and enhance the parents' understanding.

SIBLING GROUPS

The final category that can define a child as having "special needs" that make adoptive placement more challenging is sibling group membership, and the necessity of siblings being placed together. As often as possible, siblings who need to be adopted are placed into the same adoptive family. Sometimes a sibling group is too large to make this feasible. Other times, the needs of the siblings combined would be too much for one adoptive family to handle. Sometimes children have a history of incestuous relations or a long pattern of good kid/bad kid relations and placement together would not serve any sibling. For these and other reasons, siblings may be separated prior to adoption.

Usually every attempt is made to keep siblings together. Adults should not underestimate the power of the sibling relationship, and the older people become, the more precious sibling relationships become. Children whose parents have abused and neglected them often find comfort and understanding in their brothers and sisters who share their plight. If separated by adoption, siblings suffer a double loss—that of their parents and of their siblings.

Adopting siblings presents more of a challenge than adopting one child at a time, simply because there are more children present making more demands on parental time and energy. In general, however, outcomes and satisfaction for parents who adopt sibling groups are about the same as those of parents who adopt one child at a time (Rosenthal & Groze, 1992).

There are positive aspects of adopting siblings that do not exist in single child adoption. Siblings can help each other adjust to a new family simply by virtue of being present with one another during a traumatic move. As well, older siblings can comfort younger siblings, who will receive the comfort from a brother or sister that they are not yet ready to receive from a new adoptive parent.

When adopting sibling groups incrementally, Vera Fahlberg recommends placing the oldest child or the one with the most emotional problems first, followed by those who will take less energy (Fahlberg, 1991). If a child is in residential treatment and her siblings live in a foster family home, though, the younger children may be moved first instead.

TWINNING THROUGH ADOPTION

When a child already in the adoptive family gets a new adopted sibling of the same age or school grade, it is called "twinning" through adoption. Both Anne and Rita have "twinned" one or more sets of siblings in our families through adoption, and Rita has a set of "triplets"—three brothers, unrelated biologically, who are only a few months apart in age. This unique experience is more common in special needs adoption than many people realize.

Becoming a twin through adoption has its ups and downs. Kids enjoy having a same-age playmate who shares like experiences at the same time: The first day of school, first Holy Communion, summer camp, or Little League. However, unless the parents make a genuine effort to spend time with each "twin" individually, the "old" twin may resent the "new" twin's presence in the home. Before adopting a same-age sibling, parents should consult the child who will be twinned, explain the positives and negatives, and ask for the child's input. On the other hand, the newly adopted "twin" may feel that he is constantly playing "second fiddle" to the same-age sibling who arrived in the family before him. We cannot emphasize enought the value of spending time alone with each child in the family, especially when that child has been twinned through adoption.

Every adoptive twin and triplet set is unique, and how well they get along will vary from family to family and from time to time. Parents should allow the twinned children to decide how much togetherness and differentiation they want.

Parents should not allow school districts to underestimate or overestimate the closeness of adopted age-mates. They should give the children themselves a say in whether or not they learn in the same classroom with the same teacher, or if they prefer to be in different rooms.

Psychologists tell us that children who are less than three years apart in age fight more often than children who are more than three years apart, and that children who are a year apart in age or less tend to quarrel frequently. The exception to this is identical biological twins, who tend to be very close. While being an adoption twin can foster a great deal of closeness, parents report that it usually means a great deal of competition and bickering. To minimize this problem, parents must regularly physically and verbally reassure each child that she is equally loved and is very special. Twins need to hear as well as experience these reassurances throughout childhood, especially in those cases in which one "twin" is adopted and the other is Mom and Dad's biological child.

Rita's father helped her fighting siblings understand that their love-hate relationship would bloom into closeness years into the future. He told them about how he and his own brother, Wally, had fought "like cats and dogs" as children. However, as they grew older, and especially after their parents died, the brothers became very close indeed. They even moved into houses next door to each other after retirement to spend more time together. Families should remind their children that the day will come when the sibling relationship will be one of the most important in their lives.

LIVING WITH A DISABLED FAMILY MEMBER

Reactions of Primary Caretakers

While biological parents whose children are born with a handicap often experience shock, guilt, dismay, and shame over the child's handicap, adoptive parents enter the relationship with their special needs child with their eyes open. They have chosen to adopt a child with special needs, do not feel responsible for causing those needs, and do not begin parenting with a sense of shock or dismay. In many ways, adoptive parents of disabled children are initially better equipped emotionally to parent the child.

Eventually, though, parents begin to deal with the day-to-day reality of parenting a child with physical or emotional disabilities. Medical or emotional crises add a new burden to a family that may already have other children present. Even when the child with special needs is the only child, pre-existing relationships with a spouse or partner will change dramatically and permanently with the entrance of a child into the family. The adoptive parent must learn how to deal with the crisis of an illness, disability, or emotional relapse at the same time that they must carry on with relationships with healthy family members.

Parents of emotionally disturbed or mentally ill adopted children, in particular, find themselves living in a state of constant vigilance for symptoms of relapse in the ill person. Parents must learn to live with symptoms such as aggression, resistance to authority, withdrawal, silence, rage, and suicidal gestures. They learn to live with a child whose whole life is predicated on the assumption that anyone who cares is a "target."

Children with an attachment disorder that is untreated or unresolved, like those with mental illnesses or personality disorders, catapult their parents into a life that progresses from school misbehavior and playground skirmishes in middle childhood to dealing with police, crisis teams, incarceration, or involuntary commitment later in life. Adopters may stop being parents and start being "case manager" or "therapists" to their own child.

All this takes a toll on a marriage. Partners lose touch with one another, stop communicating, are less intimate, and have little or no unburdened time together. Sometimes the stress is too much, and one partner opts out of the relationship. Besides all this, parents must try to live normal lives, make decisions about the future when everything is uncertain, and devise financial plans for a family member who is chronically ill or disabled and may never live independently. Many special needs adopters think that these worries are only shared by parents who adopt severely handicapped children, but this is simply not the case. We have met many parents who adopted children as young as age two, three, five or six who developed chronic behavior problems that had just the same impact as if they had adopted a 15-year-old diagnosed with a mental illness, or an 11-year-old attachment disordered child.

In spite of the challenges to the adoptive family, we do not discourage parents from adopting such children because these children need parents, and because raising them can be so rewarding. Waiting children need parents who are as prepared for the griefs of adoption as they are for the joys. Parents must enter special needs adoption with their eyes open. Once they have counted the cost to their lifestyle, marriage, intimate relationships, other children, selves, and pocketbooks, they are then, and only then, ready to become adoptive parents. Having counted the cost, they will not be as shocked or dismayed when the hard times come. Rather, they will have had the wisdom to prepare for the hard times beforehand—and also to anticipate the great joy and satisfaction that come from loving and helping the child with special needs.

Sibling Reactions to a Handicapped Child

It is not only adoptive parents who are affected by the adoption of a handicapped child. Siblings, too, are affected. The new adopted child is welcomed into the family with excitement, hope, and joy. For a while, it seems that every day is like waking up to Christmas morning, and a sense of happiness and anticipation pervades the family. Eventually, though, the family settles into a routine and the child becomes a full-fledged family member. If the adoption is same-race, others will come to treat the adoptive family like any other family with a disabled family member. If the adoption is transracial, the family will be singled out for special attention and curiosity from time to time, which becomes a normal part of the special needs family's life.

Once the newness of the relationships has worn off, siblings will be emotionally and cognitively affected by having a disabled sibling. If there are other children in the home, they may be embarrassed by the handicapped child and try to escape physically or emotionally from the family or the new child, particularly if they felt ambivalent about the adoption. When a chronic illness is involved, the "old kids" may experience frustration over not being able to change the illness or disability. They may have trouble building a relationship with the disabled or ill sibling based on fear, shame, or anger surrounding the disability or illness. Siblings may alternate between feeling sorry for the disabled sibling and feeling angry about the sibling's disability.

When an adopted child has behavioral or emotional problems, or mental illness, the periodic emotional outbursts (or psychotic episodes) will be terrifying for the child's siblings. In the case of attachment disordered adopted siblings, younger sibs become ready targets for the child with AD and can be threatened, assaulted, or molested by the sibling who was supposed to come into the family and become a full-fledged, caring family member. When extreme chaos results from a child's emotional problems, the nondisturbed siblings may become "perfect" children who overcompensate for the disturbed child in an effort to make things easier for Mom and Dad. When a sibling has a chronic illness or disability, older siblings worry about the caretaking parents dying and the ill family member becoming the sibling's responsibility.

How Parents Can Help

Parents should understand that the illness or disability of the adopted child has an effect on everyone in the family. They should help other children in the family understand the disability before, during, and after the new child's placement. As much as possible, they should make other children in the family a part of inviting the new member into the family.

Parents should be realistic about the illness and give other family members the facts about it as a way of reducing anxiety and fear and empowering each family member. Parents should talk about how they feel about the new child, the illness or disability, and regularly ask other family members to do the same.

We believe that parents of emotionally handicapped children should not turn the family home into a residential treatment facility when other children are living at home. If the family's peace, dignity and well-being cannot be maintained with a mentally ill or emotionally disturbed child or adolescent living at home, the ill child should be moved to another safe place.

Finally, living with, loving, and caring for an ill or disabled child is challenging, rewarding, and also exhausting. Parents must practice active relaxation and manage their own stress and the stress level within the family. Through good diets, rest, and recreation the family's physical and mental health should be guarded. The worst thing that can happen in the special needs adoptive family is to allow the entire family to revolve around one ill family member. Sometimes, in a crisis, the whole family will focus on the ill family member—but this should by no means become a way of life.

CHAPTER 8

Finances

I cannot afford to waste my time making money.

— Agassiz

Agassiz may have been referring to an offer of money in return for some speaking engagements, but many special needs parents will tell you that they can't afford to waste time making money because they are too busy being mommies and daddies. And yet, special needs adoption is expensive. The adoption process is expensive, and raising children, especially children with disabilities, is expensive. That's the bad news.

The good news is that there are many kinds of financial help available that make the costs affordable, even for middle-class families. There are two types of assistance, each of which will be discussed in this chapter—non-subusidy assistance and subsidy assistance. Parents must take the time to educate themselves about what is available. No one is going to hand them this important help on a silver platter.

SPECIAL NEEDS DEFINITIONS

Section 473(c) of the Social Security Act defines a child with special needs as one who meets the following conditions:

1. The child cannot or should not be returned to the home of his or her parents, and
2. The State has determined that (A) there exists with respect to the child a specific factor or condition (such as his ethnic background, age, or membership in a minority or sibling group, or the presence of factors such as medical conditions or physical, mental, or emotional handicaps) because of which it is reasonable to

> conclude that such child cannot be placed with adoptive parents without providing adoption assistance . . . and (B) that, except where it would be against the best interests of the child because of such factors as the existence of significant emotional ties with prospective adoptive parents while in the care of such parents as a foster child, a reasonable, but unsuccessful, effort has been made to place the child with appropriate adoptive parents without providing adoption assistance.

In addition to the federal definitions of "special needs," states may establish their own guidelines for state-funded adoption assistance. These definitions will vary from state to state. Parents can obtain a copy of their state's definitions from the state agency, NACAC, or by consulting their state statutes at the local library.

ADOPTION ASSISTANCE PAYMENTS

Money. No one wants to be accused for adopting "for money" or of being a "charity case." However, parents who do not investigate subsidies carefully before making a decision are risking nothing less than bankruptcy. Adoption Assistance Payments, or AAP (also known as subsidies) are not welfare, charity, wages, or anything except temporary funding to help expensive-to-raise kids find permanency in homes with tight budgets.

Disruption prevention research has shown that special needs adoption subsidies prevent disruption (adoption failure) and save money in the long term for that reason (Barth & Berry, 1988). The federal subsidy law was designed to remove disincentives to adoption by normalizing subsidy and foster care rates. Unfortunately, actual subsidy rates average one-third that of foster care rates. The average adoptive parent is not well informed about subsidies and this lack of information is strongly linked to difficulty in placements. These problems are just two of the reasons subsidies continue to be underutilized.

This lack of information about subsidies not only hurts kids and damages families financially, it costs taxpayers a great deal of money. Foster care is more expensive for society than subsidized adoption both in terms of real dollars and in lost productivity (Barth & Berry, 1988). Successfully adopted children are more likely to go to college, be gainfully employed, and stay out of trouble than children who remain in the child welfare system.

THE THREE TYPES OF ADOPTION ASSISTANCE PAYMENTS

There are three types of AAP: basic rates, specialized rates, and state-funded subsidies. Specialized rates are for more seriously disabled children, and state-funded subsidies are reserved for those children who do not qualify for federal AAP for reasons not related to their disabilities.

Where do subsidies come from and how are they funded? The state from which the child is adopted is the source of the subsidy. The federal government reimburses states for more than half of each subsidy dollar, plus administrative costs. AAP amounts vary a great deal from state to state, and may also vary from county to county. The monthly amount also depends on the child's special needs and age group. AAP begins at about $250 per child, and can exceed $1,200. They stop when the child is 18 to 22 years old, if the adoption disrupts, or if the state or federal government stops funding the AAP program.

In the United States, basic AAP rates can range from Alabama's low of $205 monthly to Connecticut's high of $637. In addition, at least half the states have higher "specialized" or "difficulty of care" rates for more severely disabled children, ranging from New Jersey's low of $312 to Wyoming's $2,000 per month. The national average basic AAP rate is $328, while the national average specialized AAP rate is $731.

Medicaid is another important benefit that continues until the child is grown. Many states will also pay extraordinary medical expenses not covered by Medicaid. Such expenses may include medical equipment, therapy, wheelchair ramps and lifts, and computers.

Title XX services (not available to adoptive families in all states) offer various benefits such as respite care and medical mileage to special needs children. Before adopting a child with special needs, adoptive parents will need to ask whether such services are available in their state of residence, or through thte placing state.

BASIC AND SPECIALIZED RATE SUBSIDIES

The *basic monthly rate* is available to any child who meets the definition of "special needs" and who does not meet the criteria for the specialized monthly rates. These may start at any amount from $250 per month per child to $600 or more, depending on the state and its definition of special needs. Generally, the rates increase as the child gets older (and, sometimes, when rates are raised in any category).

The *specialized monthly rates,* when available, are applied to children whose special needs are more severe and expensive. There may be one specialized rate, or several.

Using Oklahoma as an example, one can see how the rates differ.

Table 8.1
Basic and Specialized Oklahoma Subsidy Rates

Basic OK Monthly Rates by Age		Specialized Monthly Rates by Age			
Age	Basic Rate	Level I	Level II	Level III	Level IV
0-5	$300	$350	$400	$450	$525
6-12	$360	$410	$460	$510	$585
13-18	$420	$470	$520	$570	$645

STATE-FUNDED SUBSIDIES

Children who qualify for basic and specialized rate subsidies must first qualify as Title IV-E-eligible according to federal law. This means that their birth parents were AFDC-eligible, or that the children or their birth parents are SSI-eligible. Sometimes, a child with special needs will not qualify as IV-E-eligible. Such children may then try to qualify for a state-funded-only subsidy (IV-B). Parent should be sure and ask their adoption agency for a determination of IV-E or IV-B eligibility for the child or children they adopt. Children who do not qualify for either program cannot obtain AAP.

Post-Finalization Subsidies

While subsidies are usually applied for prior to placement, a few states provide for their availability after finalization out of state-only funds. Parents should research this carefully. In Oklahoma, for example, children with pre-existing conditions that were discovered after the adoption was finalized may be eligible for post-finalization adoption assistance when the condition is severe.

ROADBLOCKS TO OBTAINING AAP

Financial disincentives for the adoption of U.S. born children with special needs ended in the late 1970s with the passage of landmark federal legislation called P.L. 96-272. Why, then, does research tell us that relatively few families make full use of available assistance, even when they desperately need the help? Following are a few of the reasons.

Lack of training. Social workers have not been properly trained, in some cases, to understand how crucial subsidies and related benefits are to placement success, or to properly educate parents about subsidy availability.

Misperceptions. Agencies may neglect to inform parents about adoption assistance, specialized rates, Medicaid and more because of the "hassle" to the agency, because they are not themselves informed, or because there is no immediate benefit to the agency to do so. Agencies do not earn income from these programs, and if the family appears financially sound, an agency worker may assume the family doesn't need a subsidy. Parents must ask for information and help whether they are adopting through the state or a private agency.

Attitudes. Parents and social workers sometimes don't understand the major financial implications of adopting a child with special needs, or they mistakenly view subsidies as "charity."

Misinterpretation. The federal law, P.L. 96-272, is not only widely misunderstood in both content and intent, it is unintentionally violated by a host of local policies and regulations. This is one reason why parents regularly win subsidy decisions on appeal. Maximizing the effectiveness of the subsidy program means sharing information about what it is, what it is meant to accomplish, and how it works.

NON-SUBSIDY FINANCIAL AID

Nonsubsidy forms of financial assistance are available to most adopted children with special needs. They include different programs that vary from state to state and even from county to county, such as:

- The federal program called SSI, or Supplemental Security Income,
- Medicaid,
- Non-Medicaid state medical assistance payments, and one-time funding to buy wheelchair ramps and lifts, or computers,
- Nonrecurring Adoption Expenses Reimbursement,
- Purchase of Services (POS) to lower the cost of the adoption process,
- Miscellaneous assistance, such as clothing allowances, tutoring funds, etc.,
- Federal Title XX services, such as, professional respite care and reimbursement for medical mileage costs.

Supplemental Security Income (SSI)

In the United States, the federal government pays monthly disability checks (Supplemental Security Income, or SSI) to disabled workers under age 65 and their families, to some never-employed disabled individuals over age 18, and to some individuals who are disabled before age 22, including children. Title IV-E of the Social Security Act establishes Adoption Assistance Payments (AAP) for children who either qualify for SSI or whose parents qualified for AFDC at the time the child entered the child welfare system. Establishing SSI eligibility is a very important first step for prospective adopted children with disabilities.

The Social Security Administration has regulations delineating which conditions in adults and children qualify as disabilities. These regulations are available to the public through the Freedom of Information Act and can be inspected at any Social Security office. Prospective adoptive parents considering the adoption of an infant or child with a disability would do well to obtain information from the SSA regarding possible SSI benefits if the child's eligibility has not already been established.

In 1996 President Clinton signed into law H.R. 3734, the Personal Responsibility and Work Opportunity Reconciliation Act. This law eliminated Individual Functional Assessments (IFA) for children. Children who were formerly qualified for SSI under an IFA will be reevaluated to determine if they meet the new definition, which requires that the child have a medically determinable physical or mental impairment that results in marked and severe functional limitations of substantial duration. Many adopted special needs children receive adoption assistance benefits as a result of SSI eligibility, and adoption advocates were concerned about the negative impact this law might have on adoptable children with special needs. Indeed, within months after the law was implemented, we began to hear of adoptable children denied SSI, and thus IV-E AAP eligibility, because the individual functional assessments were discontinued.

The Department of Health and Human Services had not clarified the impact of H.R. 3734 on past and future special needs children as this book went to press. The best information about the impact of these laws will be available through the North American Council on Adoptable Children (NACAC), the Department of Health and Human Services, and the National Center for Youth Law.

Applying for SSI

Anyone wanting to receive SSI benefits must first apply. Either the foster or prospective adoptive parents or an agency social worker or director may apply on a child's behalf. The representative payee for the child may either be the agency, in the case of a child whose custody is retained by an agency, or the foster or adoptive parent, depending on thechild's circumstances and that of the family. The SSI application is available at the local Social Security Administration office. Applicants can also have the application mailed and can complete much of the process over the telephone. Once the application has been completed and returned to SSA, the local office will arrange a personal or telephone interview, whichever is more convenient for you, regarding the child's circumstances. The complete application is then sent to the Disability Determination Service (DDS) in your state, where the decision will be made as to whether the child is disabled as defined under the law.

A disability evaluation specialist from the DDS and a medical doctor will consider the facts of the child's case based on the application and information given by all the doctors, clinics, hospitals and professionals who have treated the child. When medical records are needed, the government will pay a reasonable charge for them. Physicians are asked to provide the medical history of the child. If the history is incomplete or the DDS team needs more information about the child's condition, additional examinations or testing may be required. The SSA will pay for the additional examination or testing and for some travel expenses related to the testing.

Once the entire application has been submitted, it takes two to three months to process the disability claim. If it takes more time to receive the child's medical records or additional examinations or testing are required, the process may take longer.

When a decision has been made, the SSA will send you written notification about their decision. If the decision is favorable, the notification will show the amount of the child's check and the date when payments will begin, including the number of back payments that will be sent. Usually, payments for the eligible disabled are dated from the time of the first application. Included with an approval notice will be an award letter and an SSA publication stating the child's (and your) rights and responsibilities.

If the child's claim has been denied, or if you or the adoption agency or the child's physician disagree with any part of the decision, the decision can be questioned or appealed. A reconsideration can be requested, at which the DDS team considers information it had not considered previously. The appeals process is described in the information sent by SSA at the time the determination letter is sent.

Unlike AAP, the costs of SSI are covered entirely through federal funds, so some states will ask parents to forgo a subsidy in favor of SSI. Parents should be careful before agreeing to this. They should determine which amount, SSI or AAP, will be higher, and whether or not there are planned increases in the near future for either amount. Also, parents should know that since SSI is tied to parental income, this assistance could be lost if the income increases, and it is difficult in many states to apply for post-finalization AAP. Furthermore, SSI rules restrict the amount of money parents can put into savings and retirement accounts. All things considered, AAP is a better choice than SSI for most families, but each case is different and must be thoroughly investigated by the parents.

Medicaid

On the initial application for basic adoption assistance, parents are given the opportunity to apply for Medicaid, or Medical Assistance, that continues until the child is 18, or in special circumstances until the child is age 21. It is a good idea to apply even if the family has health insurance in the event that the health insurance is ever lost.

After placement, the Medicaid cards of children adopted from another state are converted to the Medicaid system of the state where the adoptive family resides. In other words, a child from Alabama who is adopted by a family in Georgia will ultimately have a Medicaid card from the state of Georgia. (Subsidies, however, continue to be administered from the state where the child came from, in this case, Alabama.)

Adoptive parents do not have to meet any financial means test in order to receive Medicaid. If special needs adoptive parents are asked to fill out a standard Medical Assistance application form, they should write *"adopted child only application"* across the top of the application. They should *not* answer the income questions, but instead write *"no means test for parents of special needs children receiving adoption assistance payments"* across each page. If the child has any resources or property, you should include the child's resources, however.

If you already have health insurance coverage, you should indicate that on the Medicaid form. However, your health insurance company will be billed first, and Medicaid will only pay what is not covered by your primary insurer.

An almost unbelievable bureaucracy has sprung up around Medicaid in some states. One adoptive parent told us that most months, at least one of the five Medicaid cards that were supposed to arrive at her house, never arrived. A chronic computer glitch sends one or more of these cards to an unknown address. No matter how many times the address is corrected, the problem eventually reoccurs. About once a year, the computer cancels the coverage of at least two of her children, who must then be reinstated. Her pharmacist is not always paid by Medicaid in a timely manner, and every now and then his check arrives in the adoptive family's mail box. He, however, is most patient. In 1996, children on Medicaid in this state were re-assigned to a series of HMOs (Health Management Organizations) with new doctors and clinics. No sooner had this been done than a letter was sent to adoptive families explaining that their children had been re-assigned in error, that all adopted children would stay on the old system. This created medical havoc for many families.

Many states have begun using managed care systems to deliver medical services to their Medicaid clients, including foster and adopted children. Adoptive parents who have long-standing relationships with specialists who treat their adopted children are finding it increasingly difficult under managed care systems to advocate for their children's continued treatment by the same specialists. In addition, physicians or mental health professionals may choose not to accept Medicaid any more, leaving adoptive parents to search for help from professionals who are not as conveniently located or who do not have long-standing professional relationships with the adopted child.

Dealing with the Medicaid system requires patience, understanding, and a sense of humor. It is important to understand that Medicaid workers are usually overworked and sometimes undertrained. Parents will receive better help if they show understanding with a firmness of purpose, rather than anger and impatience. Parents must advocate fiercely for their children without acting fierce toward the people who are supposed to help.

Non-Medicaid Medical Assistance

Non-Medicaid Medical Assistance refers to available funds for medically challenged children that are not provided through the Medicaid card. Such help is available in most states, but must be negotiated by the parents prior to placement and whenever the need arises. Parents must ask about this type of help or they may never know what is available.

What is covered by non-Medicaid medical assistance varies from state to state, but may include, among other things residential treatment, medical equipment, counseling, therapy, wheelchair ramps and lifts, orthodontic braces, orthotics, prostheses, burial expenses for children with a known limited lifespan, specialized summer camp costs (such as camps for children with asthma), diapers for older children and teens, certain types of over-the-counter medication and nutrition supplements, and personal computers for children with communication and coordination difficulties.

Parents adopting children with disabilities should ask if there are funds available in their own state to assist parents (not just adoptive parents) with the cost of raising disabled children. Such programs are called Crippled Children's Services or Aid to the Disabled in many states and are income-based, just like SSI.

Parents should also investigate services offered by private organizations such as Shriners' Hospitals, Crippled Children's Services, and others. Major cities have referral organizations that list all of these groups and institutions. Parents should check with their NAATRIN or NACAC representatives to find out more about such referral groups.

NON-RECURRING SPECIAL NEEDS ADOPTION EXPENSES

There is help for the expense of adopting a child with special needs. This is one of the few programs that parents of internationally born special needs children can apply for in many states. Although each state may set the cap below $2,000, the federal reimbursement maximum for nonrecurring (one-time) special needs adoption expenses is limited to $2,000 per child.

Parents should save all receipts associated with the costs of adopting the child—from receipts for the cost of buying this book, to the long distance phone bill. Parents should ask their social workers for the form that must be filled out after placement in order to access these funds. After returning the form with receipts, reimbursement can take anywhere from two weeks to several months to arrive.

Parents of internationally adopted children with special needs will have to show that their child meets the federal definition of a child with special needs. Several federal policy interpretations (PIQs) of P.L. 96-272 have established that a judicial determination must prove that a child cannot or should not be returned to the home of his parents. This means that a court of competent jurisdiction, either in the child's country of origin or in the United States, must have determined that the child could not be returned to his parents.

The second requirement an internationally born child must meet is that there must exist, with respect to the child, a specific factor or condition because of which it is reasonable to conclude that the child cannot be placed with adoptive parents without providing assistance. Finally, a reasonable, but unsuccessful, effort must have been made to place the child with appropriate adoptive parents without adoption assistance.

Federal PIQ-92-02(b), issued in 1992, defined "reasonable efforts" this way:

> In an effort to find an adoptive home for a child, an agency should look at a number of families in order to locate the most suitable home for the child. Once the agency has determined that placement with a certain family would be the most suitable for the

child, then full disclosure should be made of the child's background, as well as any known and potential problems. If the child meets the State's "special needs" definition, then the agency can pose the question of whether the prospective parents are willing to adopt without subsidy. *If the parents say they cannot adopt the child without assistance, the agency then would meet the requirement in section 473(c)(2)(B) that they made reasonable, but unsuccessful, efforts to place without subsidy.* (Emphasis that of DHHS)

Some states deny nonrecurring adoption expense reimbursement to internationally born children by assuming that the agency did not make reasonable efforts to place the child without assistance. In more than one fourth of the states, nonrecurring expenses are reimbursed for internationally born or adopted children. We believe that as the adoptive parents of internationally born children with special needs challenge states that deny benefits to such children, either through administrative or judicial challenges, more and more states will reimburse nonrecurring expenses to international adopters.

Reimbursable expenses include adoption fees, attorney fees, court costs, adoption homestudy fees, costs of obtaining health and psychological information about family members, photolisting book subscriptions, some home and transportation preparation fees (such as a car seat), costs of supervising the adoptive placement, Life Book creation costs, and transportation, food and lodging during the placement process. If a parent is in doubt whether a certain expense is covered, it never hurts to ask. One dad was reimbursed for a high chair for his new two-year-old son who took a great deal of time to feed because of a chewing problem. Normally, a high chair is not a reimbursable expense, but in this child's case, it was a necessary expenditure reflective of his special needs, so it was allowed.

PURCHASE OF SERVICE

Purchase of Service (POS) is provided when the state agency with custody of a child agrees to pay some or all of the fees of the private agency that will actually provide professional post-placement services and court reports until the adoption is finalized. POS is not paid between two state agencies, but, rather, from a state agency to a private one. For example, prospective adoptive parents working through a licensed private adoption agency in Montana who find a waiting child in Maine may be able to obtain POS for their agency from the state of Maine. In this way, the parents do not have to pay those fees, which frees up their resources so that they can raise the special needs child. Properly utilized, POS can result in a low-cost or no-cost special needs adoption.

The amount of POS a state will pay to a private adoption agency in-state or out-of-state varies from a few hundred to several thousand dollars, and may include coverage of the application and homestudy fees, placement fees, and post-placement follow-up fees. Parents working through private agencies should ask whether their adoption agency can obtain POS from the state with custody of the waiting child, and, if so, how much will be paid.

MISCELLANEOUS ASSISTANCE

In some states, assistance is available to help with certain non-medical miscellaneous expenses such as tutoring, respite care (specialized babysitting for special needs kids), vitamin supplements, speech therapy, clothing, and post-secondary educational expenses. Again, not every state provides this help, and other sources in the community must be used before the states will make such funding available (i.e., the school system, Medicaid, Indian Health Services, etc.). If the child has a need, parents should ask if there is help available to fill that need.

When Rita adopted a little boy from Kentucky who was repeating the first grade, she was offered a tutoring allowance, which she did not think she would need. As it turned out, her son required a great deal of intensive individualized tutoring to teach him how to read, more than he could get in special classes at school. Rita provided what she could at home and then used the tutoring allowance to get him additional help. He did finally learn how to read, and the tutoring allowance was discontinued by the time he reached middle school.

Respite care is a type of specialized babysitting for children with special needs. It is designed to give parents a break so that they can "recharge their parenting batteries." In many states, it is common for adoption contracts to include a certain number of hours of respite care. Respite caregivers are reimbursed for their services directly by the placing state.

Title XX Services

Federal Title XX assistance (not available to adoptive families in all states) offers various services such as respite care, day care, and medical mileage to special needs children, whether adopted or not. Sometimes, these are tied to parental income or AFDC.

Title XX may pay for nothing or for a great many miscellaneous services. Again, each parent should ask about Title XX and be prepared to research what is available through Title XX in the state from which their child or children arrived.

AAP APPLICATION

For many parents, the application subsidy process goes unnoticed because the child's social worker takes care of all the paperwork. Even in these cases, however, parents should be familiar with the federal laws, state laws, and subsidy policies and regulations of the state from which their child came.

Many parents don't know that subsidy contracts are designed by law to be negotiated. States are forbidden to create "cookie-cutter" subsidy arrangements. Each child and each adopting family is unique, and to the extent the law allows, each AAP contract should reflect this diversity. Parents should work with social workers in negotiating the best possible contract for their child and their family. Familiarity with the process is also important because AAP contracts are meant to be renegotiated later as the special needs of the child change.

When to Negotiate

For most adoptions, negotiations begin after the first visit between adoptive parents and the child or children. By then, the adoptive parents know more about the child's special needs and what expense will be involved in dealing with those special needs. The parents should have already spoken at length to the foster parents, as well, about their costs and expenses, and about the various types of assistance the child has been receiving to date.

The contract is usually signed at placement and is resigned every one to two years. However, parents can elect to renegotiate any part of the subsidy contract at any time. For example, if it becomes apparent one month into the placement that the child needs more tutoring than the school or family can provide, parents may ask for financial assistance to hire a tutor to come to the house.

The Parts of the Application

Of course, no two states have the same AAP application requirements. The federal government has issued model agreements, though. In addition, adoptive parents should attach information to the application that will give the state complete information about a child's special needs. The essential parts of an application include:

- *The subsidy application* provided by the state department of human services (or its equivalent),
- *Medical records or letters from professionals* documenting the child's condition, diagnosis, its severity, its duration, the prognosis, and how long treatment will continue.
- *Supplemental documentation* as needed from a physical therapist, teachers, respite workers, day care workers, psychologist, etc.
- *Copies of bills* for medical equipment, rentals, or other expenses not covered by your insurance. These are useful if you have them, but not critical to the application.
- *Copies of articles* about the child's condition, especially if the condition is unusual. These can be found in medical encyclopedias, medical journals, parenting magazines, books about the condition, or publications from national disability foundations.
- *Proof of the child's adoption.*

- *Proof of the child's prior custody by a licensed child-placing agency,* such as a court order for temporary custody.
- *SSI award letter,* if applicable.
- *AFDC eligibility proof,* if applicable. Children whose birth parents received AFDC, or were Medicaid-eligible when the child was born, *or* children who are eligible for SSI due to a handicap are automatically eligible for Title IV-E adoption assistance payments, which makes the application process easier and more likely to succeed. If either of the child's birth parents received AFDC when the child was born, or if the child's birth was covered by Medicaid, submit proof of this along with your application.

If a child's first application or first renegotiated application is denied by the state or by the state subsidy committee, a second, more detailed and better-documented application should be written and submitted. The approval process for these "unofficial" appeals, as well as for official appeals, is high, and the applications, often approved. In one year when Rita tracked the success rate of appeals for the families with whom she spoke, the success rate was 75 percent. It is important to remember that when granting an assistance request is both within the realm of the law and in the best interests of the children, most subsidy committees are anxious to say "yes."

ADOPTION ASSISTANCE ADVOCACY

Tips for Negotiating and Re-Negotiating

- Talk to your adoptive parent support group and to your own state's NAATRIN expert first, to save time and frustration. You should also call the state's NACAC representative.
- Ask at the local state adoption office for a brochure or booklet describing adoption subsidies and benefits in your area.
- Contact NAIC, the National Adoption Information Clearinghouse, for a free catalog. Free copies of federal and individual state adoption laws and much more are available from the clearinghouse.
- Get a second opinion on your subsidy questions from social workers and adoption advocates. As in medicine, second opinions can yield very different answers!
- Consider appealing denials informally and, if necessary, formally. Explore the "due process hearing," which may not cost you any money. A hearing can be held over the telephone without hiring legal representation.
- If your state's policies and regulations are in violation of the spirit or word of the federal law, rally other adoptive parents to change things. Class-action lawsuits and letter-writing campaigns have been highly effective in several states.
- Don't forget to contact your state's department of mental health. Sometimes it will pick up where adoption services leave off, especially in the areas of respite care and residential treatment for emotionally and behaviorally disturbed kids.

- Quietly refuse to give up. Children with special needs cannot advocate for themselves and must depend on their parents for this. If you get a no, find out why and try again.

OTHER QUESTIONS

Inevitably, questions will arise. Are special needs adoption subsidies considered income? Can I list them on a loan application? What about taxes? The answers are not always clear so parents should consider what they read here to be a starting point only. Further research on the policies and laws of the parent's own state of residence is highly recommended.

For most purposes, AAP or adoption subsidies should not be considered parental income, but, rather the child's resource. The IRS does not consider it taxable income (in most cases), but reimbursement. There are no W-2 forms sent out in January listing subsidy totals for the year.

It is strongly recommended that parents consult IRS publications each and every year to discover what changes, if any, have been made to the way subsidies are viewed by the IRS. Parents who have any questions should ask for clarification in writing from the IRS. As of this writing, subsidies are not usually considered to be taxable income because of the support rule. However, subsidies may prevent parents from claiming the child as a dependent. The following story tells how.

A Tax Scenario

Steve legally adopted Jane, a little girl who has multiple disabilities and high medical bills. Steve's income is $1,500 per month, and Jane's adoption subsidy is an extra $800 per month. She also has a Medicaid card.

Steve does not have to list the subsidy (or Medicaid benefits) anywhere on his tax return, but his local IRS agent advised him to be careful about listing Jane as a dependent because of the support test. Steve must be able to prove that he provided more than 50 percent of the cost of any claimed dependent's support.

His monthly income, divided by the number of people in his household, two, is $750 per month per person. But Jane's subsidy is higher than $750 per month. Therefore, Steve is not providing more than 50 percent of her support. Steve can "play it safe" and not list Jane as his dependent. Alternately, he may list her as a dependent even though he failed the support test, but must also list her subsidy as income.

Steve realizes that he uses much more of his income each month to support Jane than he uses on himself, and he has the receipts to prove it. He can document the fact that he spends more each month from his personal income on Jane's support than her $800 subsidy provides. He spends about $900 per month for Jane, and $600 for himself. Since $900 is more than Jane's $800 subsidy, Steve can list his daughter as a dependent after all, without making any mention of the subsidy on his tax forms.

Of Loans and Lunches

What about loans? Using our same example, if Steve went to buy a car, could he list Jane's subsidy as part of his income? For purposes of obtaining a loan for something from which Jane will benefit, the answer is yes. Occasionally, the loan officer will ask to see the subsidy contract as proof.

What about applying for reduced or free school lunches? When Rita wrote to federal authorities in Washington D.C. with this question, the somewhat ambiguous answer came back that "no reason can be determined at this time for not including adoption subsidies in the parental income column."

Depending on where you live, the local public school district may or may not include adoption subsidies when considering a family for free or reduced cost lunches under the federal lunch program. However, parents should always make school districts aware of this type of income so that the school district can make that determination on an annual basis. Honesty really is the best policy.

There are at least three ways that school districts throughout the United States have handled the subsidies and lunch application question:

1. Counting the subsidies as parental income,
2. Counting the subsidies as the child's income and completing a separate form for each child who receives AAP (adoption subsidies derived from foster care payments originally. Foster children are always considered to be a "family of one" with their foster care payments figured as their own income, when determining free or reduced lunch eligibility),
3. Not counting AAP as income at all.

Divorce, AAP, and Child Support

Should AAP be considered in the calculation of child support when adoptive parents divorce? Again, the answer will vary.

Occasionally, the noncustodial parent will resist paying child support for adopted children, especially for those children who receive adoption assistance. It is illegal and immoral to refuse to support a child simply because the child is adopted. In fact, the law gives adoptees one additional protection in some states that biological children do not enjoy: Adopted children cannot be disinherited.

The subsidy exists to help defray the enormous costs associated with raising a child with special needs. It was never designed to be a substitute for child support and maintenance, but rather, a supplemental financial aid. And there is no guarantee that subsidies won't be legislatively decreased or eliminated before any child is grown. Indeed, prospective adoptive parents are expected to prove financial stability and must be able to show that they can afford to care for another child before an adoption application is approved.

Before going to court, parents should check state law, or have their lawyers and mediators do so. In some states, means-tested public assistance cannot be included when considering parental income for purposes of child support. For example, if a parent is receiving AFDC or food stamps, that amount of money cannot be considered in the calculation of child support. The question arises if adoption subsidies are means-tested public assistance or not. They are indeed public assistance, and are not taxable income in the vast majority of cases. In one sense, they are also means-tested. Federal law clearly states that means tests to determine eligibility for adoption subsidy are illegal, but means tests to determine the amount of the subsidy are not. This is why most parents receiving subsidies must send in their tax returns, W-2s, and even household budgets to the state sending the subsidy every year or two.

Of course, it is also important for the custodial parent to help the judge understand what subsidies are meant to do. They are not meant to provide funds to raise healthy children, and are not available to people who adopt a healthy infant. Subsidies are designed to reimburse the parents for the higher costs associated with raising children who have special needs. Subsidies are not guaranteed by either the states or federal government. In fact, a recent Congress almost voted to do away with adoption assistance as a federal entitlement program, and many states have frozen their rates.

In some situations, the case for child support may be bolstered by a tax return, since anyone who claims an adopted child as a dependent on a tax return has proven that the child is indeed dependent on him or her for support, whether an adoption subsidy is available or not.

SUBSIDY ADVOCACY INFORMATION RESOURCES

- NACAC, The North American Council on Adoptable Children, is the premier resource. Ask for the name of your own state's NACAC or NAATRIN Representative, their newsletter, *AdopTalk,* and their publications: *The Adoption Assistance and Child Welfare Act of 1980 (P.L. 96-272): The First Ten Years,* and *NACAC: User's Guide to P.L. 96-272.* Available from NACAC.
- National Adoption Information Clearinghouse, or NAIC. Ask for a free catalog. Free copies of federal and individual state adoption laws and lots more is available from the clearinghouse.
- ICAMA, Interstate Compact on Adoption and Medical Assistance, issue brief series. These include state-by-state breakdowns of subsidy and nonsubsidy special needs adoption benefits. Each available for a small fee each from the American Public Welfare Association.
- *Adoptive Family Magazine* subsidy article reprints. Send a self-addressed stamped envelope with your request for the three subsidy articles by Rita Laws to *Adoptive Families Magazine* at Adoptive Families of America.
- Your local library. Look for articles and books by the professionals who research and write about adoption subsidies and special needs adoption: Joe Kroll, Roberta

Frank, Judith Anderson, Richard Barth, Marianne Berry, Victor Groze, and Alice Bussiere, to name a few.

SUMMARY

America has long used temporary financial subsidies as a means to effect positive and cost-effective long-term goals. Permanency for special needs children is a top priority, yet sometimes we forget that our children truly are our most important resource. A NACAC representative from an agricultural state, weary from battling for fair subsidy procedures, once remarked, "In my state, we readily subsidize corn, but not special needs kids. But it's not crops that will lead our nation into the future!"

There is a solid national law in place to help big-hearted people raise very expensive and challenging children. It is up to each adoptive parent to see that the law is implemented fully for the benefit of waiting children. Once accomplished, far fewer children will be waiting for a forever family than is now the case (Bussiere, 1990). For every child who receives the priceless gift of a permanent family, our nation is a stronger, better place for generations to come.

CHAPTER 9

Working with Educators and Schools

> Better build schoolrooms for the boy, than cells and gibbets for the man.
>
> —Eliza Cook

Dealing with schools and school systems can be one of the most rewarding or frustrating experiences parents encounter, depending on how well equipped the school system is to deal with kids who have special needs. Like much of the population, school administrators and teachers generally know little about adoption issues, and even less about special needs adoption. Teachers are usually not given preparation during teacher training to deal with the unique needs of foster and adopted students.

Adoptive parents often must educate the educators about special needs adoption, while at the same time advocating for their children within a system that is often unresponsive to the needs of adoptees. The good news is that it can be done. Most people who work in education genuinely love children. Once educators understand that a child's needs are not being adequately met, they are usually anxious to improve the situation. Many adoptive parents find that advocating for their special needs children in the schools becomes easier and easier each year.

ADVOCATING IN THE PUBLIC SCHOOL SYSTEM

Advocacy for the newly adopted school-age child begins with enrollment. When to enroll the child is up to the parents, who should decide based on the child's needs. If the child is anxious to enroll, great. If the child wants bonding time and time to get to know the community, waiting a few days or even weeks will cause no harm. Some adoptive parents choose to home school for a few months, at least. Others enroll each child from an adopted sibling group several days apart.

Parents have the right to enroll the child under the adoptive family's surname even though the placement is not finalized. In this way, the child can adjust to using his new last name right away. School officials and schoolteachers should be told about the child's adoptive status so that they can be sensitive to the child's emotional needs.

Expecting a few roadblocks when working with teachers is realistic, since most teachers are inexperienced with special needs adoption. Another roadblock is that there is a little bit of the elementary student in us all, and that inner pupil makes advocating with teachers more daunting than advocating with other types of professionals.

Teachers may be either too understanding, or not understanding enough. For example, in some transracial adoptions, the child may be the only child of color in a classroom. A few teachers have been known to ignore the child's rules infractions in an effort to "prove" their lack of racism. Sometimes, the teacher spoils the child because of pity stemming from his difficult pre-adoptive early history or due to racial stereotypes. One African-American child in a predominantly Caucasian classroom was upset by her teacher's assumption that she would be an expert on the history of slavery in America. She felt humiliated having to tell the teacher that she knew no more about the subject than any other child in the class. In other situations, a middle school coach expected an African-American adoptee to be a gifted athlete, and a math teacher expected a Korean-born adoptee to be her star pupil. Parents can educate the educators in situations like these and point out racial stereotyping, prejudice, or pity.

A teacher who is not understanding enough ignores situations that may upset or depress the newly adopted child. Assignments involving family trees, art projects for mother's and father's day, and reading literary works about abused children are all activities that can be amended to help the adopted child feel more comfortable.

When meeting with a teacher to discuss difficulties, try to avoid sitting in student desks, but rather, sit on chairs or sofas where everyone is on an "equal psychological footing." Practice what you want to say in advance and if you think you may be intimidated, take a parent advocate with you for support and help. Follow up the meeting with a letter, if desired, summarizing what was said and agreed to. If you do not come to a resolution, ask to speak to the principal, and then to the superintendent only as a last resort. Following the chain of command is the most efficient route for the parents and the least threatening to school officials.

Printed Resources

Excuse the pun, but no parent can advocate in the schools effectively until he does his homework. Doing homework means gathering up printed resources first, and contacting state and local educational advocates second. Printed resources that you should obtain include a copy of all school laws from the state of residence and a copy of policies and procedures for special education. Depending on the state, these materials may only be published once every two years and are available, usually free of charge, from the State Department of Education or its equivalent. Ask for a copy of the current school laws.

Local printed resources include a copy of parents' rights, special education policies and procedures for the local school or school district, the school handbook, and any other documents from the local school that outline current policy and available services. Parents should read the Parents' Rights in special education sheet very carefully. Not only does it explain their rights and the due process procedure, it may list important local advocacy resources, as well.

Locating Educational Advocates

Advocating for one's child can be an emotional experience. Parents understandably feel passionate about what is best for their child. New advocates may feel intimidated by school authorities. For these reasons, it is important to locate and contact local educational advocates as soon as possible after the adoption of a child with special needs.

Every school district has several experienced parents who know how to advocate within the system. To locate one, adoptive parents should ask other parents whose children receive special educational services if they know of an experienced parent advocate. Usually a phone call to such a parent is all it takes to learn more about parental options. Also, ask other parents about local support groups for parents of children in special education.

Federal Laws

A basic understanding of federal laws is useful to have. Federal law 99-457 encourages all public school districts to provide services to developmentally at-risk children, from birth through three years. Many districts have early intervention programs in place at regular public schools by contract with private institutions or through agencies such as the United Cerebral Palsy Association, the Easter Seals Society, or Head Start. Parents can call their local school district for more information. Evaluation for developmental delays is provided for under this same law, so often a child can receive an excellent free language assessment, even if it turns out that the child does not need services.

What about the school-aged child? Federal law 94-142 says the child aged 3 through 21 years must be provided services if the disability will impact school performance. (In some districts, treatment, but not evaluation, is allowed between ages three and five years.) Language deficits qualify under Federal law 94-142. The child does not have to be attending public school to receive services, but parents may have to transport the child to a public school or some other center to receive therapy.

Section 504 is another federal law that can help special needs adoptees. In general, it requires schools to provide whatever is necessary to educate those children whose special needs are not covered by other legislation or programs. When Rita could not get individualized tutoring and supervised transportation on the special education bus for her children with ADHD under existing district guidelines, she was able to use Section 504. She drew up a handwritten contract on each child that was between her and the school district. The contract called for lab classes or one-on-one tutoring when group learning proved ineffective, and for special education bus transportation, "as parent sees fit." In this way, when grades dropped or behavior on the regular bus was a problem, Rita's children were able to receive extra services for the length of time such help was needed. Section 504 contracts are usually reviewed once a year, and modified when necessary.

TESTING

The first step in determining whether a child is eligible for special education services is testing. The school or school district will schedule a time to have the child tested. There are hundreds of different standardized tests that can be administered. These measure physical coordination, mental abilities, achievement levels, and many other things. Parents should make sure that the appropriate tests are given and that they are administered by a qualified person in a proper setting. For example, some tests are designed to be administered by classroom teachers, while others require the services of a school counselor, psychometrist, or psychologist. Each test will list the uses for which it is appropriate, and describe how, where, and by whom the test should be administered. Parents can ask to see this information. If there is anything about the test or the test scores that parents do not understand, they should ask the person who tested the child for an explanation of the test scores.

Two children in a family we know were denied gifted and talented services for their very bright children due to improper testing. The district used a group test that was clearly marked "not to be used for gifted and talented eligibility." After parents complained to the Superintendent, the school district agreed to use individualized tests designed to determine gifted and talented status. The children easily qualified for the program with the new testing.

THE INDIVIDUALIZED EDUCATION PLAN (IEP)

The Individualized Education Plan, or IEP, is the core of special education services in the United States of America. Once testing determines special education eligibility, an IEP follows. Federal law requires that each child with special educational needs have an IEP on file. Parental input is actively sought in the creation of an IEP.

Parents usually receive written notice that an IEP is being developed. Parents participate in the writing of the educational goals and objectives, and meet with every member of the special education team. At any time, the parent or school can initiate changes to the IEP to better meet the needs of the child. All IEPs are reviewed at least annually.

Parents should remember that the "I" in IEP stands for "individualized." This plan must be designed to meet the *specific* needs of the child, even if creative solutions have to be developed. IEPs can include anything that supports the child's ability to learn, including everything from a "lunch buddy" to help with feeding problems to a bus monitor, to clean intermittent catheterization or diapering for incontinent children.

WHEN ADDITIONAL ADVOCACY IS NEEDED

If a parent's best efforts to develop an appropriate IEP for the child have failed, it may be time to call for additional outside help. The local special education support group or other parents in the same school district may know how to proceed.

Parents can also call local referral and information organizations that specialize in disseminating advocacy information. The local Department of Human Services or the State Department of Education may have the name of such an organization.

The most important resource, especially if a parent needs to due process (sue) a school district over educational services, may be the local Disability Law Center (formerly called Protection and Advocacy Centers). These are law offices set up by the federal government to assist people and the parents of people with disabilities, including physical, mental, emotional, and learning disabilities. There is no charge for these services.

Parents seeking to find their closest Disability Law Center should read the Parents' Rights handout (usually given to all parents of children needing special education services), or ask at the local school district. If these measures do not work, contact the State Department of Education for this information.

One Family's Due Process

When Joe, a newly adopted, emotionally disturbed seven-year-old, was struggling to learn in second grade, his parents first tried to negotiate an adequate IEP by themselves. The school system did not agree that he needed more one-on-one attention. The staff seemed unconcerned by Joe's growing list of rules infractions and violent misdeeds.

Calling in a local educational advocate did not help, so the mom and dad hired tutors to help their child. Time passed, and Joe's behavior and grades worsened. They finally turned to their local Disability Law Center. When Joe was in fifth grade, the Center first wrote a letter on behalf of the parents explaining that Joe needed special services called SED classes (Severely Emotionally Disabled). They included documentation from several mental health professionals who agreed that the child could not function or learn in a regular classroom.

The school district did not agree that the problems were severe enough to warrant special services, even with the child's failing grades. Finally, the Disability Law Center filed a due process lawsuit against the school district. However, before it went to court, Joe was accepted for admission to a residential treatment facility. The due process was dropped.

After Joe was terminated from that facility and several others a few years later, his parents brought him home while continuing the search for another treatment facility. During the months their now high-school-aged son was at home, he attended SED classes. The school district readily provided this violent youth with these services. There was no disagreement as to what Joe needed now that he was big and strong enough to be perceived as a serious threat to the safety of others. Joe was eventually transferred to a school on the grounds of a psychiatric hospital.

We encounter many similar situations, and we believe that part of the problem can be summed up by explaining a difference in perspective between parents and school districts. Parents by nature are pro-active, seeking to prevent problems before they start. School districts are by nature reactive, preferring to deal with problems only after they are well established.

Adoptive parents are not temporary guardians or babysitters. They are permanent moms and dads and, therefore, they must plan ahead. They know when their children are not learning well. School districts, on the other hand, live more in the short term. If the child is performing satisfactorily most of the time, even some of the time, there may not be a rush to do anything different. It is this difference of perspective that causes many problems between concerned parents and school officials who face shrinking budgets.

What to do? Keep trying to work it out. Don't give up. Consider the long-term perspective for your child's needs because no one else will. Be polite but persistent. Use all of the resources available. Children cannot advocate for themselves. They depend on their parents to do it for them.

PRIVATE AND PAROCHIAL SCHOOLS

Private and parochial schools have an important advantage and an obvious drawback. The advantage is that, unlike public schools, these schools can pick and choose who is admitted. There are usually fewer discipline problems in private and parochial schools for this reason, mainly because discipline is traditionally an important part of this type of educational system.

The disadvantage of private and parochial schools is that they may not have access to the special education programs and services offered by the public schools. Parents may have to look longer and harder for a private or parochial school with a comprehensive special education department. In spite of monetary limitations on building special ed programs, parochial schools, in particular, seek to be as inclusive as possible of all kinds of children. If a Catholic school can meet the needs of a special needs child, every effort will be made to do so.

Parents considering private or parochial schools should inquire about tuition discounts and waivers for large families and for families who adopt children with special needs. It never hurts to ask, and many schools are willing to find creative ways to make their program affordable.

HOME SCHOOLING

Legalities

Sometimes adoptive parents decide to home school their newly adopted child because he has had many breaks in bonding and they want to reduce the effects of this history. Given the difficulty of raising children with attachment problems, parents may be biting off more than they can chew when they decide to home school. However, each of us has home schooled newly adopted children along with other children in the family and found that time away from school can have many positive effects in the child's life.

Home schooling begins when the parent decides to become a child's teacher as well. Home schooling is legal in all 50 states, though states differ in how they apply home schooling laws. Parents should call a local home schooling group, their state Department of Education, or the Home School Legal Defense Association (HSLDA) to inquire about laws for their home state. They should also check on the legality of home schooling a child whose adoption is not yet finalized (if applicable).

Some states require that parents notify the school system that they will be educating a child at home, while others have strict requirements such as mandating a certain level of education for the home educator, periodic testing, or monitoring by the local school.

Parents should read about home schooling while learning about the laws of their own state. Contacting a local home schooling support group is a good idea, and parents can find a group in their state by contacting the HSLDA or by checking the appendix of home schooling books. Once a parent has decided to home school, it is only the beginning of the decision-making process.

The style of teaching (structured or unstructured), curriculum or materials, and school calendar must all be decided.

Why Home School?

Why do people home school their children? Home schooling adoptive parents say that their home schooled children tend to spend more time around adults, observing adults in social and business situations, which gives children increased exposure to adult role models. This, they believe, is a plus for adopted children who have been improperly socialized by poor adult role models or who have spent time in institutions. They say that spending as much time as possible with the adoptive parents will encourage the child to attach more quickly and strongly than he would if distracted by public or private school. Other parents home school for religious reasons, or because of the poor quality of their local public schools.

Adoptive parents of children with special needs are some of home schooling's biggest fans. They say that home education works great for kids with special needs because they need so much one-on-one attention. Children with learning disabilities or ADHD are less likely to become the target of the teacher's irritation or the butt of their peers' jokes. As well, since they are competing with themselves, their self-esteem soars.

Once parents have decided to home school, they must decide on the style of teaching to be used. Some parents use a school-at-home approach that is structured and mimics the public school within the home. Others use "unit studies," studying one topic in-depth and thus covering all academic subjects through one topic. An eclectic approach combines unit studies with "unschooling" or interest-initiated learning. Parents have the freedom to choose which style and material best suits their child, which can promote better learning and higher self-esteem in the long run.

UNSCHOOLING

Unschooling is a term created by a former middle school teacher, Grace Llewellyn. She has written two books that are considered classics in the world of home schooling about a third alternative to high school. *Unschooling* is about dropping out of traditional high school and teaching yourself what you need to know to do the job or jobs you love to do, so that you can earn a living. It's about how to learn math, science, history, and foreign languages doing real things in the real world. It's about how to go to college and grad school without ever finishing high school. It's about finding unique ways to learn valuable job skills, such as internships and apprenticeships. Unschooling is not for everyone. But if an adopted child cannot make it in regular school, special education, or in home school, unschooling might be the answer.

Who Unschools

We have noticed that many (not all) unschooled adoptees have one of two characteristics in common. The first group is very bright, and just as restless. For gifted and talented kids, boredom is agony. Boredom haunts their lives, and they will do almost anything to avoid it—even disciplining themselves enough that they can teach themselves what they need to know, and take charge of their own education. Give these kids a copy of the unschooling books, and watch them go. Watch them grow!

The second group, usually kids who have suffered abuse and neglect prior to being placed into the foster care system, have grappled for many years with behavioral and emotional problems. Some suffer from mental illness that has not yet been diagnosed or successfully treated. These kids have usually dropped out of regular high school, home school, alternative high school, night school, and even GED (General Equivalency Diploma) classes. These are kids who are determined to go their own way and who will unschool whether anyone likes it or not, parents included. These kids will need help to make sure unschooling adequately prepares them to earn a good and interesting living. These kids may need to read, or have read to them, the unschooling philosophy- more than once. They must not be allowed to confuse unschooling with "slacking off." Properly unschooled kids become successful working adults, not chronically unemployed or under-employed drifters.

The Unschooling Bibles

The two can't-do-without unschooling books, both written by Grace Llewellyn, are called *The Teenage Liberation Handbook: How to Quit School and Get a Real Life and Education*, and *Real Lives: Eleven Teenagers Who Don't Go to School*. Like salt and pepper, they complement each other so beautifully, it's difficult to make do without one or the other. The first book is like a blueprint for unschooling, reassuring for parents. The second book, with its actual stories of actual teens, reassures kids. Many libraries and bookstores carry these titles, or they can be ordered from Lowry House Publishers, P.O. Box 1014, Eugene, OR, 97440-1014. The phone is (503) 686-2315.

SCHOOL BEHAVIOR AND EMOTIONAL PROBLEMS

Classes for children with severe emotional and behavioral problems go by different names and acronyms. Commonly, they are called SED classes (Severely Emotionally Disturbed). These classes are much smaller, have a much smaller student-teacher ratio (i.e., 3 to 5 students per teacher or teacher's aide), offer more counseling opportunities, and provide more structure and behavior modification for students. Each student has his or her own IEP and receives a great deal of individualized attention and instruction.

SED classes are expensive because of the small student-teacher ratio. To save money, many small school districts combine their SED students into one lab. This means that a child may need to be bused to the next town to receive SED services. However, SED students are entitled to the services of the special education bus when needed. This makes transportation much safer and more pleasant because special ed busses are usually equipped with seat belts and safety harnesses, and the driver is assisted by an additional adult.

Since SED classes and transportation are both expensive and relatively uncommon, parents requesting these for their children may initially be told that such options do not exist or are not available. Parents should persist with their advocacy since SED classes are the only way that some disturbed children will receive an appropriate education.

Before You Adopt

Parents considering the adoption of a child who will need SED, or who *might* need SED, should contact the agency *prior* to placement. A child who has already been identified as needing SED services can be easily transferred into a similar program after adoption. The adoptive parents of children not yet identified as needing SED face an uphill battle getting these services started in many parts of the country. Parents should insist on an SED identification and placement process for children identified as having emotional and behavioral problems before the adoption so that they have that educational option after adoption. We have also heard from a few parents who complained of the exact opposite in their area: that SED classes were overused.

A harmful aspect of SED classes is that they may contribute to an initial increase of some undesirable behaviors, such as the use of profanity or oppositional behavior. SED classes instruct the most challenging children in any school district. Some of the kids are violent or act out of control. Each parent must decide if the good that comes from small class sizes, individualized attention, and extra counseling outweighs the disadvantages of exposing the child to a classroom of children with like behavior problems.

Admission to SED classes requires a process that differs from district to district. Generally, however, parents must produce a recommendation from a mental health professional indicating that the child should receive SED services. The child must also have a record of emotional or behavioral difficulties in the school setting. When a child is denied these services, parents can appeal the decision.

WHEN YOUR CHILD FAILS IN SCHOOL

It may be stating the obvious, but if a child begins failing in school, it is time for parents to examine the reasons for the falling grades. Poor grades are a red flag. They won't magically disappear with pep talks alone. Immediate action is needed before the child falls so far behind that catching up seems an impossible task. If the parents and school determine that the child can do the work, but refuses, counseling options should be examined. If it is felt that the child wants to do the work but cannot, remedial programs, lab classes, tutoring, and other special education options should be explored.

The Homework Hassle

For most children, homework is an irritation, but it gets done. For parents of some older adopted children with emotional and behavioral problems, homework is the Mother of all power struggles. We have heard many stories from parents in the middle of the homework hassle. They describe adopting older children who had never been taught to do homework by former caregivers. These children strongly resist developing good homework habits and find many ways to manipulate their way out of doing homework. They forget the assignment, the textbook, or the backpack itself.

Even when the homework is completed, the power struggle is not over. Some children will destroy, hide, or "lose" their homework before reaching the classroom. This problem can stubbornly persist for years, and have a terrible effect on grades.

Fortunately, there are things a parent can try. Following are two different approaches that have worked for special needs families.

Recipe for Homework Completion

Ingredients list:
1 child who refuses to do homework, no matter what
1 or 2 frustrated and concerned parents
1 or more concerned and involved teachers
1 small notebook
1 pen or pencil
1 duplicate set of textbooks (optional)
1 or more Mozart CDs, cassette tapes, or record albums (optional)

1. Mark the notebook with a name such as "Assignment Book" or "Homework Lists."
2. Date each page for the next few weeks with a separate date or day of the week, i.e., Monday to Friday.
3. Write up and post on the wall or refrigerator a list of rewards and consequences for the completion of each day's or week's Assignment Book entries. For example, rewards include snack treats, local outings with Mom or Dad, trinkets, or a small toy. Consequences may include early bedtimes, loss of playtime, extra chores, or loss of phone privileges.

4. Make note of the work and the home telephone number of the child's teacher.
5. Require the child to show the notebook to his or her teacher each day. The teacher will write down or check the child's list of all outstanding homework, and sign the page. Ask the teacher to check the child's backpack or book bag to ensure that the child has the proper textbooks. (When "I forget my book" becomes a constant refrain, parents should investigate the possibility of borrowing a duplicate set of textbooks to keep at home until the end of the school year.)
6. If necessary, assist the child until all homework is completed. Persistence counts. It helps to set aside a quiet place for doing homework. All televisions and loud music should be turned off. (Note: Homework Time is a great time to play a little classical music. Some researchers believe that the music of Mozart, for example, helps the listener to think more clearly. This is called the Mozart Effect.)
7. Require the child to show the notebook and school work to a parent after completing the homework so that the parent can sign below the teacher's name. This tells the teacher that the homework was completed and checked by the parent.
8. If a daily entry is not signed by the teacher (or substitute teacher), call the teacher at school or at home to obtain the homework assignment.
9. Continue as above until child has developed a new homework habit.

Cooking time: anywhere from 2 weeks to several years!

As with any recipe, this one is not guaranteed to work every time. Some children will continue with the homework power struggle for as long as they remain in school. However, this recipe is worth trying when other, less restrictive methods have failed.

The Love-and-Logic Approach

Attachment Disorder expert Foster Cline, M.D., and educator Jim Fay have a different approach to the homework hassle. In their book, *Parenting with Love and Logic*, the authors say that parents are responsible only to give their children the opportunity and place to do their homework, but that children must decide whether they will spend their time doing homework, or thinking about doing homework (Cline & Fay, 1990). They say that parents cannot force their children to learn.

Parents who use this style of parenting believe that children who do not want to learn or who resist it are probably showing signs of emotional disturbance, attachment problems, learning disabilities, or some other undiagnosed problem. Sometimes professional help, such as counseling or special education, is needed.

One parent we know tells his children that they should feel free to fail a grade if they want to, explaining that some children like their teachers so much they are unwilling to move on to the next grade. Others point out the advantages of being held back in school: The pupil will be able to enjoy a whole class of children who are a year younger, will be the oldest and biggest kid in the class, and will not have to advance with any disliked peers of their own age. One adoptive mom, Harriet, told her son with a sympathetic smile and a shrug of the shoulders, "Honey, even if you outgrow the desk, they will probably let you sit at a table or be able to find a chair big enough to fit you." Harriet's son took his mom seriously because Harriet had become a mother who didn't try to control his life, only allow him to have responsibility for what was truly his business. These parents do not see holding a child back as having long-term negative consequences for their family.

Because Anne has long been a home schooling mother, she tells her children that school failure and misbehavior may be a sign that a child needs more "mom time," and that because she cares so much for them, she will bring them home for schooling any time the child's grades or behavior suffer for more than 18 weeks. This has worked well with even her most challenging children, because the message is delivered with caring and a calm attitude in a matter-of-fact way that lets the child know that even if the child will not take responsibility for herself, mom still will take responsibility as a parent. Children who have had many control issues in their lives also may benefit from the opportunity to choose themselves whether to school at home or school.

WHEN YOUR CHILD IS TRUANT

Truancy, whether it be day-long unexcused absences or chronic tardiness, can be just as frustrating a problem to deal with as the Homework Hassle. Some older adopted children with emotional and behavioral difficulties develop a habit of skipping school, a difficult habit to break.

Schools are not prisons, and any child with average intelligence who wants to skip classes or skip school is likely to find many creative ways of doing so. Parents of such children often find that no sooner do they plug one hole in the truancy dam that another leak develops somewhere else.

For some children, increased vigilance on the part of parents and school officials is enough to eradicate the problem. Escorting the child directly to the teacher, picking the child up from the teacher, and keeping in close contact with school officials throughout the day are all helpful.

For other chronic truants, it is necessary to find and eliminate the cause of and motivation for the behavior. A counselor or family therapist can help your child explore the reasons for the truancy. Does he hate school? Is he unsuccessful with grades? With friends? Is he being picked on by a bully? Does he dislike his teachers?

Professionals can also explore the motivation that makes truancy a habit. Does she have a friend she likes to be truant with? A boyfriend? Is she engaging in criminal activity while truant? Does she use drugs when she is not at school?

With ongoing counseling and treatment, some truant kids can learn a new habit of regular attendance. For those that do not, alternatives to regular school should be explored. These include residential treatment, day school in a restrictive setting such as a mental health facility, SED classes, home schooling, unschooling, and GED classes.

YOUR CHILD THE BULLY

More than a few adoptive parents of older children who have emotional and behavioral problems have had to deal with the reality of their son or daughter acting like a bully. This is a complex behavior in most cases, and a problem that is not solved by reasoning with the child. Bullies tend to be insecure, show little or no sincere remorse, are sometimes unattached, may abuse siblings, and often don't believe they are doing anything wrong.

What to do? Try your library first. Bullies have received a great deal of attention from psychologists in recent years, and there are some very good books available on the results of bully studies. Also check out books on sibling abuse and Attachment Disorder to see if the information applies to your child.

If reading up on the research does not equip you to deal effectively with the problem, seek professional help for your child right away. Ask your therapist to work with the school to develop ways to stop your child's negative behavior.

Above all, do not ignore the problem. Bullies don't simply stop being bullies. They get bigger and stronger and meaner. Some of them grow up and abuse spouses and their children. Bullies need help.

WHEN YOUR CHILD DROPS OUT OF SCHOOL: THE GED

As the old adage goes, "You can lead a horse to water, but you can't make it drink." The same can be said of teenagers and school. Beyond a certain point, usually ages 14 to 18, some teens are going to drop out of school. Parents of children with emotional and behavioral problems are at higher risk of having to deal with this problem.

If a child announces his intention to drop out, or if he simply refuses to go to school, parents should stay calm. Panic will not help the situation. Forcing a child to go to school may work with a few kids, at least in the short term, but will eventually fail as a strategy with very determined teens. For parents who have tried alternatives to regular school, such as residential treatment, day school in a mental health facility, SED classes, and home schooling, GED classes may be the only answer left.

GED stands for General Equivalency Diploma, a term that varies in name from area to area. The concept, however, remains the same. All GED-type exams are designed to help people who cannot graduate from high school in the traditional way to earn a diploma in a nontraditional way, via exam. GED diplomas are completely legal and valid high school diplomas, and can even be used as a basis to apply for admission to many colleges.

Commonly, GED diplomas are sought by prison inmates, mature working adults, teenaged parents, chronically ill students, and even senior citizens. When Rita taught GED classes for Native American students, one of her students was old enough to be her grandfather. He attended night time GED classes for only a few weeks and passed his exam the first time he took it. His great-grandchildren took him out to dinner to celebrate the arrival of his diploma.

Some adoptive parents will find themselves in a position of needing to know more about GED for their teens who have dropped out of school. A call to the local school district administration office or to the State Department of Education, or its equivalent, is all it takes. A brochure is usually sent to the parents outlining local rules and regulations regarding the GED.

GED How-To

Generally, a sample test is available on request. There are also many wonderful books and software products available to help people study for the exam. Any library, bookstore, or computer and electronics store will have some of these titles.

People wishing to take the GED examination often take a pre-test to determine their strengths and weaknesses. The pre-test, like the actual GED exam, is divided up into sections such as history, math, and English. If a GED student scores high in math and low in history, for example, there is no need to study for the math portion of the exam, and all efforts can be put into studying for the history segment.

Parents must encourage their child to study regularly for the classes, either independently or in GED classes, and must stress the importance of having a high school diploma in today's society. Happily for teens who may not have studied diligently, the GED exam can be taken more than once.

COLLEGE BY DISTANCE LEARNING

The same kids who found regular high school unappealing may find traditional college classes, or the college environment, to be no better for their needs. They may find, as have millions of people around the world, that nontraditional college is the answer. Distance Learning (DL) is the college equivalent of home schooling. There are no commutes or uncomfortable wooden desks! While generally reserved for "mature adults," there are a growing number of programs that serve teens and young adults, too. Of course, DL is also an ideal way for busy adoptive parents to finish a degree, or earn an additional one.

Distance Learning also goes by the name Distance Education, and Nontraditional Education. DL is common and widely-accepted in Europe, Asia, Africa, and Australia, but is a relatively recent phenomena in the United States. Some Americans know only one form of DL well: the correspondence course.

DL is simply learning from a distance, usually from home, or from a conveniently located off-campus site. DL allows people to earn college credits, even entire degrees from the AA to the Ph.D., without ever leaving home. DL makes use of many different education delivery methods: The ever-popular mailbox, the Internet, software, modems, TV stations, two-way television using fiber optics, microwave, digital phone lines, satellites, radio, ham radio, and videocassette and audio tape.

DL also refers to on-campus classes where the professor is not physically present, but communicating with students at several sites simultaneously via television, modem, or some other electronic means. A broader definition of DL includes noncredit courses, workshops, seminars, and career credits like CEUs (continuing education credits). Additionally, DL is an exciting and growing part of public and private schools from elementary level through high school in many areas such as math, science, and languages.

Guides that are essential for Distance Learners are *College Degrees By Mail,* and *Bear's Guide to Earning Non-Traditional College Degrees* by John Bear, and *The Independent Study Catalog* from Peterson's Publishing.

CHAPTER 10

Transracial Adoption

> We *feel* and *act* like any other normal everyday family, so we keep forgetting that we don't look like one.
>
> —Timothy Laws-Rodriguez, age 12

Transracial adoption is one of the most controversial issues in adoption, second, perhaps, only to the open adoption records debate. There is no single take on this issue that satisfies all of the people all of the time. This chapter offers both an overview of the issue, and a practical how-to for parents who have already or who are now adopting transracially. Specifically, the chapter is divided into these sections: the history and the controversy, and what adoptive parents need to know.

Transracial adoption is the adoption of a child of a race different from the adoptive parent. In America, this almost always means Caucasians adopting minority-race children. Adult members of minority groups are seldom encouraged to adopt transracially. This one-way transracial adoption exists partly because a disproportionately high number of minority race children are waiting to be adopted. However, racism is also undoubtedly to blame for the lack of transracial adoptions involving the adoption of Caucasian children by minority race parents. Some of the same agency workers who allow Caucasians to adopt children of color, hesitate to allow Caucasian children to be adopted into minority communities by adults of color.

Transracial adoption, in principle, is allowed only when waiting children do not have access to same-race placements, however the supply-and-demand principle found in economics is also a factor. There is a much larger supply of young at-risk mildly disabled children and small sibling groups of color, than there is of their Caucasian counterparts. Adults of all races prefer to adopt younger children with few or minor disabilities, when possible.

IF YOU ARE A MINORITY RACE ADOPTIVE PARENT IN AMERICA

If you are an American who is African-American, Hispanic, Asian, Native American, or of mixed races, you will probably find that your road to adoption of a healthy same-race infant will be different. You may find many agencies anxious to place a child with you. You may well adopt the first child you apply for, instead of the tenth or the twentieth.

There are agencies that specialize in minority placement, and in some states healthy infants and toddlers are available for adoption to you through the state public agency. For example, Hispanic people will have more success in states with large Hispanic populations, such as Florida, Texas, and California. Native Americans may adopt soon after contacting their tribes or looking in states like Oklahoma, South Dakota, and New Mexico. African-American families can contact One Church, One Child or their state Department of Human Services for more information about adopting a child of the same race.

On the other hand, if you are an adult of color who is interested in adopting transracially, go for it. Ask your local special needs adoption support group where you can find an agency that can help you. A friend of ours who is African-American and an experienced same-race adoptive parent is also very knowledgeable of Native American culture. She has been a foster mother to several Native American children. We have encouraged her for years in her desire to adopt an older Native American child, as she would be an excellent and culturally sensitive mother to such a child. There are many older Native American children and older sibling groups who have waited so long for permanency that many tribes would gladly consider a transracial placement.

TRANSRACIAL ADOPTION: THE HISTORY AND CONTROVERSY

Columbus

What was probably the first transracial adoption in America occurred in 1492 when Christopher Columbus kidnapped a Taino Indian child, made him his official interpreter, and later adopted him. The child was named Diego (this was also the name of Columbus's biological son), was baptized into the Christian faith, and traveled widely with the Admiral. Because Diego was forcibly removed from a loving family, and because he witnessed horrible atrocities against his own people by the Europeans, he felt torn between his famous adoptive father, to whom he eventually became attached, and the Taino people.

Columbus justified the forced adoption through a belief that he was saving Diego's immortal soul. Ironically, this same type of arrogance continued well into the 1970s until passage of the Indian Child Welfare Act (ICWA). Indian babies were routinely removed from Indian reservations not by American Indians, but by Caucasian adoptive parents, many of whom believed the baby would be "better off" away from the Native American culture.

Attitudes are different today. Most people believe that transracial adoption is justified solely when it is the only way to find a home for a waiting child within a reasonable amount of time.

TRANSRACIAL ADOPTION TODAY

More than one-half of the children in substitute care today in America are children of color—a number nearly twice that in the general population (U.S. Census Report, 1993). In cities such as Chicago and New York, children of color may constitute as many as 80-90 percent of the child welfare population. Such alarming figures have resulted in increasing numbers of transracial adoptions in the United States. The 1990s saw systemic barriers to transracial adoption dismantled through federal legislation such as the Multi-Ethnic Placement Act of 1994 (MEPA) and the Adoption Promotion and Stability Act of 1995 (APSA), and H.R. 3734, the Personal Responsibility and Work Opportunity Reconciliation Act of 1996.

Transracial adoption, like all types of adoption, is rife with myths and misinformation. Some private agencies and attorneys who place children of color, particularly black and biracial infants, have long told white adoptive parents that not only did the birth family of the child they will adopt not want the baby, but neither did the child's ethnic group.

Not surprisingly, members of these same minority communities tell a different story. In the Kellogg Foundation-supported *Families for Kids of Color* report, minority race dialogue participants painted a "remarkably uniform picture . . . of the current child welfare system, a system they described as too often insensitive, ineffective, fragmented, and remote" (*Families for Kids of Color*, p. 6). Dialogue participants from the African American, Latino and Hispanic, and Native American communities all agreed that America's child welfare system not only does not serve children of any race well, but it particularly treated children of color as "second-class" citizens and treated birth and prospective adoptive families of color with an array of "prejudice-driven practices" (*Families for Kids of Color*, p. 6). The roots of this systemic prejudice were traced to America's historical mistreatment of minorities and to the origination of our adoption system as one catering to middle- and upper-class white families seeking to adopt white, healthy infants. The Kellogg report participants did acknowledge "the importance of later reforms such as those advocating on behalf of special needs children," but "also pointed out that those movements had not typically empowered families of color" (*Families for Kids of Color,* p. 6).

Among the barriers identified by people of color were:

- The early child welfare system developed without the participation of people of color.
- Minority races continue to be underrepresented in the child welfare workforce, especially in leadership and administrative positions.
- Ignorance and fear of cultural differences.
- Insistence that families and children of color adopt middle class white norms.
- Differences of race, ethnicity, and class between adoption workers and families often cause mutual mistrust and misunderstanding.
- The current system is driven by a "protection and removal mentality" that is crisis-driven, precluding effective permanency planning.
- The current system "often fails to recognize the long-term damage caused by severing or limiting contact between children and their biological families" *(Families for Kids of Color,* p. 8). Narrow definitions of "family" limit placement to either reunification with birth families or legal adoption into unrelated families rather than exploring open adoption placements, kinship care by extended family or friends; foster care adoption; legal guardianship or subsidized guardianship; single parent adoption, and coparenting involving more than one family.
- Fiscal underpinnings of the system are rigid and do not allow for flexibility or creativity at the casework level when designing appropriate placement plans for children.
- Bureaucratic convenience, rather than real outcomes for children, drive today's child welfare system, leading to an absence of child-centered standards for adoption, post-adoption services, and reunification.
- Adoption and foster care case workers have case loads that are unmanageable, worker turnovers are too high, and child protective services (foster care) and adoption (permanency planning) units are divided, compromising worker effectiveness.
- A lack of advocacy for children of color has led to a lack of support for children in temporary care.
- Unemployment, economic breakdown, youth violence, drug, and alcohol or gambling addictions in minority communities result from widespread despair, long-term poverty, and oppression in these communities.
- The federal government has concentrated its resources in large, centralized bureaucracies to the detriment of smaller neighborhood-based networks and community development.
- The lack of a mandated, funded child welfare data collection and analysis system was named as the single most important barrier to effective, coordinated, national advocacy efforts on behalf of all children in substitute care and adoption, and especially to children of color.
- *African-Americans.* Fees for the adoption of children bring to mind the practice of removing the ancestors of African-Americans from their families for sale to slave owners, leading to the opposition to such fees, on principle, by many African-Americans who can afford to pay adoption fees.
- *The Latino and Hispanic* cultures in the United States are comprised of Spanish-speaking groups from more than 21 countries, leading to an increasing

diversity within the Latino/Hispanic community. Culturally competent and bilingual adoption workers are lacking at every level of service delivery, erecting barriers between the system and families and children.

- *Native Americans* have an incredible diversity of cultures, with 500 federally recognized tribes, many other tribes recognized by state governments, and over 100 Alaskan Native villages—with a variety of languages, value systems, and cultures. This variety and wide geographical dispersion makes effective advocacy difficult.

TRANSRACIAL ADOPTION TRENDS

Approximately 8 percent of all U.S. adoptions, including international adoptions, are transracial (*Families for Kids of Color*). The National Association of Black Social Workers (NABSW) and other professional and grassroots child advocacy groups have taken positions opposing the transracial placement of children. Opponents of transracial adoption have called the practice "cultural genocide" and offer convincing arguments against the practice. All of the delegates to the Kellogg Foundation's *Families for Kids* dialogue were opposed to transracial adoption based on the belief that

> children of all cultures are best nurtured within their own cultures; and . . . . a sufficient supply of families of culture would be available to care for children of color if child welfare agencies developed positive, collaborative relationships with communities of color, and recruited more aggressively and effectively. (*Families for Kids of Color,* p. 15)

The success of specialized, culture-specific adoption agencies and programs such as Spaulding for Children, One Church, One Child, and Homes for Black Children supports the latter contention. Such programs have been able to establish community relationships quickly and have attracted large numbers of prospective, same-race adoptive families.

In spite of the success of such programs, current trends in child welfare have seen federal legislators convinced that transracial adoption is the solution for children of color waiting to be adopted in America. Prospective adoptive parents and foster parents prevented from adopting children of color due to racial matching policies, with the support of the National Council for Adoption, persuaded legislators to develop, sponsor, and pass legislation in the late 1990s that limited (and in some cases made illegal) racial matching in adoption. The protestations of organizations such as the Child Welfare League of America, North American Council on Adoptable Children, and many professional and ethnic advocacy groups have resulted only in modifications to laws that have made transracial adoptions easier for middle-class Caucasians and done little to remove the systemic barriers to same-race adoption.

Thus, while only a small percentage of all U.S. adoptions have historically been transracial, the trend toward transracial adoptive placements is thought by many to be on the increase as traditional and transracial adoptions are promoted—accurately or inaccurately—as the best solutions for a child welfare system in crisis. The families who adopt children transracially, the professionals who help them during and after the process, and the adoptees themselves need support, education, and information regardless of the motivation for transracial adoption.

CULTURAL COMPETENCE

Cultural competence has been defined as "a set of congruent behaviors, attitudes, and policies that come together in a system, agency, or group to work effectively in cross-cultural situations" (The Robins Training Group, 1991). Cultural competence is more than the absence of attitudes and behaviors that are culturally destructive or incapacitating. While most adoptive parents and adoption professionals probably would recognize racial or cultural prejudice in themselves or others, some argue that many transracial adopters and adoption workers fall prey to a prevalent cultural blindness.

Believing that "color or culture make no difference and that all people are the same" (cultural blindness) also does not express cultural competence (The Robins Training Group, 1991). Other expressions of cultural blindness are that

> Values and behaviors of the dominant culture are presumed to be universally applicable and beneficial. It is also assumed that members of minority cultures do not meet the cultural expectations of the dominant group because of some cultural deficiency or lack of desire to achieve, rather than the fact that the system works only for the most assimilated of the minority group. (The Robins Training Group, 1991, p. 2)

James Mahoney, a Washington-based therapist who specializes in treating adoption issues, notes that most adoptive parents begin the transracial adoption process "color-blind," asserting that race is not an issue (Melina, 1994). This color-blind approach to adoptive parenting denies the experience of people of color, a reality that comes home to adoptive parents only when they and their children encounter racism from the dominant culture. Adoptive parents who are unprepared to handle racism and teach their children both a solid sense of racial identity and skills for handling racism put their children at risk for poor self-esteem and self-hatred. Ill-prepared adoptive parents also risk decreased openness in communication as their transracially adopted children mature, encounter racism from the dominant culture, and find they cannot turn to their dominant-race adoptive parents for help.

Joseph Crumbley, a Philadelphia therapist, says that children who have been raised to be culturally blind not only tend to accept negative racial stereotypes of their own races and feel bad about themselves, but they also

> end up feeling alienated from the white culture they grew up in because others don't see that they belong there, as well as from the culture of their own race because they

don't feel that they fit in there—or may not want to because they see only the negative stereotypes. (Melina, 1994, p. 2)

ISSUES FOR CHILDREN

Jan McFarlane writes that the transracially-adopted child "will have many more issues to resolve about who they are than children growing up in their biological families. Our children must learn not only basic developmental tasks, but also the following: what it means to be adopted, what it means to be a member of a minority, what it means to be a minority growing up with parents of the majority race and culture, and what it means to integrate pieces of the biological heritage—the birth family and its culture—with the culture of the adoptive family" (McFarlane, 1992, p. 25).

Children begin to notice racial differences at around the age of three years. One adoptive mother, Evelyn, worried about her African-American daughter, Amy's preoccupation with her skin color. Amy often asked Evelyn, "When will my skin turn white like yours, Mommy?" Like other adoptive mothers of different-race children, Evelyn learned that she must develop age-appropriate answers for her daughter's questions. One way parents prepare their children is through the use of children's books about adoption. Another is to make the words "adoption" and "adopted" a regular part of the family vocabulary. Yet another way is through the use of the child's baby book or Life Book and through same-race mentors. Finally, the adoptive family may find attendance at a support group for adoptive families of transracially adopted children a valuable aid in introducing the language of adoption to the adopted child.

WHAT ADOPTIVE PARENTS NEED TO KNOW

Different Needs

Although transracial adoption by itself is not a "special needs" adoption, adopting a child of a race that is different from one's own does present special responsibilities and challenges to the adoptive parents. The adoptive parents should try to find same-race mentors for their children to help with this, and the family should live in integrated neighborhoods and attend integrated churches or find other ways of immersing the child in her culture.

Transracial adoptive parents should read about and be prepared for the normal stages in the racial identity process, a process all children experience to some degree. Many libraries and college bookstores have psychology books about the stages of racial identity. Being prepared for these normal stages enables the parent to help children deal with their feelings more effectively. For example, some minority race children will first over identify with the race of their adoptive parents, and then go to the other extreme and vilify that same race before finding a healthy middle ground of tolerance for all races.

When it comes to adopting African-American children, transracial adoptive parents must learn about the specific skin and hair care needs of African-Americans. Most Caucasians don't know, for example, that the skin will need moisturizing nearly every day, or that the hair of most Black children should not be washed more than twice per month, and that the hair will need regular conditioning. Mentors can help with grooming tips and hair care.

Transracial adopters should celebrate and incorporate into family life the customs, traditions, and celebrations of all races and cultures represented in the family. For example, the African-American celebration of the New Year called Kwanzaa takes place right after Christmas. This week-long celebration of values and family-centered principles is easy to learn about. Public libraries carry many different Kwanzaa titles.

Love Is Not Enough

Adoptive parents have learned that "love, by itself, would not be enough" (McFarlane, 1992, p. 25). Transracial adoption is more complex than that. Transracially adopted children also need cultural education and contact with members of their own racial group, both in and out of the adoptive family.

Families should give serious consideration to adopting transracially at least twice or to adopting a sibling group when they adopt transracially, so that the transracially adopted child has a same-race family member with whom she can grow up.

Transracial adoption that is sensitive to cultural and racial issues requires time and effort on the part of adoptive families. However, this sensitivity is crucial if the child is to grow up feeling comfortable in the culture of both his birth and adoptive families. Prospective transracial adopters should ask themselves how comfortable they feel in the culture from which they hope to adopt a child. Do the prospective adoptive parents have close friends, colleagues, or neighbors of that race or culture? Are they willing to make the effort to build such relationships? Any prospective parent who is not willing to take the time, and make the effort, should reconsider transracial adoption.

It is critically important that adoptive parents understand the history of relations between the culture of the adoptive family and that of the transracially adopted child, and understand the affect of this history on the present-day interactions between the adoptee's culture and that of the adoptive parents. Adoptive parents also must realize that they may misjudge the actions of their child or members of the child's race based on learned expectations.

Finally, parents ought to teach their transracially adopted children coping strategies and interventions that respond to conflicts and confusion resulting from differences. They also need to teach their transracially adopted children how to respond to prejudice from members of other cultures.

THE AUTHORS' EXPERIENCES

Since in some parts of the United States being open to the possibility of transracial adoption can mean the difference between waiting a few months for a placement and waiting a few years, prospective parents should carefully consider this option. When an agency has made *genuine* but unsuccessful efforts to place a child in a same-race family, transracial adoption should be considered for the benefit of the child. Permanency, no matter what the race of the kids or parents, is far more important than any other consideration.

We have adopted transracially and feel that the experience has been and continues to be a highly positive one. Our families are multi-cultural as well as multiracial. We have experienced the best of many worlds. Our initial experiences with transracial adoption are typical of those we have seen over the years helping thousands of other families adopt special needs kids.

The Initial Reaction

We did not set out to adopt transracially, only to remain open to considering children of all races. Each adoption process found us applying to adopt a variety of children of all races, including children from our own race. The first child or sibling group officially offered from that group was the one we took home.

Both of us received a mixed reaction from our families and in-laws regarding our transracial adoptions. Our own parents and most relatives were supportive. However, each of us heard from a few relatives, neighbors, and friends who were hostile toward the idea. As often happens in transracial adoption, those people eventually "came around" and accepted our minority race children. For some, it was a natural process, and for others, showing tolerance and acceptance was the only way to be able to continue a relationship with us.

Community Acceptance

No one can predict the level of community acceptance for a special needs adoptive family and, sometimes, assumptions about it are just plain wrong. Close friends of ours, Dan and Brenda, live in a small, rural, middle-class, almost all-white community. Several friends and relatives warned the couple that bringing African-American children into the town would be bad for the children. However, the community has been accepting and warm to this multicultural family and the children have fared well. In this family's case, the dire predictions failed to come true.

On the bus and at school, an occasional bully has muttered a racial slur, something that can happen anywhere, sadly. A close family friend and African-American mentor to the children helped them learn how to deal with this without anger or violence. Whenever such behavior was reported by Dan and Brenda's kids, the school system showed zero tolerance for it, and punished the bully.

Anne's family lives in a large, multiracial and multicultural university community. Their neighborhood is integrated and she and her husband predicted that their children would find ready acceptance. The family was stunned when a nearby neighbor decided to move because Dirk and Anne had adopted African-American children. Their experience proves that racism exists in all types of communities. Transracial adoptive parents should never assume that, because they live in integrated neighborhoods and communities, they and their children will never experience racism.

Prospective adoptive parents should keep an open mind about the level of acceptance they will find. It helps to talk to other families in the same community who have already adopted, and to ask about their experiences. Some agencies call these experienced families "Buddy Families" and will be happy to introduce new adopters to a few of them.

THE RESIDUE OF PREJUDICE IN OURSELVES

After dealing with the reaction of friends, relatives, neighbors, and the community transracial adopters have to deal with their own unreasonable fears. Most people raised in America, regardless of skin color, have to deal with the residue of prejudice in themselves. It is perfectly normal for a parent to wonder if the bond with a different race child will be as strong and beautiful as the bond with a same-race child. It is normal to wonder, and it is normal to watch those fears dissipate quickly after meeting the child.

It is also normal, if one has not grown up around people of other races, to wonder if race will hinder the bonding process. It does not. Like any other parents, transracial adopters quickly grow to love every feature of their child.

And what if race does adversely affect a parent-child bond? Obviously, the adoption should not continue. It is very rare to encounter a situation in which an adoption is damaged or disrupted only because of race differences. Perhaps this is because people who adopt transracially are not racists to begin with, or they would not attempt such a placement.

When a Parent Is Not Ready for Transracial Adoption

The authors have both come across a few people asking for help with a special needs adoption who claim to be open to children of all races, but who, in fact, are not. These people are easy to spot because they'll ask if any "light-skinned" Indian or Mexican children are available, or any part-Asian children who have "round" eyes, or any biracial Black children who favor the Caucasian parent. It is not acceptable to walk into an agency asking about only those minority race children who are "white-alike." Children of color should not be raised by people who have not faced and successfully dealt with any vestiges of racism they may have in their hearts. Anyone concerned about skin tones should stick to same-race adoption. Adoption agencies basically work with only two types of people: Those who prefer same-race placement, and those who are open to children of other races. There is no in between.

Anyone who cannot picture him- or herself kissing or hugging an adult of another race had better not adopt transracially, because the adopted child always grows up. The cute little baby will one day become a grown man who will walk down the street in the adoptive parent's neighborhood, date the neighbor girls, and, if African-American, possibly be mistaken for a criminal simply for walking down the street in a predominantly Caucasian neighborhood.

AN ORDINARY FAMILY

In time, parents can hardly believe they ever worried about bonding. They find that loving a child of a different race is the same as loving a same-race child. Even though they celebrate the dual cultures within their families, they may find themselves mildly surprised that people sometimes stare in public, at the mall, or at the grocery store. Transracial families feel and behave like any other family. They just look different.

REACTIONS AND QUESTIONS FROM STRANGERS

All transracial adopters develop stock answers to the questions they hear in public, some of which are rude, and some of which are well intentioned. Many transracial adopters, for example, started thinking about adoption after speaking to an adoptive parent they ran into at the store. For this reason, many transracial adoptive parents keep a supply of adoption agency and support group business cards in their wallets. When a stranger shows an interest in adopting, it is easy to hand a card to that person, and doing so may result in a waiting child finding permanency.

Americans are a curious lot, and it seems, there will always be those who ask, "Is this your child?" The correct response is, of course, "Yes." Inevitably, a second question follows, "No, I mean is this *your real* child?" Rita's stock reply is, "Some of my children were born to me and some were adopted, but they all *my* children." It is wise to discuss such exchanges with those kids who overhear them, no matter what is said. Some children shrug it off, but some need to discuss their feelings about questions from strangers, and the replies offered.

Transracial adopters should be prepared to hear ridiculous or rude questions from strangers occasionally. Some of the most common include:

- Are you going to tell her she's adopted?
- Are you going to teach him English?
- Does she know she's Black? (or Korean, or Indian, etc.)

- (Nodding at same size children of different races) Are they twins?

Sarcasm and rudeness are not the right tools to use in dealing with intrusive questions because they set an inappropriate example for the children who witness the exchange. Rather, a well-planned direct response is best. Some parents simply say, "Excuse me. I do not wish to discuss my family."

Stares

Many a transracial family, built through adoption or not, has been surprised to find that some people will stare at them in public, even throughout an entire meal in a restaurant, or do a "double-take" when a child calls, "Mom" or "Dad" to a different-race adult. These stares can make a family feel very uncomfortable.

Experience has shown us that there are two effective ways to deal with staring: indirect and direct. The indirect method is not as easy as it sounds. It involves ignoring the stares and encouraging the children to ignore them as well. Sometimes this doesn't work. However, the impulse to stare back in a rude way should be avoided. This could lead to an ugly confrontation.

The direct method of dealing with stares is not only more effective, it has the added benefits of setting an example of kindness, especially toward those people who are staring because they themselves would like to adopt waiting children.

The direct method is simple: Smile at the people who stare at you. Look them in the eye for a few moments—that's all it takes—and smile a little smile. Smile, and you disarm the person staring. You catch them off guard. They can respond only one of two ways, both of which are positive: They can stop staring, or they can smile back.

Your Public Face

Transracial families do well to be more cognizant of what they say in public to each other, and how they discipline their children. The reason is that people may not assume a parent-child relationship between two people of different races. The results can be tragic. A few examples:

- A Caucasian adoptive father is arrested at a department store for "kidnapping" a little girl who is African-American. He is handcuffed and put in the back of a police car because he cannot produce a family photo "proving" that they are father and daughter.
- A stranger reports a license tag number to police for suspected child abuse because a Caucasian woman standing next to the auto was wagging her finger at and speaking sternly to a child who was African-American. The mother was upset because the child had just destroyed a trash can in the bathroom of the restaurant at which they

had just eaten. The behaviorally challenged child was out of control because he could not have cherry pie for dessert.

- A doctor reports an adoptive couple for child abuse because their Korean-born infant has dark purplish spots on his buttocks. The parents must endure an investigation of child abuse before convincing child protection services that the spots are "Mongolian Spots," a harmless birth mark common to children of color.
- A mother is screamed at by a stranger in a mall because she slaps her son's hand after he pinches his baby brother. Since the mother and sons were of different races, the stranger had no idea they were a family, and calls the mother a liar when she explains.

NATIVE AMERICAN SPECIAL NEEDS ADOPTION

> There is no formal adoption ceremony among Native Americans, no word for "orphan" no such thing as a child without parents, because the Native American extended family is so important.
>
> —Jim Cadwell, Project Director,
> The Native American Child and Family Resource Center

As this book was being written, legislation modifying ICWA, the Indian Child Welfare Act of 1978, was considered before Congress. Though no major changes to the federal law were enacted, ICWA has increasingly come under attack as opponents seek to make the transracial adoption of off-reservation Native Americans easier than it is under ICWA.

Rita is a member of a federally recognized American Indian tribe and has helped many people adopt waiting special needs Indian children. The number one misconception she has found that exists regarding ICWA is that prospective adopters of special needs children must physically look like American Indians, or be full-bloods.

The truth is that when it comes to healthy Indian children, there are just as many or more infertile Indian couples vying for these children as there are Caucasian couples applying for scarce healthy Caucasian infants. However, this nation has not yet recruited enough Indian families for waiting *special needs* Indian children. Because of this, agencies that have the support of the children's individual tribes may place these children into homes where there is little or no provable Indian ancestry. They may also place them into non-Indian homes.

In general, the older the child, or the more severe the disability, the more likely it is that non-Indian applicants will be considered. However, it always helps to document any Indian ancestry, no matter how slight, that might exist in a family. ICWA gives tribes the opportunity to become involved in adoptions involving their children. The tribes seek to find families who will be culturally sensitive, however, the tribes do not have to follow the hierarchy of considering tribal member applicants first, other-tribe Indians second, and people with no provable ancestry or no Indian ancestry at all last.

In Rita's family, ICWA has worked for and against the children. When she and her husband adopted a child from South Dakota who is half Native American and half African-American, Rita's membership in an Oklahoma Indian tribe was a plus. However, when they went back later to adopt some of their son's full-blood half-siblings, the tribe placed the children with a Caucasian family instead. They did this because the family lived on the Reservation and there was a better chance that the children would stay on the Reservation if they did not move hundreds of miles south to Oklahoma.

ADOPTING A SPECIAL NEEDS AMERICAN INDIAN CHILD

Anyone interested in adopting special needs Indian children who believes he or she may have some American Indian ancestry should trace their ancestry before trying to adopt a Native American child. Once the proof is in hand, the tribe should be contacted for details about enrolling. Some tribes only enroll people who are one fourth or more Indian, while others place no blood quantum restrictions whatsoever on membership. If tribal membership is not available, then the proof of Indian ancestry should be given to the adoption agency for inclusion in the homestudy.

Prospective parents, whether part-Indian or not, should document their interest in and involvement with Indian peoples and cultures as part of the homestudy. They should make a list of Indian books and periodicals they have read, Indian events attended, and the like. This tells the tribe how culturally aware and involved a family is and can increase chances for a special needs Indian child adoption to occur.

Once the homestudy is complete, prospective parents should send copies of their homestudy to their own tribes first, and other tribes second, with a cover letter stating an interest in children with special needs. Since tribes receive many letters from people hoping to adopt healthy babies, it is crucial to highlight the words "special needs." Homestudies should also be sent to organizations that exist to match waiting Indian children with appropriate homes. It is also a very good idea to subscribe to photolisting books from states with high Native American populations, such as Oklahoma, South Dakota, Texas, Colorado, New Mexico, Arizona, Florida, or California.

TRANSRELIGIOUS ADOPTION

In the movie *Gandhi,* based on the true life story of peace-activist Mohandas K. Gandhi, the Mahatma advises a Hindu who has murdered a Muslim in a riot to adopt a Muslim orphan and raise the child as a Muslim. In this way, the Hindu can atone for his crime, learn to appreciate other faiths, and help a child as well. The appreciation and acceptance of the worth of other faiths is an absolute pre-requisite to trans-religious adoption.

Adopting transreligiously means adopting an older child of a different religion. Technically, this term encompasses the adoption of special needs infants as well, although in the vast majority of cases the infant grows up practicing the faith of the adoptive parents. In such cases, however, adoptive parents would do well to make sure their child grows up knowing something about the faith of the birth parents. After all, this is part of the child's past, and part of the legacy from her family of origin.

Every effort is made to match children to same-religion adoptive parents, especially when the birth parents request an adoptive family of a certain faith. Church-run adoption agencies of every major religion exist to help find same-faith families for waiting babies and children.

Sometimes, however, it comes down to a choice between a child waiting too long and choosing a family of a different religion. Again, permanency has to be the first consideration for the sake of the child. When transreligious adoption occurs, it is imperative for the adoptive parents to be sensitive to the rights and needs of the child.

Here are some things the transreligious adopter can do:

- Study and learn about the child's religion.
- Buy some books about the child's faith and about your faith that speak to the child on his level.
- Attend services at a church, synagogue, or mosque that serves worshipers of the child's faith.
- Talk to the foster parents, the social worker, and most important, to the child about what the child wants to do regarding religion.
- If the child wants to convert to the faith of the adoptive parents (which is very often the case), be sensitive to the transition and careful to show respect for the faith the child is leaving.
- Be patient. The older child may wish to take the conversion process slowly.
- If the child decides not to convert, or changes her mind, be prepared to be a two-religion family. Forcing an older child to convert to a different religion can only cause resentment in the long run.
- Find a mentor for the child who shares his religion, and who might be interested in taking the child to worship services.
- Attend worship with the child, even if you do not participate. This sets an example of tolerance and acceptance.
- Be open to the child practicing a hybrid of the two religions that may mean going to services with you at times and going to services of her first faith at others. This dual religious identity may be a precursor to conversion to the faith of the adoptive parents, or it could be a permanent situation. Stay open to both possibilities.
- Show respect for all religions at all times.

CHAPTER 11

International Special Needs Adoption

> Six years ago, I was living at Howrah Train Station without a family, and this year I got to shake the hand of the President. That's pretty special.
>
> —Marjeena Griffin, adopted daughter of Elaine Griffin, 1995 National Teacher of the Year

International special needs adoption at its most practical level (that of raising the children) is similar to domestic special needs adoption. However, some very important distinctions exist. Those who adopt internationally are generally not able to access Adoption Assistance Payments (AAP) for internationally born children. Some exceptions are in states in which Title IV-B or state-paid adoption assistance payments are available to all children with special needs, or to those who have been adopted through licensed child placing agencies. If the internationally adopted child was ever in the actual legal custody of a United States licensed adoption agency, and the state of residence offers adoption assistance state-funded payments to such children with special needs, then the adoptive family may be able to apply for AAP before or after the adoption has been finalized. This is the exception, rather than the rule.

Most of the children available for adoption internationally come from Asian and Latin American countries, although children from Eastern European countries are increasingly more often available for adoption. The United States Immigration and Naturalization Service (INS) requires that a child must be an orphan, abandoned, or have only one living parent before the child can enter the United States for the purposes of adoption. Although independent adoption (without the assistance of an international agency) is possible, all children entering the United States for adoption must meet INS requirements. INS offers a free book called *The Immigration of Adopted and Prospective Adoptive Children*, available to anyone who requests it from an INS office.

Many children with special needs are available for adoption internationally. As well, many children who have been placed as "healthy" infants and toddlers from foreign countries have later been found to have special needs. Adoptive parents adopting from foreign countries must be willing to risk medical, behavioral, and emotional problems in the adopted child. Some conditions that are not considered as "special needs" in the United States are considered "special needs" in foreign countries. These conditions include, but are not limited to, low birth weight, developmental delays, cleft lip or palate, birth marks, lazy eye, and other correctable, by U.S. standards, medical problems.

The cost of an international adoption ranges from a low of around $8,000 to a high of over $20,000. Some financial assistance or fee reductions may be available through different agencies when adoptive parents are willing to accept the referral of a child who has special needs.

Another consideration in international special needs adoption is that of the language difference when the child is older at the time of adoption. Prospective adoptive parents considering the international adoption of an older child should learn about English as a Second Language (ESL) in order to prepare for such an adoption.

CHOOSING INTERNATIONAL SPECIAL NEEDS ADOPTION

Why do people choose international adoption over domestic adoption? There are probably as many reasons as there are parents. Some parents are unaware that there are young waiting children in the United States who can be adopted across state lines. Others have tried to work with states that have had policies discouraging transracial adoption. Yet others have waited for years for a placement through their home state and have been unsuccessful. Single parents are finding that if they can afford the expense and travel time, infants are available for adoption in several countries, while in the United States married couples are often given preference. A small number of international adopters are fearful of the birth parents of a child and think that by adopting internationally they can avoid thinking about or dealing with an adopted child's birth family. Some parents have lived in the countries from which they adopt, or feel a special place in their hearts for a culture. Some may have a parent, grandparent, or ancestor of a certain race or culture and may want to adopt from that country.

Parents who choose international adoption should know at the outset that the international adoption process is challenging, often takes a long time, and has its pitfalls just like domestic adoption. International adoptions rarely fall through because birth parents change their minds, but they may fail when a child dies, a government falls, or the international adoption program is closed. In such cases, the agency almost always offers adopters another child and works with the family regarding fees.

International adoption is as rewarding as domestic adoption, and long-term studies of internationally adopted children show good outcomes in terms of the adoptee's self-esteem and the parent-child attachment. When someone adopts an internationally born child with special needs, however, there is almost never a financial "safety net" as there is with domestically adopted children. The financial aspects of international adoption are discussed in a later section.

THE INTERNATIONAL ADOPTION PROCESS

International adoption begins when the prospective adoptive parent contacts an agency specializing in international adoptions and completes the initial application. Usually such agencies assign a staff or contract social worker to complete a homestudy. Either the agency or the parents complete the paperwork required by the INS. Some paperwork must be completed or signed by an agency representative.

The homestudy process in international adoptions is similar to that in domestic adoptions, although it may involve more adoptive parent preparation specific to adopting transracially and transculturally. If a child is to be adopted in the United States, the homestudy must be approved by a licensed state or private adoption agency or person qualified to approve the adoptive home under the receiving state's laws. If the child is to be adopted in a foreign country, the homestudy must be approved by a licensed state or private adoption agency in or out of the United States or person qualified under state law to write homestudies and approve adoptive homes.

There are a few requirements for prospective adoptive parents. Married prospective adopters must be U.S. citizens; single prospective adopters must be citizens and at least 25 years old. The adoption agency and foreign adoption program may impose other requirements.

Orphan Immigration Process

When a child has not already been located in another country, usually adoptive parents file an advance petition, the I-600A, with INS that contains all of their information and the adoption homestudy and their FBI fingerprint cards so that INS can pre-approve the adoptive parents. The FBI fingerprint check is mandatory. Parents can be fingerprinted at their local police station and must send two sets of clear fingerprints to INS, although many parents obtain four sets just in case their prints are lost or misplaced. The advance petition is sent to INS along with proof of the prospective parents' U.S. citizenship, marriage, prior divorces (if applicable), a favorably recommended homestudy, and a filing fee. The filing fee and documents are good for one year from the date of filing.

Under INS laws, a child must be an orphan in order to be adoptable. *Orphan* is defined as any child whose parents have died or abandoned the child; whose sole surviving parent is unable to provide for the child, and who is under age 16 when the orphan petition is filed.

Once a child is referred to the parents, they file the *Petition to Classify Orphan as an Immediate Relative*, the I-600 form, with INS. This is filed with a proof of the orphan's age (usually a birth certificate), death certificate(s) of the orphan's parent(s) if applicable, proof that the orphan's surviving parent cannot provide for her or that the orphan has been abandoned to an orphanage, and proof that the pre-adoption requirements of the state of the adoptive parents' residence have been met. If the orphan has been adopted overseas, proof of this is also required. Once the petition has been approved, the orphan is considered to be an immediate relative of a U.S. citizen and does not have to wait to receive an immigrant visa. The child is instead issued an orphan visa and enters the country as a legal, permanent resident of the United States. The child is *not* a U.S. citizen upon entry, however. All internationally adopted children must be naturalized.

In rare cases the petition is not approved. This may be because the child does not qualify as an orphan for some reason, or because INS determines that the adoptive parents cannot give proper care to the child. If a couple is not approved, they will be notified about the reasons and have the opportunity to appeal the decision.

ETHICAL QUESTIONS

The INS requires that full disclosure of an orphan's disabilities or illnesses be set forth in the orphan petition and signed by the adoptive parents. Failure to disclose the known details of a child's medical, social, and behavioral history and any diagnoses is unethical.

Another ethical issue in international adoptions is fraud. Periodically in the media we see stories about black market baby-selling in foreign countries. Knowing that many Americans want to adopt healthy babies, unscrupulous attorneys or agencies have sometimes stolen babies or young children from their parents then sold them into adoption in the United States. INS has even discovered a black market for fraudulent documents supporting orphan petitions. Sometimes adoptive parents have paid thousands of dollars to adopt a child who was never placed. Others have received ill or disabled children when they had not planned a special needs adoption.

There are also rumors that circulate in some countries that Americans adopt children in order to use their organs for transplants in the United States. This rumor, though untrue, turns up like a bad penny time and time again and has delayed some adoptions. In a few extreme examples, international adopters have been detained or attacked because of local fears for the adopted child's safety.

All international adopters should take care to work with reputable adoption agencies or facilitators so as to avoid truly unethical adoption practices.

FINANCES

As has already been mentioned, international special needs adoptions present more financial risk to adoptive parents than domestic adoptions. Children adopted in-country can receive federal- or state-paid adoption assistance, medical assistance, or SSI based on disability. In most cases, internationally born children do not qualify for such benefits.

If a child was not adopted in a foreign country but entered the United States in the custody of a licensed child placing agency, that child may qualify for adoption assistance payments at the federal or state level. Although very few internationally born children have qualified, we know of several who have. These children qualified under laws pre-dating H.R. 3734, the Personal Responsibility and Work Opportunity Reconciliation Act of 1996. Under this law, noncitizens who are not U.S. military veterans or who have not worked and paid taxes in America for at least 10 years cannot receive SSI or food stamp benefits. As well, legal immigrants also cannot receive most federal benefits during their first five years in the country.

At the time this book went to press, it was unclear how the provisions of this law would affect internationally adopted children. Since IV-E adoption assistance eligibility is predicated on either SSI or AFDC eligibility, it may be that the non-naturalized foreign-born child will be ineligible for either program and thus ineligible for IV-E adoption assistance. Since so few children were found to be IV-E eligible under the former law, this should have little impact on international adoptions. It may have an effect on children who are legally adopted but not yet naturalized, however. Even children who have qualifying disabilities and whose families qualify by income for SSI could not receive the federal benefit under the new law. As well, H.R. 3734 eliminated Individual Functional Assessments (IFA) for children, which will significantly reduce the number of children who are SSI eligible. Parents who want more information should contact NACAC, the federal Department of Health and Human Services, or the National Center for Youth Law.

Nonrecurring Adoption Expense Reimbursement

Internationally born or adopted children are eligible for nonrecurring adoption expense reimbursement up to $2,000 per child under P.L. 96-272 in nearly half of the states. We believe that the states that actively seek to disallow nonrecurring adoption expense reimbursement for internationally adopted children with special needs will come into compliance with the spirit and letter of the federal law as adoptive parents challenge these states through administrative and judicial appeals.

In order to be eligible for nonrecurring adoption expense reimbursement, the adopted child must meet three tests under P.L. 96-272 (c): A judicial determination must prove that the child cannot or should not be returned to the home of his parents; there must exist, with respect to the child, a specific factor or condition because of which it is reasonable to conclude that the child cannot be placed with adoptive parents without providing assistance; and a reasonable, but unsuccessful, effort must have been made to place the child with appropriate adoptive parents without adoption assistance.

Federal policy interpretation PIQ-92-02(b) defined "reasonable efforts" thus:

> In an effort to find an adoptive home for a child, an agency should look at a number of families in order to locate the most suitable home for the child. Once the agency has determined that placement with a certain family would be the most suitable for the child, then full disclosure should be made of the child's background, as well as any known and potential problems. If the child meets the State's "special needs" definition, then the agency can pose the question of whether the prospective parents are willing to adopt without subsidy. *If the parents say they cannot adopt the child without assistance, the agency then would meet the requirement in section 473(c)(2)(B) that they made reasonable, but unsuccessful, efforts to place without subsidy.* (Emphasis that of DHHS)

According to *Issues in Adoption Advocacy,* some states

> continue to interpret the third section of the federal special needs definition in a much too literal and selective fashion. Such states employ a narrow interpretation to disqualify some families from receiving reimbursement for non-recurring adoption expenses, as well as for ongoing IV-E adoption assistance. International adoptions have been particularly subject to this treatment.
>
> Ironically, foreign children are often available for adoption by American parents only because they are unadoptable in their native countries. For those children, a "reasonable, but unsuccessful effort" has been made to find a family without an adoption subsidy. Federal law does not indicate that the reasonable, but unsuccessful effort must be made in the United States. When one considers that many foreign children are difficult, if not impossible to place in their own countries, their status as waiting children becomes virtually indistinguishable from that of children waiting for adoption in the United States. (International Adoptions and "Reasonable Efforts," *Issues in Adoption Advocacy,* Nov/Dec 1996, p. 2.)

In its final ruling on the nonrecurring expenses reimbursement program under Title IV-E of the Social Security Act, the Department of Health and Human Services (DHHS) ruled that all children who meet all the requirements of section 473(c) without violating state or local laws were eligible for nonrecurring adoption expense reimbursement (DHHS,1988). DHHS said that children adopted through public or private agencies or adopted independently, including those adopted internationally, were eligible for reimbursement of nonrecurring adoption expenses by the state agency. Although DHHS received complaints from agencies and states arguing that internationally adopted special needs children should not have their nonrecurring expenses reimbursed, DHHS ruled that reimbursement for internationally adopted children was not an optional provision. They furthermore ruled that eligibility for Title IV-E adoption assistance (meaning the child must be SSI or AFDC eligible also) is *not* a requirement for the reimbursement of the nonrecurring expenses of adoption of a child with special needs.

Also in this ruling, DHHS emphasized that Congress "intended to encourage the adoption of special needs children by expanding the reimbursement of nonrecurring expenses to parents who adopt any children with special needs, not just those who meet the categorical eligibility requirements of Title IV-E foster care" (DHHS, 1988, p. 50217). Knowing the intent of the Congress is important for adoptive parents of special needs internationally adopted children, since more than half the states currently deny nonrecurring expense reimbursement to international adoptees. These denials are open to challenge, and until further administrative rulings, policy interpretations, or new laws signal a new intent of the government, special needs adoptive parents can rely on the fact that the federal government supports special needs adoption. In challenging state administrators of IV-E funds, adoptive parents should point out the intent of the law.

Perhaps the most critical finding of DHHS relating to nonrecurring expense reimbursement can be found in the following statement relating to international adoptions:

> In our reexamination of the statue and legislative history, we found that there was no basis for excluding reimbursement for intercountry adoptions based on the Immigration and Naturalization Act. We further concluded that exclusion of intercountry adoptions as a group cannot be a state option. That is, the statute provides no basis for excluding these cases if they otherwise satisfy the statutory requirements. (DHHS, 1988, p. 50218)

If the internationally adopted child meets the section 473(c) requirements, the child qualifies for nonrecurring adoption expense reimbursement regardless of her country of origin. Adoptive parents should be aggressive in advocating for their internationally born children with special needs, even if the state initially denies nonrecurring expense reimbursement. In most successful cases that we know of, the parents prevailed only after appealing an initial denial.

State Subsidies for Internationally Adopted Children

We wrote elsewhere in the book that adoption subsidy committees are generally eager to approve adoption assistance payment requests for children with special needs. Unfortunately, state administrators who have oversight of such committees are sometimes not so eager to work with special needs adopters. We have heard from hundreds of adoptive parents across the country applying for adoption assistance who faced their fiercest opposition from administrators of state and federal adoption assistance funds. One mother told us that her state adoption subsidy administrator was "like a dragon, guarding the gold belonging to these kids, gold that she mistakenly thought belonged to her."

The authors have been directly involved in many appeals of adverse adoption assistance payment rulings involving U.S. and internationally born children. We have learned how to overcome barriers by fighting those states that seemed intent on erecting them for us. This has been nowhere more true than in our experience with international adoption.

Our state, Oklahoma, like several others, allows state-paid subsidies for special needs children who have been in the custody of a licensed adoption agency. The law applies to all children adopted in these states, regardless of their country of birth. Children whose adoptions were finalized in their country of birth are usually ineligible for such assistance, but those whose adoptions must be finalized in the United States may qualify for state-funded subsidies. These children must meet the state definition of "special needs" and the other provisions of the law relating to adoption assistance. If they do, adoptive parents should advocate for equal treatment of their internationally born child.

The authors have helped several adoptive parents of internationally born children receive state-paid adoption assistance in Oklahoma. The state initially denied every application on the basis of the child's foreign birth, a clear violation of the final DHHS ruling on nonrecurring adoption expense reimbursement. In that ruling, DHHS issued a clear finding that states could not deny special needs adoptees assistance strictly based on their national origin.

The state then said that, because international adopters often are required to sign an "Affidavit of Support" either for the adoption agency or INS, they have promised that the internationally born child will not become a public charge. The subsidy program administrator claimed that nonrecurring expense reimbursement and state-paid subsidies made the adoptee recipients "public charges." Adoptive parents argued that no child receiving adoption assistance of any kind is a "public charge," since a public charge is a child in the custody, care, and control of the state. Adopted children are in the custody, care, and control of their adoptive parents.

The third argument the state administrator levied against adoptive parents of internationally born children with special needs was that the parents had signed a statement indicating that they would provide for the medical and other needs of the child being placed for adoption, making the children ineligible for state assistance. Adoptive parents argued that every decree of adoption issued in the state of Oklahoma, including those for children who receive federal adoption assistance payments, decrees that the exclusive care, custody, nurture, education and control of the adopted child is vested exclusively in the adoptive parents and all of the rights, duties, privileges and other legal consequences of the parent and child relationship will exist between the adoptee and the adoptive parents. Such language, adoptive parents contended, exists in every adoptee's adoption decree, a document required by every state for review with each subsidy application, yet the language is never construed to mean that adopted children are not entitled to adoption subsidies. That adoptive parents sign such agreements or are protected by such decrees does not relieve the state of its legal responsibility to adhere to the requirements of federal and state AAP laws.

Finally, we have seen the state argue that all the requirements of the federal adoption assistance law should be applied to internationally born children applying for AAP, even when those children are applying for state-paid subsidies only. Children applying for state-paid subsidies clearly do not qualify for federal AAP (i.e., they are not SSI or AFDC eligible), yet the state administrator attempted to apply federal standards to a state-paid subsidy application on an internationally born child with special needs. Such actions are clear violations of the intent and letter of the federal and state laws supporting needy children with special needs. We hope that by becoming informed, adoptive parents of special needs, internationally born children will advocate for their children and prevail against states with such unfair practices and prejudices against international adoptees.

THE EFFECTS OF INSTITUTIONALIZATION

When an internationally-adopted child has been institutionalized for any length of time, parents should prepare themselves for adoption by reading about the profound effects of institutionalization. Post-institutionalized children exhibit a wide array of problems, ranging from simple developmental delays to profound emotional and behavioral problems. Chapter 7, Living With Disabilities, discusses some of these issues, and the Appendix offers information about other contacts.

The essential problems experienced by children who have been institutionalized for much of their lives include attachment disorder, communication difficulties, and problems giving and receiving affection. The attachment problems of institutionalized children can be more profound and primitive than those commonly seen in domestically adopted children.

Barbara Bascom a pediatrician associated with the Romanian Orphans Social, Educational and Services project (ROSES), described her first visit to a Romanian orphanage:

> I walked into a room full of about 80 babies and found complete silence. No crying, no talking, nothing at all. Just the eerie creaking of rusty cribs rocking back and forth. When I approached the children, they raised their hands to shield their faces. It was almost a reflex. We named it "the orphan salute." (McKelvey, 1994, p. 2)

Prospective adoptive parents can receive a "Foreign Adoption Information Sheet" from the Attachment Center, detailing the symptoms many institutionalized children share and resources for treatment. The address is the Attachment Center at Evergreen, P.O. Box 2764, Evergreen, CO 80439.

ENGLISH AS A SECOND LANGUAGE (ESL)

English as a Second Language (ESL) will be an issue for all internationlly born children who were adopted past infancy. Children immersed in another language at the pre-verbal stage may be delayed in developing English. Those who are already fluent in their native tongue will have ESL issues.

Older internationally adopted children usually begin trying a few words of English right away. Once immersed in the new family and environment, an initial phase of trying to communicate may be followed by one of despair. The child may totally stop speaking for a short time, then begin mimicking others. Within a few months, most children are speaking in phrases and some sentences. Some speak well within three or four months of arriving; others take many more months. There are almost certainly lags in receptive language. Some children do so well with English socially that their parents and teachers come to believe that they have mastered the language. Good social use of English only demonstrates competence in communicating, not mastery of the language or adequate receptive language skills.

There has been little research surrounding the acquisition of language by internationally adopted children. Language acquisition is usually studied in biological families who have moved to a new country, or in families who use two languages. ESL programs have been developed based on what researchers have learned through such studies.

Children who have been adopted internationally do not share the same relationship to language as those who move to an English-speaking country or those who are raised by parents who speak two different languages. Intercountry adoptees have been gestated in a language, spoken to in infancy and, if older, in early childhood in their native tongue. Then they are suddenly adopted and a complete break with the original culture and language is made. Other ESL children have the opportunity to continue speaking their original language at home, within the family. Adopted children do not. All this combined makes international adoption even more traumatic for the young child. He does not speak the language, cannot be helped to make sense of what is happening to him, and is suddenly immersed in a culture in which the smells, sights, tastes and sounds, including the sounds of language, are different.

In spite of these challenges, intercountry adoptees seem to do well with language acquisition. Many do have ongoing troubles with receptive language. Some are later diagnosed inaccurately with learning disabilities because no one recognizes a problem as one related to ESL. Yet other children have their very real learning disabilities and delays mistakenly attributed to ESL, when they have both ESL issues and learning disabilities. A parent of an intercountry older adoptee should have his child evaluated for speech and language services in the schools within the first six months after arrival. In many districts without ESL programs, intercountry adoptees can qualify for speech and language help, and we know many adoptive families who report excellent results.

Helping Your Child with ESL

How can you help your new child learn English and use language adaptively? Here are some suggestions from parents who have been there:

- Make use of board books, simple books designed for very young learners, and flash cards for learning language.
- If the local school system will test your child and offer services, make use of them or hire someone to tutor your child in speech and language.
- As soon as your child has learned the name for one object, activity, or feeling, give him a synonym. Once he has learned the second word, add a third. Thus, ice cream is "yummy," then "good!" then "delicious."
- Teach classes first ("bug"), then members of a class ("cricket").
- Use open-ended questions to give the child opportunities to talk about experiences, wishes, and ideas. "Tell me about the animals you saw at the zoo," rather than, "Did you see an elephant at the zoo?"
- When your child describes objects, people, places, or activities to you, give her additional language by repeating what she said and then rephrasing it using different words.
- Make use of any available programs for children learning a second language. Adoptive mom Adrienne says that intercountry adoptees need these even though they are now in an English-speaking home. This is because such children will not be able to complete development in the first language. They have had to stop development in one language and start all over in a new language. It will take a long time to reach the level of proficiency they had in the first language. They will lag behind their peers in language development until the task is completed some seven to eleven years after starting the second language development.
- If adequate progress is not made, have your child tested for learning problems and visual and auditory processing problems.
- Read often to your child, and have her look at the words while you are reading. Read a variety of books, from Dr. Seuss to Winnie the Pooh.
- If you have a computer at home, add a sound card and buy some of the talking programs on the market for kids, such as "Reader Rabbit," "Kid Talk," and "Once Upon a Time." There are many to choose from and they are particularly appropriate for use by children and parents together (to correct any mispronunciation). They make wonderful use of the areas of sight and sound for language learning. Some of the programs allow the child to compose a story using the keyboard and then have the story read back to him by the computer. Some programs even come in Spanish and English, which is wonderful for children from Spanish-speaking countries.

RAISING THE TRANSCULTURALLY ADOPTED CHILD

Parenting the internationally adopted child shares many of the same issues and concerns as transracial adoption. Parents should make full use of culture camps and every other aid available to help them to instill in their children a sense of cultural, racial, and religious identity. For more information on transracial adoption, see Chapter 10.

PART IV

FOR BETTER OR FOR WORSE

CHAPTER 12

When Things Go Wrong

> There are times when parenthood seems nothing but feeding the mouth that bites you.
>
> —Peter DeVries, U.S. author

Special needs adoptions are riskier than traditional healthy infant placements. Sometimes there will be difficulties involving out-of-home care, a child's acting out that endangers others or the child, and even the failure of the adoption. This chapter takes a look at what happens when things go very wrong in adoption.

FALSE ABUSE ALLEGATIONS

Marilyn Anthony was playing with her quadriplegic adopted son in their backyard. As she rolled her paralyzed son down the grassy slope of their backyard with her feet, his shouts and laughter filled the air. Their game was one of her son's favorites, allowing him the rare opportunity to move unfettered for a few short moments. A few hours later, the police and a county social worker knocked on her door to investigate complaints by a neighbor that Marilyn had been abusing her child. She had been seen, they said, "kicking" a motionless child around the yard. The child was examined for bruises and even though none were found, and her frightened son corroborated her story about their game, he was almost taken from the home. Only intervention by Marilyn's lawyer was able to prevent her son's removal. After spending several hundred dollars on legal fees, missing work to cooperate with investigators, and learning that her child had been removed from class for social worker interviews, Marilyn was told that the complaint would be dropped due to lack of evidence.

Children should be protected from the crime of child abuse, and every American has a clear obligation to report suspected abuse whenever and wherever it is encountered. Most allegations of abuse are never substantiated, however, and many innocent people suffer from the fear, humiliation, shame, and expense of fighting a false abuse allegation. Some adoptive parents have spent their life's savings fighting false abuse charges, and a few have even spent time in jail before being vindicated.

Adoptive parents need to know that foster and special needs adoptive parents are more likely to be charged with child abuse than other parents. Transracial or large special needs adoptive families attract more attention and scrutiny. Foster and adoptive families of emotionally disturbed children can be victimized by children who use child abuse allegations as a way of hurting and alienating families that genuinely care. Ironically, adoptive parents are statistically less likely to actually be abusers than other parents, probably because of the stringent homestudy process designed to screen out those unqualified for parenting.

Sibling abuse is not a well-known problem, but it is all too common among emotionally disturbed siblings placed together into the same adoptive home. Sometimes adoptive parents are accused of abusing a child when, in fact, one child has been abused by another child in the family.

Adoptive parents who have survived the nightmare of false abuse allegations often say that it was the worst experience of their lives. To be falsely accused of something as heinous as hurting one's own child is an experience that can and does ruin lives, marriages, and can destroy entire families. When the false charges are made by the adopted children themselves, they also contribute to adoption disruption.

PROTECTING YOURSELF FROM FALSE ABUSE ALLEGATION

Mr. and Mrs. Hall adopted Jenny from a girls' home when she was 15. They knew about her long, sad history of being abused. They knew she had been physically and sexually abused by several adults in her original family, and that she had falsely accused a foster father and a male teacher of sexually abusing her. The Halls took some common sense measures to protect themselves from false abuse allegations.

Seven months into the adoption, Jenny became enraged one day when her parents refused to let her stay out past curfew. She went to her room and struck her own thighs with a rolling pin, the same object her birth mother had used to abuse her. The next morning she went to school and described a beating from her dad to the school nurse, complete with bruises on her legs for evidence. She also accused him of raping her and gave highly convincing details based on the abuse she had suffered in her birth family.

Jenny never went home that day, but was placed in a temporary shelter. Mr. Hall was visited that evening by county officials as he and his wife were

frantically calling Jenny's friends to find out where she was. After being informed of the charges and the evidence, the Halls promptly produced letters from Jenny's social worker and from her long-time therapist. These letters explained her history, cautioned that she had made false abuse allegations before and might do so again, and offered details of Jenny's actual abuse history for comparison to the story she had just given authorities. After calling and speaking with the social worker, with Jenny, and with the therapist, the allegation was labeled "unfounded." Jenny came home the next day, and was reevaluated for further psychological help.

Jenny made one more false abuse allegation against her father the following year, but this time the school authorities called the parents, the therapist, and the county officials simultaneously. The charges were investigated and labeled false before any steps were taken that might have caused trauma to the family. Slowly, Jenny recovered from her emotional problems as treatment continued, and the adoption remained intact.

Jenny's parents were wise to obtain the letters in advance. Some parents suggest that such letters should be given to all caregivers, the school, local child welfare authorities, and the local police department *before* an allegation is brought. Since only some of the children who have survived abuse actually make false allegations, many parents decide to keep such letters on hand, but do not divulge such private information about their child unless absolutely necessary.

VOCAL

Victims of Child Abuse Laws, or VOCAL, is a nationwide organization of people who have survived false abuse allegations. VOCAL volunteers advocate a very important strategy for parents who are falsely accused: Tape-record or have a credible witness to every single conversation with abuse investigators. This is essential because it is important that parents not be misunderstood, misquoted, or have their words confused with those made by another accused person. If an abuse investigator asks to speak to a parent, that person should immediately reach for a tape recorder, or inform the investigator that it will be necessary first for a neighbor, friend, or some other witness to be present. This protects everyone and fosters accuracy in the investigation. The recorded tapes should be kept by the parent in a safe place, or the witness should be asked to take live notes, or to later write down what he or she remembers from the conversation.

It can be especially helpful for parents to have a professional, such as their attorney or family therapist, to accompany them to the interview with officials. If parents are accused of child abuse or neglect in court, being able to produce credible witnesses of the parents' responsible behavior will go a long way to supporting the parents and disabling the adopted child's attempt to undermine the adoption.

MARRIAGE ON THE ROCKS: DIVORCE AND SPECIAL NEEDS ADOPTION

About half of all first marriages end in divorce, and the numbers are even higher for second and third marriages. Statistics also tell us that the more children there are in a family, the less likely the marriage of the parents is to end in divorce. There are exceptions to this, of course. Rita's marriage of 20 years ended in divorce suddenly, five years after their last adoption. Overnight, she became the sole custodial parent of ten children, eight of them minors. Since no marriage is immune from divorce, all married parents should be prepared to deal with the possibility of divorce, and the possibility of ending up as a single parent. Of course, the best defense is a good offense. Any household's marriage is its greatest asset and should be guarded, protected, and nurtured as such.

It should never be forgotten that only those married people with healthy, strong marriages should enter into adoption, or parenthood of any kind, for that matter. Parenting children with special needs, especially emotionally disturbed children, is stressful to a marriage. When children with emotional problems pit one parent against the other, the marriage relationship can be compromised. A united parental front and excellent communication between parents is crucial. Usually Mom is the target and the child goes to great lengths to enlist Dad as an ally. Dad should stubbornly resist, and both parents should approach parenting as a team.

If divorce is unavoidable, parents should put the children first in all decisions, from the initial separation to the final decree. A sudden split causes unnecessary trauma, and parental bitterness and fighting are salt in a child's psychic wound.

Divorce is even more traumatic for the adoptee than for the biological child because the adoptee has already suffered the loss of birth parents. The adoptee may have also been through one or more divorces while in his or her birth family or foster family. Divorce is an additional loss, a revisiting of old hurts, and a painful ordeal at best. Counseling can help the adoptee understand that even though the marriage has ended, the parental relationships will continue.

OUT-OF-HOME CARE: RESIDENTIAL TREATMENT

She adopted him and his brother at ages six and seven years. No two children ever had more angelic smiles, or more beautiful eyes. They were healthy and affectionate in spite of having spent years with extremely abusive birth parents. The new mom found herself nearly smothered in hugs and kisses for the first few months of the placement. Everyone endorsed the placement except for the children's psychologist. He said they needed to be in a home where there were no pets and no younger children, because the boys were rage-filled and aggressive. The new adoptive mother wasn't worried. She noticed the boys were cruel to the family's cat, so she decided she would watch the boys carefully whenever they were around her infant daughter, their new sister. And the cat, well, he could defend himself, couldn't he?

The boys "tested" the rules for the first six months. They rarely minded, but Mom stayed hopeful that they would, someday. Mom was tired a lot, but she had expected to be. The baby was irritable, but she was probably teething. The cat often hid in the kitchen cabinets. Mom finalized the adoption in court and the new completely legal family went home.

That night, as the younger son removed his long-sleeved shirt and climbed into the tub, she saw the scratches on his arms, dozens of them. He had never cried, never shown them to her, never asked for medical treatment. She would discover later that the child had pulled the cat out of the cabinets almost every day, and swung it around by its tail.

She would also find out that the boys had been forcing their baby sister to eat dirt in the frontyard. The boys were hoarding food in their bedroom closet. They were stealing money from their mom's purse. They were kicking and strangling each other in play. By the time the mother knew everything that was going on, the adoption was more than a year old.

At this point, the mother did the very smartest thing she could have done: She called the social worker who had placed the boys with her. The social worker helped her find a good child testing center. Testing confirmed that they had serious emotional and behavioral problems. The professionals recommended that the brothers not be around their baby sister any more. The boys received long-term outpatient care. They lived in residential treatment for several years while undergoing treatment. Eventually, the mother learned how to parent "from afar."

The adoption did not turn out the way she had wanted it to, but at least all three of her children were safe and thriving. When an adoption goes bad, that is what parents must keep in mind: Safety first. Togetherness second.

When Residential Treatment Is Needed

It is ironic that sometimes children must live away from home in order to stay in a family, but it happens, especially in older child adoption. Sometimes children end up needing residential treatment for behavioral or emotional problems so severe that outpatient therapy is not enough, and living in a family is not a safe option. Residential treatment is usually called for when attempts such as outpatient therapy, drug therapy, school counseling, family counseling, parent training classes, behavior modification, and special education have failed.

When children live in institutionalized settings, moms and dads can and do parent from afar. It may seem as though permanency for children who cannot function in a family doesn't make sense, but experts agree that having parents on the "outside" is ultimately better for emotionally disturbed kids in residential treatment than having no parents at all.

Cost

Residential treatment is very expensive and health insurance policies usually do not cover it. Fortunately, many treatment facilities accept Medicaid, and some church-run facilities charge modestly because donations make up the difference. Some facilities will charge the parents only the full amount of the child's adoptive subsidy, while others use a sliding scale with fees based on parental income. It is very risky to adopt a young child who is emotionally disturbed *and* not eligible for Medicaid and AAP. Young emotionally disturbed children are at high risk of needing residential treatment during the teen years. To be unprepared to meet this major expense is to court financial disaster.

Finding the Right Place

When it becomes clear that residential treatment is necessary, it is best for parents to look locally first. Check the phone book for residential care facilities, or call the local mental hospital or counseling clinic for a list of residential care facilities (sometimes called children's ranches or villages). Most facilities will insist on seeing a report from a professional, such as a psychological summary, before even sending out an application. This is because many facilities specialize in helping a certain type of child. For example, one facility may cater to drug-abused youth, or to a single gender, or to kids who have been arrested, or to kids who are troubled and have never been arrested, or to a certain age group.

Parents should be prepared to talk to several such facilities before finding the right one, and they should be prepared for a series of interviews. Residential care facilities carefully screen all admissions because admitting a child they are not equipped to help can have disastrous consequences for the entire community.

Once in contact with a local residential care facility, parents should ask the admissions officer about the nearest association of children's institutions. Many states have these umbrella organizations that help set standards and which provide catalogs describing each residential care facility in the state. These catalogs are a terrific time saver and show at a glance which type of child each institution serves.

If no local residential treatment facility is available, there are at least two national resources parents can try. The first, Father Flanagan's Boys' Home, also called Boys Town, (for both boys and girls), has a nationwide network of state-of-the-art residential care centers for "troubled youth." Boys Town is recognized as the world leader in developing programs that help kids who can't function effectively in the usual family setting. If the child is accepted, they ask the family to pay only what the family says it can afford.

One more resource available in some states in the United States is the private therapeutic foster care offered by the award-winning Casey Foundation. Financial arrangements are made on a case-by-case basis.

WHEN YOUR CHILD BREAKS THE LAW

It's a sad truth, but parents of chronically troubled kids will probably deal with the juvenile justice system sooner or later. It helps to be prepared. As with so many other aspects of adoption, laws and procedures vary tremendously around the United States, but, in general, parents of kids who have broken the law can expect to receive a phone call from the police, or a summons to appear in court.

If the child is a juvenile, she will probably be taken to juvenile detention and may be released to the care of her parents. Sometimes a repeat offender is detained in a locked juvenile facility pending a hearing. Adult children will probably go straight to jail. Parents should consider deciding in advance whether they will post bail for their son or daughter. Some parents say they will bail the child out of jail once but not again; others say, "You found your way into jail; good luck finding your way out." Parents who have agreed about not posting bail for a child should notify their relatives of their decision and ask for their cooperation in allowing the child to suffer some consequences.

Once notified that their child has been accused of committing a crime, parents should immediately call the district attorney's office, or the juvenile court bureau to determine if they are required to be in court, if they are required to bring the child personally, and if they are required to hire legal representation. If the child is in the physical custody of the state or of an institution, these questions should be directed to the social worker on the case, or to the institution's representative.

Consulting an attorney is also a good idea, especially to determine if the parents are in any way liable for the financial ramifications of the child's actions. Some states have passed laws making parents of minors responsible for the acts of their children.

In most cases, whether the child is living at home or not, the adoptive parents will be required to be in court when the child receives a hearing. Since the court may not be aware that the parents in the courtroom are not the ones who abused or neglected the child in early childhood or caused the juvenile's antisocial behavior, the parents may receive a stern lecture from the judge. When one mother went to court with her troubled teenage son, the judge was aware that the child's serious behavior problems pre-dated the adoption, but still said to her, "Since you failed, the state is now having to solve your son's problems!"

Once a troubled teen has established a pattern of out-of-control behavior, some parents recommend warning local officials if the child lives at home or in the area. Local officials should include police and fire department, school officials, and if necessary, local merchants. When one adoptive father notified the local police chief that his child might be involved in selling drugs and auto burglary, the chief was very happy to have received the information. The chief went out of his way to spend one-on-one time with the child and to keep a special eye on his activities.

Other parents handle trouble with the law differently. One adoptive mom we know was called to a local mall where her daughter had been caught shoplifting. When the store manager asked if she was the mother of the teen, she wanted to explain, "Yes, but she was just adopted six months ago at age 16 and I didn't raise her to steal." Instead, she looked the manager in the eye and calmly answered, "Yes, I am her mother." The incident became a claiming experience for both mother and daughter.

DISRUPTION: WHEN AN ADOPTION FAILS

Disruption is a term meaning a reversed adoption. Often it is used to describe all failed adoptions. Clinicians and researchers use the term in a more narrow way to indicate a failed adoption that has not yet been finalized in a court of law. *Dissolution* is the term used to describe an adoption that has been set aside legally after an adoption finalization. Dissolutions can occur years after the initial placement and are common when a family seeks to protect itself from an emotionally disturbed child who becomes a threat to the safety of family members. Dissolutions are much more difficult to obtain than disruptions, and dissolutions can involve high legal bills. Bad matches lead to emotionally devastating disruptions and disastrous dissolutions.

People who adopt older children are in the greatest need of accurate information because their adoptions are most at risk in terms of disruption. Disruptions can run as high as 10 to 20% in older child adoption (Barth & Berry, 1988). *This is 10 to 20 times higher than the disruption rate in infant placements,* and does not count the placements in which the troubled child is living out of the home, but is still legally part of the adoptive family.

First Steps

Parents who find that an adoption is not working should immediately contact their social worker. It is important to determine, with the help of qualified professionals, if the problem can be solved or not. If it can be solved or relief can be had, finalizing the adoption should be postponed until the parent or parents feel absolutely confident that the placement will work. If it is determined that the problem cannot be solved—that this was a match that should not have happened—it is important to reverse the adoption before it is finalized. This will relieve more anguish, suffering, and debt.

Since disruption is not unknown in more risky older child and sibling group placements, adoptive parents of such children should remind themselves of this fact if they must decide on disruption or dissolution. Guilt, on top of the anguish and heartache of such a loss, can incapacitate and demoralize adoptive parents, especially mothers. While dealing with guilt and grief, disrupting parents should also feel proud that they tried. They gave it their all.

One of the ironies of disruption is often found in the reaction of others. Sometimes the very people who discouraged the older child's adoption are the same ones who discourage a disruption. Adoptive parents shouldn't let people's unsolicited opinions hurt them. Instead, they should listen to their social worker and other professionals involved, their adoption support group, and make up their own minds.

It's All in the Matching

Many special needs adoption advocates believe that there is no such thing as an unadoptable child. They say there is a parent for every waiting child if the matches can just be made. Even children who must live in institutions due to behavior problems, or who must live in hospitals due to chronic illness, can benefit from having a forever family on the "outside" who loves and cares about them.

At the same time, everyone with any experience in the field agrees that matches cannot always work out. Matching, especially when it comes to placing older children and sibling groups, is a highly specialized art. It must be approached with caution and expertise. When adoptions go wrong, the root cause is often a bad match. Some children simply don't belong in some families. Both social workers and prospective parents need to make sure that a match is sound.

Experienced social workers make far fewer inappropriate matches than do new ones. Even experienced adoptive parents should ask seasoned social workers for their opinions on a potential placement. Many adoptive parents learn through experience that they can be blinded by love, and, sometimes, by a "rescue fantasy" mentality. All adoptive parents need the opinions of objective experts. They should listen to therapists and professionals who have experience with the types of children they plan to adopt. Grandpa's opinion is nice, but if Grandpa does not have real knowledge of special needs adoptive placements, parents need another opinion, too!

A few months into a troubled new placement, a couple we know was asked by their veteran social worker, "So when are you going to disrupt?" The couple was taken aback and offended by the worker's bluntness and pessimism and asked the agency to provide a new social worker. More than a year after the adoption of their son was finalized, the adoption was dissolved. The family had become a "war zone," according to the exhausted parents. The couple reconsidered their opinion of the social worker, wondering out loud, "What did she see that we refused to see then?"

Preventing Disruption: The Safety Net

The average stay for children at Father Flanagan's Boys' Home is about 22 months. Many children are helped by residential care facilities and return to their families and continue to improve. However, some children are not helped by any institution, and some may be terminated from a program due to infractions of inviolable rules (i.e., drug usage, sexual activity, violence, or running away).

Once a child is terminated, it may be impossible to find another residential treatment facility willing to accept the child. The second facility may say, "If the other place could not help your child, we cannot help your child." This is the situation faced by the Kelly family, Joe, Susan, and Connie. Five years after Connie's adoption, when she was 13, her parents could no longer keep her at home. They had exhausted all therapeutic options, and the state from which Connie had been adopted refused to help them find a residential treatment facility.

Finally, they found a place on their own, Connie was accepted, and she did fairly well for the first two years. After that, she began running away again, abused alcohol, and became promiscuous. After several threats to terminate her from the program, she was sent home. Joe and Susan had her admitted to a mental hospital for the maximum 90 days allowed by their state's Medicaid program. After that, she was allowed to return to her residential treatment facility, but she slid back into old behaviors and was terminated again.

At this point, no other facility would accept her. When Connie became violent and continued to be defiant about all rules, her parents found a short-term shelter for her while they applied to the state for more help. As the weeks passed, the district attorney began to threaten to sue Joe and Susan for abandonment if they did not pick up Connie from the shelter. The exhausted and nearly bankrupt parents applied for a dissolution of the adoption, the only option they saw remaining. Connie was told to leave four different shelters and to never come back by the time her hearing came up before a judge. At this point, Joe and Susan were terrified to accept her back into the home because Connie was threatening to kill them. The court placed Connie into a foster home and charged Joe and Susan child support. The court refused to allow the dissolution of the adoption because it was not likely that Connie would be readopted by another family, not at age 16, and with her history of problems. Connie remained in foster care until age 18. She retained contact with Joe and Susan. Her parents realized too late that they had adopted their high-risk troubled daughter without a safety net in place.

A *safety net* is our term for a way of protecting both children and parents when an emotionally disturbed or high-risk child is adopted. A safety net is simply a clause inserted into an adoption assistance contract that says that in the event that residential care should become needed (i.e., recommended by a mental health professional) the state placing the child will locate a facility. The safety net further stipulates that the state placing the child will pay any cost not covered by AAP (subsidy), Medicaid, or the family's private insurance, and will continue to find additional placements for the child as long as they are needed, or until the child is 18 years old. If the state cannot find any other residential placements for the child, they will place the child into foster care or some other out-of-home setting as long as it is necessary.

Over the years, we have seen states voluntarily include similar clauses in the contracts of emotionally disturbed children going into adoptive placements. We have also seen states refuse to consider adding such a paragraph. Under no circumstances would we ever encourage a family to adopt a child who is at risk of developing behavioral problems unless a safety net was part of the assistance contract. The situation faced by the Kelly family described earlier in this chapter is an all too common nightmare for special needs adoptive parents.

When Is a Safety Net Needed?

How can parents determine if a safety net is needed? The following checklist can help. The presence of just one of these factors may indicate the need for a safety net. The more factors present in a child's history, the more wary adoptive parents should be of adopting without a safety net. An adopted child is at risk of developing emotional and behavioral problems that could result in a need for residential treatment later if that child:

- Has a biological family history of mental illness, behavioral and emotional problems, or drug or alcohol abuse,
- Has had multiple caregivers,
- Has experienced any type of abuse or neglect,
- Was hospitalized or institutionalized frequently and for many consecutive days during the first 18 months of life,
- Has a drug or alcohol abuse problem,
- Engages in high-risk or illegal behaviors,
- Has a history of emotional or behavioral problems in foster care or at school,
- Has seen or been seen by mental health professionals on a regular basis, or
- Exhibits moderate to severe emotional or behavioral problems with the adoptive parents or with other caregivers prior to finalization of the adoption.

DESPERATE MEASURES WITH DANGEROUS CHILDREN

Right now in this nation, hundreds of special needs adoptive families are in crisis. In many cases, they adopted high-risk youngsters without the safety net described above, and months or years *after* the adoption's finalization, are living with a dangerous child or teen. Disruption is no longer a choice. These families are often living with incredible stress, have exhausted their savings, and are living with mentally ill or emotionally disturbed and out of control teens who threaten the safety of their families. These parents have tried the obvious solutions: Working closely with the adoption agency, intensive therapy, parenting classes for parents of difficult kids, medication, hospitalization, classes at school for emotionally disturbed children, residential treatment or private foster care. Every state and county is different. In some states, families in crisis would have access to help, in others, they are on their own. Following are some possible solutions.

Hire an Experienced Attorney

Since each state is so different, the advice of an attorney can be invaluable. Parents should ask the local NACAC Representative (see Appendix), or ask at an adoption agency or adoption support group for the names of attorneys who are familiar with adoption and juvenile law. An experienced lawyer will know the best legal way of protecting both the family and the child, while maintaining the integrity of the adoptive family if disruption is not an option.

Returning to the State of Origin

It is not likely to happen, but adoptive parents who have exhausted all other options can certainly call the child's state of origin and ask the state to accept the child back into their custody. It's rare, but we have heard of a few cases in which this worked because a birth family member or former foster parent had expressed a desire to parent the child.

Long-Term Foster Care with Legal Custody

In some states, parents of dangerous kids who have exhausted all other options may be allowed to place their children into long-term foster care. They retain legal custody but surrender physical custody. These parents work with their local Department of Human Services (DHS), or the local DHS and the district attorney's office. If parental rights and legal custody remain with the parents, the adoption assistance will probably be used to pay the required child support. In many cases, the court will set the child support amount at 100 percent of the Adoption Assistance Payment.

Relinquishment to a Private Agency

In cases involving very young children, families may also ask their private agencies to accept the child back even though they have finalized the adoption. They then relinquish their parental rights just as a birth parent would. The agency then attempts to place the child for adoption once again. If this fails, the agency places the child into DHS custody. Many private agencies will not risk taking custody of a troubled child for whom they may not be able to find another family, or may not be able to surrender to DHS, but adoptive parents can ask about this possibility.

Relinquishment to the State

Some families hire an attorney and go to court to relinquish rights. This can be done in many places if parents can document that the child is dangerous, if the district attorney agrees with the idea, and if the judge consents. Relinquishment is also more of a possibility if the child is younger than eight and thus easier to replace for adoption. Adoptive parents who relinquish children in this way always lose the adoption assistance payments, and may be charged child support until the child is adopted by another family. Child support amounts are determined by parental income using a chart. However, the judge can decrease the child support payments if parents ask and have good reason—at his or her option.

Ethical Questions

For all the talk about birth parents who "abandon" their children, many people are unaware that adoptive and foster families also may abandon the children they have contracted or promised to parent. We are a society that promises that children removed from their original families for abuse or neglect will be better served by foster care and adoption, but sometimes we cannot keep that promise. Through institutional abuse and neglect, foster care drift, inept, unprofessional, or unethical adoption practices or poor matching, adoptions fail. Children sometimes end up no better served by foster care and adoption than they would have been by remaining with their dysfunctional families of origin. Unfortunately, only hindsight can reveal what "should have been."

We know of state social workers and administrators and legal experts who have recommended child abandonment off the record as a solution to a troubled adoption. The family is advised to place the child in a mental hospital, residential facility, or shelter and then refuse to pick the child up when called. The staff then calls the police who label the child "abandoned." The police contact the district attorney who has to determine on a case-by-case basis if the family had good cause to abandon or not. Those who do are allowed to hire an attorney and work out an arrangement with a juvenile court judge for permanent DHS custody and foster care. The child is said to be "deprived" of a home. This is done to protect the family from the child. The family is usually required to pay child support based on income. Depending on the way the provisions of the AAP contract and who has legal custody, the amount of child support may simply mirror the amount of the subsidy.

The family that is not found to have good cause is told to pick up the child immediately or be charged with criminal abandonment and neglect. If the family refuses, a bench warrant for their arrest is issued and both parents are subject to arrest and trial.

Practicing without a License

We have known a few adoptive parents, and many attorneys, who practice social work without a license. Since in most states adoption independent of an agency is legal, many times attorneys with no child welfare training whatsoever place special needs and older children with disastrous results. We have known adoptive parents who dissolved finalized adoptions and took the child's replacement into their own hands. One couple whose adoption of a Romanian child was not working received the referral of an infant from another program. Not wishing to jeopardize the baby's placement, they sent their Romanian daughter across state lines to friends for adoption and lied to their adoption agency, stating that the girl was at summer camp. They proceeded with their infant adoption and justified their actions by saying both children were "better off"—in their opinion.

In her agency practice, Anne replaced several older or handicapped children who had originally been placed by local attorneys who made their living placing infants. When the opportunities to place special needs children presented themselves, the attorneys proceeded with no understanding of the needs of special needs children or their families. The families suffered financially and emotionally, and the children experienced yet one more trauma of rejection and displacement. Anne's subsequent placements of these children into prepared families were successful. The children had suffered one of life's worst traumas, increasing their sense of worthlessness and fear, all because adults acted without competence in special needs adoption.

Ethical adoptive parents and attorneys, we believe, are open to the tutelage and oversight of helping professionals who will consider the best interest of the child. Adoptive parents who take a child's placement into their own hands, and attorneys who do likewise without knowledge of child welfare, special needs and older child adoption place a child at risk for another failed adoption. We agree with the Child Welfare League of America that children are best served when child welfare professionals have oversight of adoptive placements.

Picking up the Pieces after a Failed Adoption

Parents and children are devastated by a failed adoption. Some parents have called it the "death without a death." The dream dies and the futures of the family and the child are irrevocably changed. As with a death, everyday life is experienced through a fog of sorrow. Insult is added to injury when others judge and criticize because of misunderstanding.

Although we have heard others speak harshly about adoptive parents who "give the child back because he wasn't good enough," from personal experience we both know the anguish of failed adoptions. The guilt and shame of having failed to preserve a child within the adoptive family is equal to none we know. As parents who were to improve the lives of the children we adopted, we not only failed them and became another set of parents who abandoned the child, we also exposed our other children to sexual molestation, terrorism, chaos and violence at the hands of their once-adopted siblings.

Parents who disrupt an adoption entered the placement with the same high hopes and joy of any adoptive parent. They probably had "welcome home" parties, proudly announced their child's arrival or adoption to friends and family, and lived in their faith and civic communities as family for some time before the adoption failed. They must then explain to the child, their other children, family members, friends, and the schools why the child is no longer part of their family. Becoming one more parent or set of parents who have let a child down is not easy; it is not convenient, and it is never a choice that is made without trauma and grief to everyone involved. Families need emotional and therapeutic support after an adoption failure, not criticism.

A common question after a disruption is, "What will become of the child?" Parents who have disrupted are not informed of the child's future progress as a general rule. After all, there is no longer any legal connection between them, and the law says that the privacy of children must be protected. Most parents will still worry and wonder and pray. That's normal. The good news is that many children who go through a disruption, even more than one, go on to successful placements.

ADOPTING AFTER DISRUPTION OR DISSOLUTION

Another common question is: "Will this disruption hurt our chances of adopting again?" The answer to that is, "Almost surely not." First, however, parents must grieve the loss of the child, the loss of the dream. There is no evidence that parents who have disrupted an adoption are likely to do so again, or are not every bit as qualified to parent as anyone else. We do not know any social workers who hesitate to work with parents who have experienced agency-recommended disruption. If anything, it shows that the family was aware of their limitations and took steps to correct a bad situation—for everyone's sake.

Very rarely, and the rarity of this can't be stressed enough, we learn of a couple or a single adopter who does not understand or will not accept their limitations. These people will experience two, three, or more disruptions, and continue to insist that they can parent any child. In cases like this, it will become increasingly difficult to find an agency who will accept an application to adopt—and rightly so. Unfortunately, such parents know how to abuse our loosely constructed systems and use attorneys or other facilitators to get what they want.

When parents consider another high-risk adoption, they should arrange for the safety net described earlier. If the state will not guarantee a safety net, parents can negotiate to take guardianship of a child. In this way, the child can have permanency and a guarantee of services and the family does not risk their financial well-being or long-term safety. When in doubt, parents should ask for 18 to 24 months of post-placement supervision. Many times, it takes that long to understand how a troubled child is going to impact a family and a marriage.

WRONGFUL ADOPTION

Wrongful adoption is a term used to describe adoptions in which the adoptive parents were "wronged" in some way. Typically, this means that the adoptive parents were not given adequate or truthful information about the child's risk factors, disabilities, or behavioral problems, and were placed in crisis as a result. Wrongful adoption lawsuits are very expensive and time-consuming. They are also increasing.

The Wisemans, for example, told their agency they did not want to adopt emotionally disturbed children. They were matched to and adopted Maria and Jean at ages 5 and 6, believing the children to be emotionally healthy. In fact, they had specifically asked about emotional or behavioral problems and were told the little girls had none.

The children's "honeymoon phase" (unusually positive initial behavior) ended after the couple finalized the adoption. At this point, the children began acting out in severe ways. They became defiant of household rules, acted out sexually with toys, and then sexually abused the Wiseman's third child, a toddler. Surprised and dismayed, the Wisemans began to research the girls' history. They learned that the agency has purposely withheld information about the girls' past sexual and physical abuse and acting-out and many foster care placements. One former day care provider told them that the girls had a history of sexual acting out with other children. Before the placement, when the Wisemans had written the agency and asked them if the girls had any history of sexual abuse or sexual acting out, the social worker returned a letter stating that the girls had no such history. The Wisemans learned from the former day care provider that this same social worker had been the one to remove the girls from the day care center for sexual acting out.

After trying various treatments without success, the Wisemans hired an attorney. The girls entered residential treatment. The Wisemans sued the placing agency for wrongful adoption. They asked for reimbursement of their expenses for treatment, plus legal costs and punitive damages.

The adoptive parents contended that the state agency had withheld critical information from them. They said that had they known the whole truth about the children they would never have adopted the girls. The state maintained that the information was withheld accidentally. The case is still pending.

Prevention

Preventing wrongful adoption lawsuits means that prospective adoptive parents must be absolutely certain that they have access to all of the information about the children they are adopting. Parents should insist on full disclosure, and if it is not forthcoming, should go elsewhere to adopt.

CHAPTER 13

Special Needs, Special Situations

> Everyone needs a family and a place to call "home." You don't stop needing parents just because you grow up.
>
> —Kiki, adopted at age 18

SEARCH FOR IDENTITY: WHO AM I?

Several years ago, one of the largest studies of adopted adolescents ever undertaken in the United States found that 65 percent said they would like to meet their birth parents. The majority also said they wanted to know who they looked like and why they were adopted (Benson, et al., 1994). Other research has also supported the finding that the adoptee's search for identity, often including an actual search for and connection with her birth family, is a normative aspect of growing up adopted.

Once a child understands conception and childbirth, he or she is also ready to come into a full understanding of adoption. Children adopted at older ages will probably already have understood a great deal about adoption. Children who lived with and became attached to their birth parents carry that attachment with them and sometimes later forget what life with their original parents was like. They may idealize the absent parent and long to return home. Others want to reject everything they know or remember about the birth family and deny any connection, often out of a fear that they will become what their birth parents were.

Children adopted from other countries or races may immerse themselves in their original culture, even assuming the dress, customs, or traditions of the country. Conversely, they may completely reject the country of origin and embrace America and all things American.

No matter what path the adoptee takes in building his or her identity, the adoptive parent must learn about adoption from the adoptee's perspective. This can be done through reading the works of adoptees such as authors Jean Paton or Betty Jean Lifton, or poets such as Penny Partridge. Joining a national nonprofit organization dedicated to adoption equity such as the American Adoption Congress, or attending an adoption search and support group can also be a tremendous help not only to the adoptive parent, but to the adolescent or young adult adoptee. Support groups for adopted children and adolescents such as those sponsored by agencies like Holt International can help the adoptee to see that her identity struggles are not unusual and that she is not alone.

Adoption experts agree that adoption threaten's the adoptee's sense of self. With no history and no sense of rootedness, he struggles to understand who he is, and where his future lies. Everyone experienced with adoption also suffers some loss of identity. Original parents are parents, yet they do not parent the child they lost to adoption. Adoptive parents are parents also, yet they did not produce the child and have no part in the child's innate abilities and heritage.

When adoptees have incomplete or no information about their birth families, they often tell us that they feel an incomplete sense of self. Many special needs adopted children have only negative information about their birth parents and extended families, information that does not tell about Uncle Joe, who attended Duke University on a football scholarship, or Aunt Emily, who had perfect pitch. They only know about Mom, whose alcohol addiction led to removal of the adoptee and his siblings from the home; or about Dad, who was in prison when the adoptee was born. Adoptees who have only negative information about their parents may develop a negative self-image. Adoptive parents can help by trying to give the adoptee help and understanding in seeking positive, balanced information about the family of origin.

Adoptees and the Search

Adoptive parents whose children search for their birth parents often interpret the search as a threat to the parent-child relationship. Most adoptees who search say they love their adoptive parents and do not seek to replace them. They seek, rather, to regain a part of themselves that they feel is "missing," even if what is missing is information rather than a relationship.

In her work with adult adoptees in search, Anne learned that more than half never told their adoptive parents that they were searching. They were afraid that their adoptive parents would disown them, castigate them, or be very upset and threatened by the search. Many adoptive parents actually did threaten the adoptee with abandonment if they searched!

Adoptive parents of special needs kids, in particular, can have a hard time if a teen or young adult searches for the very parent who abused or neglected the child. Many such adoptees do search and even establish relationships with birth parents who are still dysfunctional or even imprisoned. One of Anne's friends searched for and found her institutionalized mother and visited her regularly in the state psychiatric hospital until her mother died some ten years later. She never told her adoptive parents about the relationship but said that the few glimpses of her mother's real self during that decade gave her a sense of wholeness and understanding that she'd never before experienced. In her book, *Mother, Can You Hear Me?* adoptee Betty Allen describes a similar experience of finding her misdiagnosed mother in an institution.

We believe that adoptive parents must do the best they can to encourage security in their adopted children *and themselves* while they are raising minors. Once a child reaches adulthood, parents should have some faith in themselves and in the loving bond they have established with their kids. With some children there will be a stronger bond than with others; but our experience shows that consistent reliability, trustworthiness, and love always bear some fruit, even in the most wounded or disordered adoptee. Adoptive parents must learn to let go of their adopted children and of their own need to control or possess the adoptee. All adoptees have two families, even if one family did not raise the child and did not provide reliability, trustworthiness, and love. The original family provided our adopted children's roots, and when we reject those roots we reject part of our children. We adoptive parents must often work on our inner selves before we can grow gracefully into our children's adulthoods.

When an Adoptee Returns to the Birth Family

Under what circumstances might a child return to her birth family? We have known some situations in which older, disturbed children experienced one failed adoptive placement after another, went into residential treatment or independent living, and then returned voluntarily as adults to the birth family. In a few other cases, states finally admitted that they could not keep the adolescent in any facility and actually returned the child to the birth family. We have also met adult adoptees who grew up in abusive foster or adoptive families and reestablished relationships with their birth family in adulthood.

OPEN SPECIAL NEEDS ADOPTION

Open adoption exists when adoptive and birth families meet, exchange information, and establish ongoing contact. There are many degrees of "openness," ranging from meeting once, to exchanging letters through a third party, to full integration of birth and adoptive families into an extended kinship system. We define "open" literally. A truly open adoption is one in which birth and adoptive families have full and ongoing access to one another.

There are several reasons why openness may be established in a special needs adoption. Since many waiting children are adopted by their foster parents, many special needs adoptions begin with openness. Foster parents are required by the agency to support ongoing parent-child contact. Adoption is considered only when it is clear that the original family cannot be preserved. Rosenthal and Groze found that ongoing openness between birth and adoptive families was positive for most special needs adopters (Rosenthal & Groze, 1992).

Sometimes a birth family decides from the beginning that they cannot raise a disabled child. They arrange openness with an adoptive family that feels equipped to raise a child with special needs. Joanne Finnegan writes about her experience of choosing adoption for her son in *Shattered Dreams, Lonely Choices: Birthparents of Babies with Disabilities Talk about Adoption.*

Families may also open their adoption some time after it has been finalized. Anne and her husband opened most of their special needs adoptions after they were finalized, having learned about the benefits of ongoing contact for identity formation in adoptees. We know many families who maintain varying degrees of contact with the birth parents of their adopted children, including birth parents with mental illness and some who are incarcerated. When a child benefits from contact and the adoptive family and child can be kept safe, openness can be wonderful. One of the best books on the market about open adoption is Lois Melina and Sharon Roszia's book, *The Open Adoption Experience.*

LARGE SPECIAL NEEDS ADOPTIVE FAMILIES

Since the average American family contains two children, a family with more than three children might be considered a "large family." In special needs adoption, a large family has five or more children. There are even a few highly publicized special needs adoptive families who have 25, 30, or more children.

Many assumptions are made about large adoptive families, the most common being that the parents are either saintly or insane. In reality, every parent has different motivations. Some truly enjoy children, and some enjoyed growing up in large families. Some want to extend their parenting skills to help as many children as they can. And a few married into large families. A few people suggest that parents who adopt many children consider children collectibles, adopt over and over again to avoid intimacy, or have an adoption "addiction." They do not stop to consider that most American children in public schools or day care have a pupil-teacher ratio of 21 or 30 to one, and that no one suggests that one teacher cannot instruct so many children for six hours a day. Large families work by finding creative ways of living, methods of which the average family is not aware.

How Do They Do It?

How do they do it? There is no single answer to this question. We know many large families, and each is unique. Take chores, for example. In one family with above-average income, a maid and part-time cook do most of the chores. In another household, chores are scheduled and carried out at precise times every day, almost military-style. In a third home, the children clean house on Saturday and do very little the rest of the week. In another, someone is hired to clean house, and parents take turns cooking with the children.

What really matters is that each child in a large family is made to feel special. Parents accomplish this by making sure they spend time individually with each child, as well as with the family as a whole. Children spell love t-i-m-e. Parents may take each child out alone on his or her birthday, and write behavior contracts with a parental outing as the prize. Some parents cook dinner each night with a different child or take each child to the grocery store in turn, anything for a little quality time one to one.

Adding Children to a Large Family

Parents in large adoptive families often grow tired of being judged by other people's limitations instead of by their own: "I don't know how you do it with eight kids. I can't even do a good job with my two!" Sometimes, they must deal with adoption agencies and judges who reject them outright before making a careful assessment of their abilities to parent additional children.

The larger a family grows, the more delicate the balance is between functionality and chaos. In a home with many special needs children, the balance is particularly delicate. A bad match can throw the entire house into conflict as too much time and effort is centered on one new child for too long a period of time. Therefore, the larger a family grows, the more careful the parent or parents should be about the addition of other children. For example, if the children in the household are young, parents should avoid adopting older children with emotional problems who might pick on the little ones. A little research, reflection, and careful consultation with the children themselves and with the social worker can help lead to a positive match.

A Special Kind of Normal

When it comes to special needs adoption and large families, the undisputed expert among experts is Dr. Barbara Tremitiere who has not only researched this issue and placed many children into large families, she has raised such a family, including 12 adopted children and three children by birth.

In her doctoral dissertation, "The Large Adoptive Family: A Special Kind of Normal" (Union Institute, 1992), Tremitiere encourages parents building a large family to practice "preventive awareness." Preventive awareness is an ongoing objective whereby parents strive to be aware of various factors in their lives such as the

- complexities of the issues surrounding parenting a large family,
- significance of adding more children,
- crowding studies,
- experience of the child in a large family,
- limited resources of time, energy, and money,
- realistic contingency plans in case of illness, death, divorce, and other tragedies,
- and parental "burn-out," to name a few.

Parents contemplating building a large family and parents who have already done so should seek out some of Tremitiere's writings in adoption periodicals. She is a prolific writer and speaker, and her speeches and articles are a wealth of information for large special needs adoptive families.

UNIQUE SITUATIONS

Flexible Requirements

For every adoptable healthy newborn, there are hundreds of people waiting to adopt that child. For this reason, adoption agencies can afford to develop stringent standards about the people who adopt infants. Usually these standards include marriage, youth, job stability, the means to pay thousands of dollars in adoption fees, church attendance, excellent health, a nice home, and solid middle-class values.

Special needs adoption is different. Sixty to 100,000 children await permanency in the United States alone, and Americans are not fighting over them. Adoption agencies have had to be more flexible about who can adopt. While sacrificing the "ideal" family, they have also had to make sure that each and every approved prospective parent will be a good parent.

The first ideal characteristic to go was marriage. Since the 1960s singles, a fast-growing segment of the population, have been adopting special needs children and proving themselves to be terrific parents. In a few cases, agencies prefer single parents, such as with a child who has been sexually abused and does not want to have a parent of the same gender as his or her abuser.

Agencies have become flexible about age, too. People in their 50s and 60s are adopting older and teenage waiting children. Older parents tend to have a great deal of patience and are well suited to older kids and sibling groups. Some agencies are encouraging disabled adults to adopt, provided the disability does not interfere significantly with the ability to parent. Because of financial aid programs like Purchase of Services, Medicaid, and AAP, people with limited means and those who do not own their own homes are adopting special needs kids, too.

This new flexibility is great news for special needs children who wait for unconditional love and a permanent family. And it is wonderful news for the thousands of Americans who once thought no agency would accept their application. This trend continues to extend to adults who have a different lifestyle, but who could be good parents.

We frequently receive calls from people asking if they can adopt even though they are vegetarian, or home school their kids, or live in an isolated rural area, or practice an Eastern religion. The answer, happily, is yes, if you can find a special needs agency that will accept your application, and if the homestudy process reveals that you are a good prospective parent.

Gay and Lesbian Adoption

Not all agencies will give homosexual adults the opportunity to adopt. A growing number of agencies are accepting applications from gay and lesbian adults, however. If the homestudy reveals that the applicant will be a good parent, his sexual orientation is immaterial.

For all of the talk about gay and lesbian parenting, there is no evidence that one's sexual orientation makes one a worse—or a better—parent. Kids raised by gay or lesbian parents are not more likely to be gay or lesbian themselves. As one young lady being raised by her gay father and his partner put it, "The only bad part is explaining things to my friends. My parents are great, and my boyfriend gets along with them just fine."

Gay and lesbian adoptive parents can encounter difficulty finding an agency that will work with them. For this reason, and for ongoing support, networking is important. A great place to learn about special needs adoption support groups for gay and lesbian adults is the National Adoption Information Clearinghouse, listed in the Appendix. Most of NAIC's materials are free, and they have an excellent catalog. Another source of support and information is the Gay and Lesbian Parents Coalition International (GLPCI), also listed in the Appendix.

In general, most church-affiliated adoption agencies will not accept adoption applications from openly gay or lesbian parents. If a couple decides to apply for adoption and conceals the fact of a gay or lesbian relationship, such duplicity can serve as grounds for removal of the child from the home later, so openly gay and lesbian partners who consider adoption should consider their options. We do know some same-sex couples who have adopted as single parents without making their lifestyle an issue. This has been particularly successful for parents who are already raising other children.

If a state law does not preclude gays or lesbians from adopting, the state or county agency may be willing to work with such couples or individuals. In these cases, the state in which the prospective parent lives makes all the difference. Large states with many waiting children, such as New York and California, place more children in gay and lesbian families than smaller states. In nearly all states, only one parent in a gay or lesbian partnership can adopt a child. All single parents in partnerships (whether straight or gay) thus have to make legal arrangements for the care of their adopted children in the event of their death. Usually this can be taken care of by appointing guardians in the event of the adoptive parent's death.

RELATIVE ADOPTIONS

Relative adoptions are historically the most common, since in most cultures orphaned children were informally adopted by extended family members. Relatives of a child who cannot remain with his birth parent(s) are almost always considered first when adoption is necessary. The exception to this is U.S. infant adoption, when extended family members are usually not approached and asked to adopt a baby that cannot be raised by his parents. If seeking kinship placements was standard practice in this country, as it should be, we would have even fewer infant adoptions by nonrelatives. There is almost always an aunt or uncle, cousin or in-law willing to raise a baby rather than see him raised by strangers. Infants are often separated unnecessarily from their root families because U.S. adoption is more an industry than a service to children or a profession with a universal code of ethics.

When family members adopt, and we encourage this whenever parents cannot raise a child, the legal process is much the same as with nonrelative adoptions. In many states, the homestudy process is waived and the family can simply adopt the child after obtaining permission from the parents and court and termination of parental rights. There is seldom a post-placement supervision, although the court may order one.

STEPPARENT ADOPTIONS

Stepparents are among this country's largest group of adopters. State laws governing stepparent adoptions often differ from nonrelative adoptions. If a custodial parent remarries and the noncustodial parent does not support or visit the child for a certain amount of time, the court may notify the noncustodial parent and proceed to terminate parental rights and allow a stepparent to adopt. In all respects, stepparents who adopt are legal parents. Usually when stepparents adopt, there is more knowledge within the family about the original parent. Children are usually raised knowing about the original parent and a copy of the original birth certificate is available until a stepparent adoption is completed.

We do know of families who kept secret the identity of the original parent, especially when a stepparent entered the family when the child was young. Later, the adoptee nearly always learns the truth and has the same issues surrounding not knowing one parent as are experienced by other adoptees. We recommend that the parent disclose all known information to the child, including information about stepparent adoptions.

GUARDIANSHIP

Guardianship versus Adoption

When for some reason adoption is not an option for a child, guardianship can be the legal means of giving a child some stability. Guardianship allows a person to take the place of a parent, assuming the legal responsibility for the child in the absence of fit parents. As long as the original parents are alive and the child is under 18, they have the opportunity to come into court and prove they are fit parents, unless their parental rights have already been terminated. The "best interests" of the child are not considered when birth parents who still have rights ask the court to vacate a guardianship. The courthouse doors are always open to birth parents who seek to prove their fitness as parents. If the birth parents whose rights have not been terminated succeed in proving their fitness, the child is returned to them regardless of how long he has lived with the guardians, the quality of the child-guardian attachment, or the superior parenting abilities or qualities of the guardian(s). When guardianship is used rather than adoption and a state agency has custody of a child, we have found that any challenges to the guardianship are very rare. Challenges are much more common with in-family guardianships, discussed below.

Guardianship is more common in special needs placements than most people are aware. Sometimes teens and older children do not want to be adopted because they have strong ties to a birth parent or relatives and are afraid of being adopted. Visitation may or may not be court-ordered in such situations, but usually is left to the discretion of the guardian(s).

A child may be so severely handicapped that prospective adopters need all the support the state can give them for the child's care. In such an instance the state may offer guardianship rather than adoption, so that services and equipment not available for an adopted child can continue to be provided. When Anne and her husband adopted a multihandicapped Texas child, for example, the state offered them guardianship as a means of guaranteeing financial provision for their daughter. They chose adoption instead, but some years later found that the state refused to pay for expensive equipment their daughter needed and every few years threatened to withdraw some of their financial support of the child. They learned from some Texas parents who had assumed guardianship rather than adopting that the very services and equipment denied their daughter were routinely provided to children whose parents had taken guardianship.

Based on our combined experience in negotiating with states over what they will provide for children needing permanency, we recommend that adoptive parents seriously consider assuming guardianship rather than adopting their child if the child has severe medical or emotional special needs. Before making a decision, parents should consult the laws of the placing and receiving states and an attorney who has their best interests and those of the child at heart.

In-Family Guardianship

Guardianship can also become an issue in special needs adoptive families when adopted children grow up and become sexually active. Teens may become parents before they are ready to assume responsibility for a child. As grandparents, adoptive parents may find themselves in a situation requiring them to become guardians in order to protect their grandchild. This can happen when the adoptee is incarcerated and has dependent children, has a mental or physical illness or addiction, or when she is mentally handicapped and not capable of providing competent care for a baby or young child.

When grandparents see that their adult child is truly not able or willing to care for a child, the best approach is to consider guardianship as a helpful legal arrangement that protects the child and supports the parent. We know of several grandparents who have had to assume guardianship of their grandchildren and whose relationships with their adult children were sacrificed in the best interest of the grandchild. Whenever possible, grandparents should try to avoid this unless they are willing to pay the emotional and financial cost of guardianship.

When grandparents can work with their adult children and enlist their support for a guardianship plan, it is easier on everyone in the family than setting up a win-lose situation. In many such cases, unfortunately, parents may end up having to establish their own child's unfitness to parent. Any grandparents undertaking guardianship should ask themselves if the needs of the child are so great that they warrant possibly sacrificing the relationship with their adult child. Grandparents (or other relatives, for that matter) should also remember that whenever the child's parents can prove their fitness as parents in court, the child can be removed from the guardians. Court battles over the grandchild can be emotionally and financially devastating, so grandparents should seek the advice of others who have had personal and professional experience in similar situations before making the decision to assume such a guardianship.

PARENTING TEENS AND ADULT CHILDREN

Throughout this book, we have written frankly about the challenges of special needs adoption as well as of its many blessings. We would not have 13 adopted children between us were special needs adoptive parenting not rewarding. We feel fortunate to have experienced adoptive parenthood. When we write about the pitfalls and negative aspects of special needs adoption, then, we do so only because there is so much about special needs adoption that no one tells us. Common knowledge about special needs adoption tends to run to extremes: It is either wonderful and all children need is love, or special needs adoption is too risky and should not be undertaken by anyone. The reality, of course, falls somewhere in between.

When we write about parenting teens and adult children who were adopted with special needs, we do not write about the rewards of watching a challenged child grow up into a self-sufficient, responsible and caring adult, parent, and citizen. Most adoptive parents, like Bob and Dorothy DeBolt, raise self-sufficient special needs kids because most adoptive parents are able to transmit their values to kids who are, in turn, able to apply them.

Research shows that most adopted children turn out pretty well. What now follows is not written about or to the majority of adoptive parents; it is written for parents of difficult kids who do not outgrow their disturbed and disturbing behaviors. It is written so that parents of emotionally disturbed, attachment disordered, and severely disabled children will understand that the future does come and they will see their children grow into adulthood—for better or for worse.

Parenting for the Worse

Those adopted children with special needs who are most difficult to parent are the ones with severe emotional and behavioral problems, untreated attachment disorder, and mental illness. As we showed in an earlier chapter, these children comprise a minority of special needs adoptees. In our experience, these kids usually have been adopted as older kids, have had several foster care placements and a history of abuse, or come from Third World orphanages or have lived in the streets.

Parents know by the time a child is 12 to 15 when something has gone very wrong and the love of adoptive parents has not succeeded in helping the child. By this age those children who are going to become antisocial adults, or adults who always live on the edge of disaster, have had trouble with truancy and grades at school, are rebellious at home, have an undesirable peer group, and have poor communication and relationships with both adoptive parents. Sometimes they run away from home or do not come home at night.

Many parents, in spite of their best efforts, will not be able to avoid trauma or heartache. We recommend 12-step groups such as Al-Anon, support groups for parents of mentally ill children, and family therapy for such parents. Living with chaotic children can produce a chaotic environment in the household and eventually produce Post-Traumatic Stress Disorder-like symptoms in parents and siblings of difficult kids. After years of living with child-induced chaos, parents find themselves cringing when the phone rings late at night and wondering why a teen is in the bathroom so long (is she cutting herself or using the bathroom?). When a troubled teen becomes an adult, the turning of the calendar's page does not magically instill responsibility. The shoplifting that resulted in a wrist slap for your juvenile son lands him in jail after his 18th birthday.

We cannot stress enough that adoptive parents of difficult kids need to establish and maintain strong ties to other adoptive parents who will understand. They also need to establish and maintain credibility with professionals, law enforcement, and educators in their community.

Parents should never allow the difficult child to become the center of the family, a vortex that sucks everything in her direction. Married couples and long-term partners should keep their relationship first, presenting a team and a united front and not allowing the teen or adult child to play good parent/bad parent. Parents should also pay close attention to their symptoms of co-dependency and monitor their own mental, emotional, spiritual, and physical health as they parent in the trenches.

Independent Living

Parents of mentally retarded, medically fragile, multihandicapped and mentally ill young adults must come to grips with the reality that the adoptee may, and probably will, outlive the adoptive parent. Who will care for the adoptee then? Will the adoptee suddenly be catapulted from the safety and routine of the adoptive home, where many times he was not required to take responsibility for himself to the extent he was able, to the unfamiliar environment of a state institution? Will an adoptive sibling care for the adoptee willingly, and should adoptive parents expect as much?

When a disabled child turns 18, his disabilities do not disappear like smoke from birthday cake candles. His needs remain the same or increase, and the financial assistance that was paid until he was 18 or 21 disappears. Although significantly disabled adults can receive SSI, Medicaid, and other public assistance, such assistance barely provides enough to live at subsistence levels.

Group homes and public housing for the handicapped or mentally retarded are hard to find and have long waiting lists. Parents who have adopted, or consider adopting, developmentally disabled or very ill children must plan ahead for the eventuality that the adoptee will not always have Mom or Dad around. They should consult their attorney and make plans to provide for the child in such a way that Medicaid benefits are not lost.

Many adoptive parents of medically challenged children never think that the adult may be employable but remain unemployed because a business does not want to take on an adult whose health care premiums, if health care is even available, will be sky high. Employers may not want the liability of an employee with a history of mental illness or medical problems. In spite of antidiscrimination laws, the employer can probably find a way of rejecting your adult child's application without making the rejection look discriminatory.

Chronic Chaos

Perhaps the most unhappy of circumstances in the special needs adoptive family are presented by the mentally ill, personality-disordered, addicted, or emotionally disturbed adolescent and adult. Many adoptive parents have little understanding of psychiatric disorders. Parents can begin to understand psychiatric disorders by consulting the *DSM-IV*, the *Diagnostic and Statistical Manual* of the American Psychiatric Association, which should be a fundamental part of every special needs adoptive parent's library. The *Physician's Desk Reference* and a good medical encyclopedia are also recommended.

Parents need a good understanding of psychiatric illnesses because childhood disorders can develop into adult disorders. Children diagnosed with conduct disorder or attachment disorder, for example, sometimes later are diagnosed with full-blown personality disorders such as Antisocial Personality Disorder (formerly called "psychopathy" or "sociopathy") or Borderline Personality Disorder. Often individuals with personality disorders also have an addiction. The combination of a personality disorder and an addiction can literally be deadly. Parents of adults diagnosed with multiple disorders will have to act in ways that protect their safety and sanity and those of their at-home children first, and then in ways that might help the diagnosed adult child.

Sometimes parents have to wait 20, 30, or 40 years before their chaotic adult child finally recovers. Sometimes parents have to bury a chaotic child who died violently as a result of risk-taking behavior or through suicide or addiction. Sometimes parents visit their adult children in prison or in mental institutions. Sometimes parents watch as their adult children remain chronically unemployed, marry abusive, addicted, or disordered spouses, or have their own children removed by child protective services. None of these outcomes are what we expect when we adopt waiting children. We all hope that our children will live legally and sanely in the world after leaving home. Most of us hope that our children will not return home to live and that we will not have to raise their children. But some of us will have our hearts broken time and time again. We will need to do grief work, keep ourselves healthy, and find ways of allowing joy and love to flow through our lives by not allowing our chaotic kids to become the focus.

ADOPTING AN ADULT

The adoption of adults is legal in all states, though the process varies. In most states, adult adoptees give their own consent to adoption, no homestudy is required, and birth parents are not notified of the adoption.

Adult adoptions occur when birth parents will not or cannot give consent to an adoption, when a teen is placed at age 16, 17, or 18 and the family agrees to finalize in adulthood, or when for some reason a child's special needs are so great that guardianship is preferred prior to adulthood. Sometimes families are also made when a young adult has been emancipated after long-term foster or group care and has developed a relationship that leads to adult adoption. Other times, foster families adopt an adult after state assistance with the young person's special needs is no longer available.

Anne's oldest child approached her and her husband and asked to be adopted, having lived with them for only seven months as a foster daughter at age 16. Their relationship had continued while her birth family relationships deteriorated. When asked why she would want to be adopted in adulthood, she replied, "Everyone needs a family and a place to call 'home'; you don't stop needing parents just because you grow up."

AFTERWORD

Throughout this book, we have strongly encouraged all prospective adopters to take an educated, active role in their own adoptions. We have showed how adopting and advocating for the special needs child are two halves of a whole. We related what the research shows, what our experience working with thousands of families for a combined three decades has taught us, and what our personal experiences with our own more than 30 adopted and foster children reveals. But we cannot tell anyone what his or her experience will be. No one can. Every child and every family has a unique story, a story written in human hearts.

Appendix: Resources

NATIONAL SPECIAL NEEDS ADOPTION AND ADVOCACY ORGANIZATIONS

Special Needs Adoption and Advocacy organizations are peopled primarily by adoptive parents and adoption professionals and are dedicated to the support and education of adoptive families, as well as to advocacy for permanency planning for children in need of families worldwide.

Aask America (Adopt a Special Kid), 2201 Broadway, Suite 702, Oakland, CA 94612. Tel. 510-451-1748. Founded by special needs adoptive parents/advocates Bob and Dorothy De Bolt. Chapters or affiliates in many states. Special needs information, referrals, and low-cost adoptions. Hosts regional conferences and publishes newsletter.

Adoptive Families of America (AFA), 2309 Como Avenue, St. Paul, MN 55108. Tel. 800-372-3300, 612-645-9955. Fax: 612-645-0055. Web—http://www.adoptivefam.org. Publishes *Adoptive Families Magazine* bimonthly. Hosts annual conference. For $4.95, AFA will send 80-pp. adoption booklet including information needed to make adoption plans, including information about 242 agencies, resources for parents and children, information on independent, special needs, and intercountry adoption, listing of 350 adoptive parent support groups, and tips on choosing an agency or attorney. Dues, including magazine, are $24.95 annually U.S.

American Public Welfare Association (APWA), 810 First Street, N.E., Suite 500, Washington, DC 20002-4267. Tel. 202-682-0100. Fax: 202-289-6555. Issue Brief Series. These include state-by-state breakdowns of subsidy and non-subsidy special needs adoption benefits. Available for a small fee each.

CAP Book (Children Awaiting Parents), 700 Exchange Street, Rochester, NY 14608. Tel. 716-232-5110. Fax: 716-232-2634 Web—http:// www. ibar. com/adoptions.html. A photolisting book of children awaiting adoption nationwide. $75.00 annually.

NACAC (North American Council on Adoptable Children), 970 Raymond Avenue, Suite 106, St. Paul, MN 55114-1149. Tel. 612-644-3036. Fax: 612-644-9848. The best-known special needs adoption organization in the U.S. and Canada. Publishes *Adoptalk*, many publications, and hosts an annual conference. Focuses on adoption of waiting U.S. and Canadian children, and post-placement advocacy. AAP/Subsidy hotline: 800-470-6665.

National Adoption Center (NAC), 1500 Walnut Street, Suite 701, Philadelphia, PA 19102. Tel. 215-735-9988. Fax: 215-735-9410. e-mail: nac @adopt.org. Web—http://www.adopt.org/adopt. Free and low-cost brochures, pamphlets, newsletter, and resource list available. Computer matching of waiting children and prospective adoptive families.

National Adoption Information Clearinghouse, 5640 Nicholson Lane, Suite 300, Rockville, MD 20852. Tel. 301-231-6512. e-mail: naicinfo @erols.com. Web—http://www.workstation.com/naicinfo/. Free catalog, free information about all aspects of adoption, especially special needs adoption, including state and federal adoption laws.

National Council for Single Adoptive Parents, PO Box 15084, Chevy Chase, MD, 20825. Tel. and Fax: 202-966-6367. Single adults can adopt, too. Free brochure, quarterly newsletter, publishes *Handbook for Single Adoptive Parents.*

National Resource Center for Special Needs Adoption (see Spaulding for Children).

Spaulding for Children/National Resource Center for Special Needs Adoption, NRCSNA, 16250 Northland Drive, Suite 120, Southville, MI 48075. Tel. 810-443-7080. Fax: 810-443-7099 e-mail: sfc@ic.net or HN4778@handsnet.org. Free catalog and newsletter. Publishes adoption resources, offers training, and makes referrals.

U.S. Department of Health and Human Services, Children's Bureau, 200 Independence Avenue SW, Washington, DC 20201. Tel. 202-619-0257.

Youth Law Center, Alice Bussiere, 114 Samford Street, Suite 900, San Francisco CA 94104. Tel. 415-543-3379 or 415-543-3307.

OTHER SPECIALIZED ORGANIZATIONS

Black Adoption Committee, 1631 Kessler Blvd., West Drive, Indianapolis, IN 46208. Tel. 317-253-1918.

Boys Town Hotline: 800-448-3000. Boys Town, Nebraska, 68010. Perhaps the most valuable phone number for parents of emotionally disturbed

children. Boys Town has helped more kids with emotional and behavioral problems than any organization on the planet.

Children's Defense Fund, 122 C Street NW, Suite 400, Washington DC 20001. Tel. 202-628-8787.

Child Welfare League of America, 440 First Street NW, Suite 310, Washington, DC 20001. Tel. 202-638-2952. Fax: 202-638-4004. e-mail: books@cwla.org. Web—http://www.cwla.org. Consultation, training, research, books, pamphlets, and advocacy.

Committee for Hispanic Children and Families, 140 West 22nd St., Suite 302, New York, NY 10011. Tel. 212-206-1090.

Council of Three Rivers American Indian Center, COTRAIC (formerly, NAARE, Native American Adoption Resource Exchange), 200 Charles St., Pittsburgh, PA 15238. Tel. 412-782-4457. Fax: 412-767-4808. The Indian Exchange program helps match waiting special needs American Indian children to families. Also publishes COTRAIC newsletter, and hosts annual Native American Pow Wow.

FACE Facts, Families Adopting Children Everywhere, P.O. Box 28058, Northwood Station, Baltimore, MD 21239. Tel. 410-488-2656. FACE publishes a magazine, provides adoptive parent training, and hosts an annual adoption and foster care conference.

FAS (Fetal Alcohol Sydrome) Adolescent Task Force, P.O. Box 2525, Lynnwood, WA 98036. Tel. 206- 778-4048.

FAS (Fetal Alcohol Syndrome) Diagnostic Clinic, 4800 Sand Point Way NE, P.O. Box C5371, Seattle, WA 98105. Tel. 206-528-2660

Fetal Alcohol Syndrome, National Organization On FAS, 1815 H St. NW, Suite 710, Washington, DC 20006. Tel. 1-800-666-6327

Gay and Lesbian Parents Coalition International (GLPCI), P.O. Box 50360, Washington, D.C. 20091. Tel. 202-583-8029 or 201-783-8029. e-mail: GLPC@aol.com

Hispanic Family Institute, 5800 South Eastern Avenue, Suite 370, Los Angeles, CA 90040. Tel. 213-887-1573.

Homes for Black Children, 2340 Calvert, Detroit, MI 48214.

Home School Legal Defense Association. Tel. 703-338-5600.

Institute for Black Parenting, Adoption Unit, 9920 LaCienega Blvd., Suite 806, Englewood, CO 90301. Tel: 310-348-1400.

National Center for Youth Law, 114 Sansome Street, Suite 900, San Francisco, CA 94104. Tel. 415-543-3379.

National Congress for Men and Children, P.O. Box 171675, Kansas City, KS 66117-1675. Tel. 913-342-3860, 913 342-0606, or 800-733-3237. A coalition of organizations and individuals who support father's rights and men's rights in North America; also advocates for fathers wishing to raise their children who have been placed for adoption against the father's wishes.

Native American Child & Family Resource Center, 29758 202nd Street, Pierre, SD 57501. Tel. 605-945-283. Fax 605-945-1039.

RESOLVE, Inc., 1310 Broadway, Somerville, MA 02144-1731. Tel. 617-623-0744. Fax: 617-623-0252. Education, advocacy and support for people dealing with infertility. Information about adoption and special needs adoption.

Single Parents for Adoption of Children Everywhere, SPACE, 6 Sunshine Avenue, Natick, MA 01760. Annual conference for single adoptive parents and for singles seeking to adopt.

Special Needs Adoptive Parents (SNAP), 9800 Academy Hills NE, Albuquerque NM 87111. Tel. 505-822-0921.

Special Needs Adoptive Parents (SNAP), Granville Street, Suite 1150-409, Vancouver BC, V6C 1T2 Canada. Tel. 604-687-3114 (800-663-7627 in BC). Fax: 604-687-3364.

Stars of David International. Tel. 800-782-7349. Adoption information for Jewish and partly-Jewish families. Call for address.

United States Children's Bureau, Box 1182, Washington, DC 20013. Tel. 202-205-8671.

Victims of Child Abuse Laws (VOCAL), 7485 East Kenyon Avenue, Denver, CO, 80237. Tel. 303-233-5321 or 303-430-4813. Support and invaluable suggestions for people who have been falsely accused of child abuse.

NATIONAL RESOURCES FOR THE DISABLED

Organizations

Alliance of Genetic Support Groups, 35 Wisconsin Circle, Suite 440, Chevy Chase, MD 20815-7015. Tel. 301-652-5553. Fax: 301-654-0171. A national coalition of genetic support groups, concerned individuals, and professionals increasing awareness of genetic disorders.

American Psychiatric Association, 1400 K Street NW, Washington DC 20005. Tel. 202-682-6133. Referrals and information about specific mental illnesses.

Association for Bladder Exstrophy Children, 21 West Colony Place, Suite 150, Durham, NC 27705. Tel. 919-403-1463. Fax: 919-403-8605. e-mail: A4BEC@aol.com.

Association for Retarded Citizens (ARC), 500 East Border Street, Suite 300, Arlington, TX 76010. Tel. 800-433-5255 or 817-261-6003.

Autism Society of America, 8601 Georgia Avenue, Suite 503, Silver Spring, MD 20910. Tel. 301-565-0433.

Council for Children with Behavioral Disorders, c/o Council for Exceptional Children, 1920 Association Drive, Reston VA 22091.

Disability Information and Referral Line, 800-255-3477.

Epilepsy Foundation of America, 4351 Garden City Drive, #500, Landover, MD 20785. Tel. 301-459-3700. Fax: 301- 577-9056.

Federation for Children With Special Needs, 95 Berkeley Street, Suite 104, Boston, MA 02116. Tel. 617-482-2915.

Fetal Alcohol Network, 158 Rosemont Avenue, Coatesville, PA 19320. Tel. 215-384-1133.

Learning Disabilities Association of America, 4156 Library Road, Pittsburgh, PA 15234. Tel. 412-341-1515. Fax: 412-344-0224. Web—http://www.ldanatl.org. Free packet of materials. Newsletter.

Little People of America, P.O. Box 9897, Washington, DC 20016. Tel. 301-589-0730.

March of Dimes Birth Defects Foundation, 1275 Mamaroneck Avenue, White Plains NY 10605. Tel. 914-428-7100.

National Alliance for the Mentally Ill (NAMI) and National Alliance for the Mentally Ill Children and Adolescents Network (NAMI CAN), 2101 Wilson Blvd., Suite 302, Arlington, VA 22201. Tel. 703-524-7600.

National Center for Youth with Disabilities, Univ. of Minnesota, Box 721 UMHC, Harvard St. at East River Road, Minneapolis, MN 55455. Tel. 800-333-6293 or 612-626-2825.

National Down Syndrome Society, 666 Broadway, New York, NY 10012. Tel. 800-221-4602 or 212-460-9330.

National Easter Seal Society, 70 East Lake Street, Chicago, IL 60601. Tel. 312-726-6200, TDD 312-726-4258.

National Hydrocephalus Foundation, Route 1, River Road, Box 210A, Joliet, IL 60436. Tel. 815-467-6548.

National Information Center for Youth and Children with Disabilities, P.O. Box 1492, Washington, DC 20013. Tel. 800-999-5599.

National Mental Health Association, 1021 Prince Street, Alexandria, VA 22314. Tel. 703-684-7722.

National Organization for Rare Disorders (NORD), P.O. Box 8923, New Fairfield, CT 06812-1783. Tel. 800-447-6673 or 203-746-6518.

National Society of Genetic Counselors, 233 Canterbury Dr., Wallingford, PA 19086-6617. Send SASE with request for specific information.

National Tay-Sachs and Allied Diseases Association, 2001 Beacon Street, Brookline, MA 02146. Tel. 617-277-4463.

Parent Network for Post-Institutionalized Child, P.O. Box 613, Meadowlands, PA 15347. Tel. 412-222-1766.

Prader-Willi Syndrome Association, 6490 Excelsior Blvd., Suite E-102, St. Louis Park, MN 55426. Tel. 612-926-1947.

Simon Foundation for Continence, P.O. Box 835, Wilmette, IL 60091. Tel. 847-864-3913. Fax: 847-864-9758. Membership is $15 per year. Reprints, tapes, videos, and pamphlets available. Sells the book, *Enuresis: A Guide to the Treatment of Enuresis for Professionals,* Ed. Penny Dobson, R.N.

Spina Bifida Association of America, 4590 MacArthur Blvd., Suite 250, Washington, DC 20007. Tel. 800-621-3141 or 301-770-SBAA.

Spina Bifida Center, Kennedy Krieger Institute, 707 N. Broadway, Baltimore, MD 21205. Tel. 1-800-873-3377.

Publications and Periodicals

Exceptional Parent Magazine, P.O. Box 3000, Dept. EP, Denville, NJ 07834. Tel. 1-800-372-7368. Fax: 413-637-4343. $28.00 for one year subscription.

1996 Resource Guide: Directories of National Organizations, Associations, Products & Servces. From *Exceptional Parent Magazine.* Includes national information and advocacy resources, national resources for specific disabilities and conditions, parent training and information centers, parent-to-parent programs, state assistive technology centers, disability-related electronic bulletin boards, federal and federally-funded information resources, professional organizations, and much more. Write to *Exceptional Parent,* P.O. Box 8045, Brick, NJ 08723, or call 800-535-1910.

Sharing Our Caring, P.O. Box 400, Milton, WA 98354. Down's syndrome.

ADOPTION AND PARENTING

General Interest

Brodzinsky, David M., and Schechter, Marshall (Eds.). *The Psychology of Adoption.* New York: Oxford University Press, 1990.

Clarke, Jean Illsely, & Dawson, Connie. *Growing Up Again.* New York: Harper & Row, 1989.

Eckman, Paul. *Why Kids Lie by Paul Ekman.* Charles Scribner's Sons, 1989.

Lifton, Betty Jean. *Journey of the Adopted Self: A Quest For Wholeness.* New York: Basic Books, 1994.

Lifton, Betty Jean. *Lost and Found: The Adoption Experience.* New York: Harper & Row, 1988.

Melina, Lois Ruskai. *Making Sense of Adoption: A Parent's Guide.* New York: Harper & Row, 1989.

Melina, Lois Ruskai. *Raising Adopted Children: A Manual For Adoptive Parents.* New York: Harper & Row, 1986.

Schaefer, Carol. *The Other Mother.* New York: Soho Press, 1991.

Schooler Jayne E. *The Whole Life Adoption Book: Realistic Advice for Building a Healthy Adoptive Family.* Colorado Springs, CO: Piñon Press, 1993.

Severson, Randolph. *Adoption: Charms and Rituals for Healing.* Describes the uniqueness of adoptive families and offers a ceremony for adoptive families welcoming a child into their midst. Heart Words Center, 5025 N. Central Expressway, Suite 3040, Dallas, TX 75205. Tel. 214-521-4560.

Severson, Randolph. *Raised Right: A Spiritual and Philosophical Guide to Discipline in Adoptive Families.* HeartWords Center, 5025 N. Central Expressway, Suite 3040, Dallas, TX 75205. Tel. 214-521-4560.

Sorosky, A. D., Baran, Annette, & Pannor, R. *The Adoption Triangle.* San Antonio: Corona Publishing, 1989.

Verny, Thomas. *The Secret Life of the Unborn Child.* New York: Summit, 1981.

Verrier, Nancy. *The Primal Wound: Understanding the Adopted Child.* Baltimore, MD: Gateway Press, 1993.

ADOPTIVE BREASTFEEDING

La Leche League International, Center for Breastfeeding Information, 1400 North Meacham Road, P.O. Box 4079, Schaumburg, IL, 60168-4079. Toll free: 800-LALECHE in U.S. or 800-665-4324 in Canada. Tel. 708 519-7730. Fax: 708-519-0035 Web—http://www.prairienet.org/LLLI/homepage.html. LLLI is the recognized premier resource world-wide for breastfeeding and adoptive nursing information. Thousands of volunteers in North America. Write or call for free catalog. Induced lactation and Re-lactation (adoptive nursing) pamphlets and books available for sale. See local white pages for nearest LLLI support group.

Medela Incorporated, P.O. Box 660, McHenry, IL 60050-0660. Tel. 800-435-8316 or 815-363-1166. Fax: 815-363-1246. Web—http://www.medela.com. Medela manufactures, rents, and sells electric and manual breastpumps which facilitate the induced lactation and re-lactation processes. They also sell many other breastfeeding aids. Many volunteer La Leche League Leaders sell or rent these breastpumps, or Medela can be contacted directly.

ATTACHMENT DISORDER

Organizations

ATTACH, 2775 Villa Creek #240, Dallas, TX 75234. Tel. 214-247-2329. Professional and lay parent coalition.

Attachment and Bonding Center of Nebraska, 10855 West Dodge Road, Suite 180, Omaha, NE 68154. Tel. 402-330-6060.

Attachment Bonding Center of Ohio, 12608 State Road, North Royalton, OH 44133. Tel. 216-843-7600.

Attachment Center at Evergreen, P.O. Box 2764, Evergreen, CO 80439. Tel. 303-674-1910.

Attachment Disorder Parents Network, P.O. Box 18475, Boulder, CO 80308. Tel. 303-443-1446.

Attachment Disorder Parents Network of Connecticut, 16 Heritage Circle, Clinton, CT 06413. Tel. 203-669-3140.

Attachment Disorder Parents Network of Massachusetts, 46 Carter Drive, Framingham, MA 01701. Tel. 508-877-5930. Support, contacts, information packet.

Center for Attachment Therapy, Training, and Education (CATTE), 101 Hawk Point Court, Folsom, CA 95630. Tel. 916-988-6233.

Evergreen Consultants, P.O. Box 2380, Evergreen, CO 80439. Tel. 303-674-5503.

Family Attachment Center, P.O. Box 50656, Provo, UT 84605. Tel. 801-223-4820.

Mothering Center, Martha Welch, M.D. 952 5th Avenue, New York, NY 10021. Tel. 212-861-6816. Attachment therapy for mothers and children.

Books about Attachment and Attachment Disorder

Barth, Richard P., and Berry, Marianne. *Adoption and Disruption: Rates, Risks, Responses.* New York: Aldine de Gruyter, 1988.

Belsky, Jay, and Nezworski, Teresa. *Clinical Implications of Attachment.* Lawrence Erlbaum Associates, 1988. For the advanced reader.

Bolton, Frank G., Jr. *When Bonding Fails.* Sage Publications, 1983.

Bowlby, John. *Attachment and Loss.* Vol. I-III. New York: Basic Books, 1969, 1980.

Cline, Foster W. *Conscienceless Acts, Societal Mayhem, Uncontrollable, Unreachable Youth in Today's Desensitized Society.* Hardcover book, 288 pages. Love and Logic Company.

Cline, Foster W., M.D. and Fay, Jim. *Hope for High Risk and Rage Filled Children.* Evergreen, CO: Foster W. Cline, 1992.

Cline, Foster W. and Fay, Jim. *Parenting with Love and Logic: Teaching Kids Responsibility.* Love and Logic Company, 2207 Jackson Street, Golden, CO, 80401, or by calling 800-338-4065.

Cline, Foster W. and Fay, Jim. *Parenting Teens with Love and Logic: Preparing Adolescents For Responsible Adulthood.* Love and Logic Company.

Delaney, Richard J. *Fostering Changes: Treating Attachment-Disordered Foster Children.* Walter J. Corbett Publishing, 1991.

Delaney, Richard, and Kunstal, Frank. *Troubled Transplants.* Portland ME: University of Southern Maine, 1993.

Fahlberg, Vera. *Attachment and Separation.* Spaulding for Children, P.o. Box 337, Chelsea MI 48118, 1979.

Harting, Barbara. *Uncharted Waters: Parenting an Attachment Disordered Child.* In manuscript form, this book was written about the adoption of a Vietnamese child, Tim, at age 2 1/2 years old, and the disruption at age 15. Available for $15.00 only through Barbara Harting, 46 Carter Drive, Framingham, MA, 01701.

Karen, Robert. *Becoming Attached: Unfolding the Mysteries of the Infant Mother Bond and Its Impact on Later Life.* New York: Warner Books, 1994.

Keck, Gregory C. and Kupecky, Regina M. *Adopting the Hurt Child.* Colorado Springs, CO: Piñon Press, 1995.

Magid, Ken & McKelvey, Carole. *High Risk: Children without a Conscience.* New York: Bantam Books, 1988.

Mansfield, Lynda & Waldmann, Christopher. *Don't Touch My Heart: Healing the Pain of the Unattached Child.* Colorado Springs, CO: Piñon Press, 1994.

Sandmaier, Marian. *When Love is Not Enough: How Mental Health Professionals Can Help Special-Needs Adoptive Families.* Washington, DC: Child Welfare League of America, 1988.

Welch, Martha G. *Holding Time.* New York: Simon & Schuster, 1988.

DISABILITIES

Bernheib, Kayla. *The Caring Family: Living with Chronic Mental Illness.* Chicago: Contemporary Books, 1982.

Bloom, Beth-Ann, & Seljeskog, Edward. *A Parent's Guide to Spina Bifida.* University of Minnesota Press, 1988.

Bodenhamer, Gregory. *Back in Control.* New York: Simon & Schuster.

Dobson, Penny. (Ed.) *Enuresis: A Guide to the Treatment of Enuresis for Professionals.* Available through the Simon Foundation for Continence, P.o. Box 835, Wilmette IL 60091.

Dorris, Michael. *The Broken Cord.* New York: Harper & Row, 1989. Fetal alcohol syndrome.

Finnegan, Joanne. *Shattered Dreams, Lonely Choices: Birthparents of Babies with Disabilities Talk about Adoption.* Westport, CT: Bergin & Garvey, 1993.

Glidden, Laraine. *Formed Families: Adoption of Children with Handicaps.* Binghamton, CT: Haworth Press, 1990.

A Guidebook for Parents of Children with Emotional/Behavioral Disorders. Parent Advocacy Coalition for Educational Rights Inc. (PACER), 4826 Chicago Ave., Minneapolis, MN 55417-1055, 1991.

Medical Facts About Spina Bifida, Kennedy Krieger Inst., and Spina Bifida Association of America. Spina Bifida Center, Kennedy Krieger Institute, 707 N. Broadway, Baltimore, MD 21205; Tel. 800-873-3377.

Money, John. *The Kaspar Hauser Syndrome of Psychosocial Dwarfism.* Prometheus Books.

Moore, Cory. *A Reader's Guide: For Parents of Children with Mental, Physical or Emotional Disabilities.* Bethesda, MD: Woodbine House, 1990.

Nutrition Care for Children with Prader-Willi Syndrome Ages 3-9 is a 12-page booklet that addresses calorie needs, supplements, diet planning and food management. $5 each through the Prader-Willi Syndrome

Association, 2510 S. Brentwood Blvd., Suite 220, St. Louis, MO 63144; 800-926-4797.

Sandmaier, Marian. *When Love Is Not Enough: How Mental Health Professionals Can Help Special Needs Adoptive Families.* Washington, DC: Child Welfare League of America, 1988.

Smith, Romayne. *Children with Mental Retardation: A Parent's Guide.* Bethesda, MD: Woodbine House, 1990.

Thompson, Charlotte E. *Raising a Handicapped Child: A Helpful Guide for Parents of the Physically Disabled.* New York: Ballantine, 1986.

Trott, Laurel. *Senseabilities: Understanding Sensory Integration.* Available through Therapy Skill Builders. Tel. 602-323-7500. Easy to understand.

DISTANCE LEARNING RESOURCES

Bear, John, and Bear, Mariah. *College Degrees* by *Mail, Bears' Guide to Earning Non-Traditional College Degrees* (12th Edition), and *Finding Money For College.* The first two list and profile DL schools, accredited and state-approved (nonaccredited), national and international, and answer common questions, such as how to obtain college credits through life and work experience. Call 800-841-BOOK (Ten Speed Press, P.O. Box 7123, Berkeley, CA 94707, USA).

Corrigan, Dan. *The Internet University: College Courses by Computer.* Describes more than 600 accredited courses and 30 schools along with 1,500 Internet sources of free study. Cape Software Press, http://www.caso.com) P.O. Box 800, Harwich, MA 02645. 508-432-2435.

Distance Education and Training Council, Washington, DC. Informative brochures, including some about life experience credits, are available from the Distance Education & Training Council, which is recognized by the U.S. Dept. of Education. Call DETC at 202-234-5100.

Education at a Distance. The United States Distance Learning Association (USDLA) publishes this magazine. Contact USDLA at 800-275-5162 or 510-606-5160.

Ellsworth, Jill H. *Education on the Internet.* Sams Publishing, 201 West 103 Street, Indianapolis, IN 46290, USA. Call. 800-428-5331. Everything you want to know about electronic educational resources from kindergarten through graduate school.

How To Earn a *College Degree in Only 4 Months* by Educational Awareness Publications, Tustin, CA. Tel: 714-832-1157. Yes, you can actually earn an accredited B.A. simply by taking GRE/CLEP tests. For more information, you can call Regents College in Albany, NY.

Lamdin, Lois. *Earn College Credit for What You Know*, Second Edition, CAEL, 243 S. Wabash Ave, Suite 800, Chicago, IL 60604. Tel. 312-922-1769. A step-by-step guide to discovering what you may be able to get college credit for, and how to go about it, plus choosing the right school, and surviving in college.

Peterson's Publishing. *The Independent Study Catalog* by Peterson's lists accredited schools that offer DL courses, as does the *Electronic University* by Peterson's. Financial issues are covered in *Paying Less For College* and *USA Today Financial Aid For College.* Many people can use their book called colleges with programs for students with learning disabilities. call Peterson's at 609-243-9111 or 800-338-3282.

Thorson, Marcie Kisner. *Campus-Free College Degrees,* 7th Edition. Thorson Guides, Tulsa, OK. Tel: 918-622-2811. This helpful guide is the 1996-1997 edition of Thorson's Guide to accredited distance learning degree programs. It lists and profiles U.S. accredited DL schools and programs, and answers common questions, such as how to obtain college credits through life and work experience.

ESSENTIAL PUBLICATIONS FOR SPECIAL NEEDS ADOPTIVE PARENTS

AAICAMA Issue Briefs, Association of Administrators of the Interstate Compact on Adoption and Medical Assistance. Tel. 202-682-0100. Fax: 202-289-6555. AAICAMA, c/o APWA, 810 First Street, N.E. Suite 500, Washington, DC 20002-4267. Issue Briefs, compiled by AAICAMA and distributed by American Public Welfare Association, explain financial and medical aspects and benefits of special needs adoption.

Adoptalk, publication of the North American Council on Adoptable Children. Also publishes *The NACAC User's Guide to P.L. 96-272.* The User's Guide will help as you seek to renegotiate your adoption subsidy contract over the years. Write NACAC at 970 Raymond Avenue, Suite 106, St. Paul, MN 55114. The phone is 612-644-3036.

The Adoption Directory, 2nd Edition, by Ellen Paul; Published by Gale Research. Tel. 800-877-GALE. Almost 600 pages of crucial information, $65. Ask at your local library, support group or adoption agency if you cannot afford this resource. This is a superb resource for agencies and support groups.

The Adoption Resource Guide, Child Welfare League of America. Tel. 202-638-2952. CWLA, 440 First Street, NW, Suite 310, Washington DC 20001-2085.

Adoptive Families Magazine, 2309 Como Avenue, St. Paul, MN 55108. $24.95 annually (bimonthly). The publication of Adoptive Families of America, the oldest adoptive parent organization in the United States, and the adoption magazine with the widest circulation.

National Adoption Information Clearinghouse (NAIC), 5640 Nicholson Lane, Suite 300, Rockville MD 29852. Tel. 301-231-6512. Fax:

301-984-8527. Web—http://www.workstation.com/naicinfo. e-mail: naicinfo@erols. com. Essential catalog, free copies of pamphlets covering all aspects of adoption, federal adoption legislation, state adoption statutes, Indian Child Welfare Act (ICWA), Adoption Directory, etc.

Reader's Guide to Adoption-Related Literature, William Lewis Gage, 805 Alvarado Drive NE, Albuquerque, NM 87108. An annually-updated bibliography of hundreds of adoption-specific books divided into categories ranging from "Adoptees—Adult Non-Fiction" to Short Fiction and Poetry. Listing is free with SASE, or available at KinQuest BBS, via modem at 505-897-0814 (8/N/1 14.4k baud).

Roots & Wings Adoption magazine, for families and friends touched by adoption. Designed for readers of all ages and stages in the adoption cycle, from prospective adoptive parents, to adoptees and birth parents. Sample issue for $3.00, or $20.00 for four issues per year. *Roots & Wings,* P.O. Box 577, Hackettstown, NJ 07840. Tel. 908-637-8828. Fax: 908-637-4259. e-mail: adoption@world2u.com. Web—http://www.adopting.org/rw.html.

GAY AND LESBIAN PARENTING AND ADOPTION

Bozett, Frederick, Ed. *Gay and Lesbian Parents.* New York: Greenwood, 1987. Chapter on adoption.

Martin, April. *The Lesbian and Gay Parenting Handbook: Creating and Raising Our Families.* New York: HarperCollins, 1993.

Ricketts, Wendell. *Lesbians and Gay Men as Foster Parents.* National Child Welfare Resrouce Center for Management and Administration, 1992. University of Southern Maine, 96 Falmouth Street, Portland, ME 04103.

INTERNATIONAL SPECIAL NEEDS ADOPTION

Organizations

Autism Research Institute, Central Auditory Processing Disorder, 4182 Adams Ave., San Diego, CA 92116.

Georgiana Society, Box 2607, Westport, CT 06880. Tel. 203-454-1221. Information about AIT therapy for CAPD (post-institutionalized children, auditory processing disorders).

International Concerns Committee for Children, 911 Cypress Drive, Boulder, CO 80303. Tel. and Fax: 303-494-8333. Matches waiting children in other countries with U.S. adoptive parents through an international photolisting book, publishes an annual Report on Intercountry Adoption, offers information.

Parent Network for the Post-Institutionalized Child, Box 613, Meadow Lands, PA 15347.

Books

Karen, Robert. *Becoming Attached.* New York: Time-Warner Books, 1994. A comprehensive history of attachment research. Every parent with a post-institutionalized child should read this book, as should every adult contemplating an Eastern European adoption.

Koh, Frances M. *Oriental Children in American Homes.* San Francisco: East West Press, 1984.

Murphy, Kay, & Knoll, Jean. *International Adoption: Sensitive Advice for Prospective Parents.* Chicago: Chicago Review Press, 1994.

Register, Cheri. *"Are Those Kids Yours?" American Families with Children Adopted from Other Countries.* Free Press, 1990.

Strassberger, Laurel. *Our Children from Latin America: Making Adoption Part of Your Life.* Tiresias Press, 1992.

Wilkinson, H. Sook. *Birth is More Than Once: The Inner World of Adopted Korean Children.* Sunrise Vent., 1985.

Wirth, Eileen & Worden, Joan. *How to Adopt a Child from Another Country.* Nashville, TN: Abington Press, 1993.

OLDER CHILD ADOPTION

Carney, Ann. *No More Here and There: Adopting the Older Child.* Chapel Hill, NC: University of North Carolina, 1976.

Fahlberg, Vera. *A Child's Journey Through Placement.* Indianapolis, IN: Perspectives Press, 1991.

Jewett, Claudia. *Adopting the Older Child.* Boston, MA: Harvard Common Press, 1978.

Kadushin, Alfred. *Adopting Older Children.* Columbia University Press, 1970.

McNamara, Joan & Bernard. *Adoption and the Sexually Abused Child.* University of Southern Maine, 1990.

Minshew, Deborah H. *The Adoptive Family As A Healing Resource for the Sexually Abused Child: A Training Manual.* Washington, DC: Child Welfare League of America, 1990.

Rosenthal, James A. and Groze, Victor. *Special Needs Adoption: A Study of Intact Families.* New York: Praeger, 1992.

ONLINE ONLY RESOURCES

On-Line resources include internet newsgroups, World Wide Web (WWW or Web) Pages, e-mail mailing lists, and electronic bulletin-boards (BBS) relating to adoption. When accessing a web page, the reader should type in the full address, including all punctuation and slashes. If an address is given as "Web—http://www.yahoo.com" the reader will have to type in "http://www.yahoo.com." The word "Web" is not part of the URL (Universal Resource Locator, or Web page address).

ADD WWW Archive. http://homepage.seas.upenn.edu/~mengwong/add/.

Adoption Advocates. http://www.fpsol.com/adoption/advocates.html. Offers current information about Adoption AssistancePayments (AAP), SSI rulings, changes in federal laws and court cases affecting special needs adoptive families, and much more.

Adoption Reform Page. http://pages.prodigy.com/adoptreform/index.htm. Everything from reform organizations, to ethics in adoption, to current adoption court cases.

AIDS KIDS. http://www.aidskids.org. This page is of special interest to those adopting HIV+ children.

Amazon.com. http://amazon.com. At over a million titles in stock, this is the Internet's largest bookstore, as well as the planet's biggest.

American Medical Association Home Page. http://www.ama-assn.org.

Autism Resource Guide. http://pages.prodigy.com/dporcari/index.html.

Center for Children with Chronic Illness and Disability. http:// www.peds.umn.edu/Centers/c3id/.

CHADD: Children & Adults with ADD. http://www.chadd.org/.

Children's Home Society of Minnesota. http://www.chsm.com/. Places children with special needs and is one of the country's oldest agencies.

Deaf Adoption News Service (DANS). http://www.erols.com/berke/deafchildren.html. Helps match adoptive parents with deaf children around the world.

Down Syndrome WWW Page. http://www.nas.com/downsyn/.

Facts for Families. http://aacap.org/web/aacap/factsFam. For parents raising children with disabilities.

False Abuse Allegations Page. http://www.vix.com/pub/men/falsereport/child.html

Growing Families Inc. of New Jersey. http://www.thesphere.com/GFI/ Information on special needs adoption, waiting children.

Holt International Childrens Services Home Page. http://www.thesphere.com/~holtbear/index.html. The country's oldest international adoption agency, places many children with special needs.

KinQuest BBS. Via modem at 505-897-0814 (8/N/1/14.4k baud modem). *Reader's Guide to Adoption-Related Literature* by William Lewis Gage can be found here, and much more on adoption.

Korea, Friends of Korea Home Page, http://members.aol.com/ForKorea/Index.htm.

Korean Adoptees Page, http://www.medill/nwu.edu/people/chappell/kor.am.adoptees.html.

The Mayo Clinics. http://www.mayo.edu.

National Center for Youth with Disabilities. http://www.peds.umn.edu/Centers/ncyd.
Oregon Adoption & Foster Care Guide. http://www.teleport.com:80/~family/02ch/02ch09.html. Information directed to adults interested in adopting waiting children.
Parents Helping Parents. http://www.portal.com/~cbntmkr/php.html. Offers wisdom for parents of children with special needs.
Rainbow House Home Page. http://www.rhi.org/.
Shriners Hospitals. http://www.pixi.com/~shriners/.
Texas DPRS Home Page. http://www.dhs.state.tx.us/tdprs/homepage.html Texas Department of Protective and Regulatory Services home page listing children waiting to be adopted in the state of Texas.
U.S. Department of Health and Human Services Page. http:// www.os.dhhs.gov.
Voices of Adoption. http://www.ibar.com/adoptions.html. The on-line national special needs photolisting of the National Adoption Center (NAC) and Children Awaiting Parents (CAP).
The Youth At Risk Gopher. gopher://tinman.mes.umn.edu:4242/. Includes research on today's youth that may be helpful to special needs adoptive parents.

OPEN ADOPTION

Anderson, Ann Kiemel. *Open Adoption: My Story of Love & Laughter.* Wheaton, IL: Tyndale, 1990.
Arms, Suzanne. *A Handful of Hope: The Promise of Open Adoption.* Berkeley, CA: Celestial Arts, 1989.
McRoy, Ruth G., Grotevant, Harold D. and White, Kerry L. *Openness in Adoption: New Practices, New Issues.* New York: Praeger, 1988.
Melina, Lois, & Sharon Roszia. *The Open Adoption Experience.* New York: HarperCollins, 1993.
Rappaport, Bruce. *The Open Adoption Book: A Guide to Adoption without Tears.* New York: Macmillan, 1992.
Silber, Kathleen & Patricia Dorner. *Children of Open Adoption.* San Antonio: Corona, 1990.

PHOTO-LISTING BOOKS AND ADOPTION EXCHANGES

Adoption of Children with Spina Bifida, 1955 Florida Drive, Xenia, OH 45385. Tel. 513-372-2040

Childen Awaiting Parents (CAP) Photolisting Book. 700 Exchange Avenue, Rochester, NY 14608. Tel. 716-232-5110, $75 per year per support group, agency, or individual, for a subscription to their national waiting child directory.

National Down Syndrome Adoption Exchange, 56 Midchester Avenue, White Plains, NY 10606. Tel. 914-428-1236.

Rocky Mountain Adoption Exchange, 925 S. Niagra, Suite 100, Denver, CO 80224. Tel. 303-333-0845.

POETRY

Cohen, Mary Anne. *Exile, A Journey.* 34 Highland Avenue, Whippany, NJ 07981. A birth mother's poetry.

Duncan, Robert Edward. *Roots & Branches.* New York: Scribners, 1964.

Johnston, Patricia. *Perspectives on a Grafted Tree.* Indianaopolis, IN: Perspectives Press, 1983.

PUBLISHERS OF ADOPTION MATERIALS

Birco Publishing, P.O. Box 341, Gladstone, MI 49837.

Boys Town Press, 13603 Flanagan Blvd., Boys Town, NE 68010. Tel. 800-BT-BOOKS, Fax: 402-498-1125. Publishes and sells many books, pamplets and videos of use to parents of children with emotional and behavioral difficulties. Highly Recommended. Free catalog.

Child Welfare League of America, 440 First Street NW, Suite 310, Washington, DC 20001-2085. Sells many excellent child welfare and adoption books oriented to professionals.

Concerned United Birthparents, 2000 Walker Street, Des Moines, IA 50317. Booklets about birth parents, adoptees, and adoption search.

Greenwood Publishing Group, Inc., 88 Post Road West, P.O. Box 5007, Westport, CT 06881-5007. Tel. 203-226-3571. Fax: 203-222-1502. Bergin & Garvey, Greenwood Press, and Praeger, all imprints of the Greenwood Group, offer adoption-specific titles, particularly of interest to special needs adoptive parents.

The Heritage Key, 6102 E. Mescal, Scottsdale, AZ 85254. Sells books, dolls, toys, and other cultural items from around the world. Great resource for international adopters.

ISC Publications, P.O. Box 10192, Costa Mesa, CA 92627. Booklets about adoption search.

Morning Side Publishing, P.O. Box 21071, Saanichton RPO, Saanichton, BC, V0S 1M0, Canada. Publications for birth parents and adult adoptees.

New Sage Press, 825 NE 20th Avenue, #150, Portland, OR 97232.

Our Child Press, 800 Maple Glen Lane, Wayne, PA 19087.

Perspectives Press, "The Infertility and Adoption Publisher," Box 90318, Indianapolis, IN 46290-0318. Tel. 317-872-3055. e-mail: ppress@iquest.net. Publications and books on infertility and adoption.

Tapestry Books, P.O. Box 359, Ringoes, NJ 08551. Tel. 800-765-2367 or 908-806-6695. Fax: 908-788-2999. e-mail: info@tapestrybooks.com.

Web—http://www.tapestrybooks.com/. Free catalog listing hundreds of infertility, adoption, and parenting books.

University Microfilms International (UMI), 300 North Zeeb Road, P.O. Box 1346, Ann Arbor, MI 48106-1346 Tel. 800-521-0600, 800-521-3042, 313-761-4700. Web—http://www.umi.com. UMI is a major source of dissertations and theses published in the United States including those dealing with special needs adoption and adoption research. Public and university libraries can access their database of titles, including the doctoral dissertations of the authors.

REFORM ORGANIZATIONS AND RESOURCES

These organizations are peopled by members from all corners of the adoption triangle—birth parents, adoptees, and adoptive parents, though adoptive parents are often a minority. Professionals are also represented. They are all devoted to adoption reform, the improvement of current adoption laws and practices.

Adoption Network Cleveland, 291 East 222 Street, Cleveland, OH 44123-1751. Tel. 216-261-1511. Fax: 216-261-1164. Web—http://pages.prodigy.com/adoptreform/anc.htm. e-mail: bln2@po. cwru.edu. Triad support group, education, newsletter.

American Adoption Congress, 1000 Connecticut Avenue, N.W., Suite 9, Washington, D.C. 20036. Tel. 202-483-3399. Web—http://pages.prodigy. com/adoptreform/aacorg.htm. Education, advocacy, publications, newsletter. Hosts annual and regional conferences. http://pages.prodigy.com/adoptreform/aacorg.htm.

American Association of Open Adoption Agencies, 1000 Hastings, Traverse City, MI 49686. Tel. 616-947-8110.

APFOR, Adoptive Parents for Open Records, P.O. Box 193, Long Valley, NJ 07853. Tel. 201-267-8698.

The Blue Book: A Directory of Adoption Groups. Birthparent Connection, Box 230643, Encinatas, CA 92023. A comprehensive listing of search and support groups, social service and adoption agencies, professional searchers, and professionals on a state-by-state and international basis.

Concerned United Birthparents, 2000 Walker Street, Des Moines, IA 50317. Tel. 800-822-2777. Newsletter, publications. Hosts annual and regional conferences.

SEARCH INFORMATION

Adoption search information is for adoptive parents, birth parents, and adoptees who are searching for someone separated through adoption. Because birth records are closed in many states, searching for birth parents, the child one surrendered for adoption, or the adoptive parents of one's child can be a challenge. The following organizations and information can help.

American Adoption Congress, 1000 Connecticut Avenue, N.W., Suite 9, Washington, D.C. 20036. Request search information for state of adoptee's birth. http://pages.prodigy.com/adoptreform/aacorg.htm

Concerned United Birthparents, 2000 Walker Street, Des Moines, IA 50317. 1-800-822-2777. Request search information for state of adoptee'a birth.

Independent Search Consultants, Inc. (ISC), P.O. Box 10192, Costa Mesa, CA 92627. e-mail: isc@rmci.net. http://www:rmci.net/isc. Consultants experienced with adoption search on a state-by-state basis. Publications for sale.

International Soundex Reunion Registry, ISRR, P.O. Box 2312, Carson City, NV 89702. Tel. 702-882-7755. A confidential and voluntary computerized identification system on a national and international scale. The service is voluntary, and free to the user. Send long SASE for ISRR registration form.

Books about Search

Askin, Jayne. *Search: A Handbook for Adoptees & Birthparents.* Oryx, 1992.

Gallagher, Helen, Sitterly, Nancy, & Sanders, Pat. *The ISC Searchbook.* ISC Publications, 1992.

Geidman, J., and Brown, L. *Birthbond: Reunions Between Birthparents and Adoptees, What Happens After.* New Horizons Press, 1995.

Gravelle, Karen, and Fischer, Susan. *Where Are My Birth Parents? A Guide For Teenage Adoptees.* Dalker and Co., 1993.

Klunder, Virgil. *Lifeline: The Action Guide to Adoption Search.* Caradium Publications, 1991.

Lifton, Betty Jean. *Journey of the Adopted Self: A Quest For Wholeness.* New York: Basic Books, 1994.

Lifton, Betty Jean. *Lost and Found: The Adoption Experience.* New York: Harper & Row, 1988.

Schooler, Jayne. *Searching for a Past: The Adopted Adult's Unique Process of Finding Identity.* Colorado Springs, CO: Piñon, 1995.

SIBLINGS AND SIBLING GROUP ADOPTION

Featherstone, Helen. *A Difference in the Family.* New York: Viking Penguin, 1980.

Hochman, Gloria, Feathers-Acuna, Ellen, & Huston, Anna. *The Sibling Bond: Its Importance in Foster Care and Adoptive Placement.* Rockville, MD: NAIC, n.d.

Powell, Thomas H., & Ogle, Peggy A. *Brothers and Sisters: A Special Part of Exceptional Families.* Paul H. Brookes, 1985.
Ward, Margaret. Full House: Adoption of a Large Sibling Group. *Child Welfare, 57,* 4. Washington, DC: CWLA. April 1978.
Wedge, Peter & Mantle, Greg. *Sibling Groups & Social Work.* Ashgate Publishing, 1991.

TRANSRACIAL ADOPTION

Grow, I., and Shapiro, D. *Black Children, White Parents: A Study of Transracial Adoption.* Washington, DC: Child Welfare League of America, 1974.
Grow, I., and Shapiro, D. *Transracial Adoption Today: Views of Adoptive Parents and Social Workers.* Washington, DC: Child Welfare League of America, 1975.
McRoy, Ruth, et al., Eds. *Transracial and Inracial Adoptees: The Adolescent Years.* C.C. Thomas, 1983.
Simon, Rita J. *Case for Transracial Adoption.* American University Press, 1993.
Simon, Rita J. & Altstein, H. *Transracial Adoptees and Their Families: A Study of Identity and Commitment.* New York: Praeger, 1987.

References

Adoption: How to begin. (1994). Minneapolis, MN: Adoptive Families of America.

Alexander-Roberts, C. (1993). *The essential adoption handbook.* Dallas, TX: Taylor Publishing.

Allen, E. C. (1983). *Mother, can you hear me?* New York: Dodd Mead Co.

Barth, R. P., & Berry, M. (1988). *Adoption and disruption: Rates, risks, and responses.* New York: Aldine de Gruyter.

Benson, P., Sharma, A., & Roehlkepartain, E. (1994). *Growing up adopted: A portrait of adolescents and their families.* Minneapolis, MN: Search Institute.

Briere, J. N. (1992). *Child abuse trauma: Theory and treatment of the lasting effects.* Newbury Park, CA: Sage Publications.

Burgess, D. & Streissgruth, A. (n.d.). *Educating children prenatally exposed to alcohol and other drugs.* Unpublished paper.

Bussiere, A. (1990). Implementation of PL 96-272: Adoption Assistance. In *The adoption assistance and child welfare act of 1980 (Public Law 96-272): The first ten years,* pp. 75-86. St. Paul, MN: NACAC.

Cadoret, R. J. (1990). Biologic perspectives of adoptee adjustment. In *The Psychology of Adoption* (Brodzinsky, D. M., and Schechter, M. D., Eds.). New York: Oxford University Press.

Clarren, S., & Aldrich, R. (n.d.). *Fetal alcohol syndrome/Fetal alcohol effects.* University of Washington: Children's Hospital and Medical Center.

Cline, F., & Fay, J. (1990). *Parenting with love and logic: Teaching children responsibility.* Colorado Springs, CO: NavPress.

Cohen, J. S., & Westhues, A. (1990). *Well-functioning families for adoptive and foster children.* Toronto: University of Toronto Press.

Cole, E. S., & Donley, K. S. (1990). History, values, and placement policy issues in adoption. In D. M. Brodzinsky & M. D. Schechter (Eds.) *The psychology of adoption*, pp. 273-294. New York: Oxford University Press.

CWLA. *The child welfare stat book 1993* (1994). Washington, D.C.: author.

Department of Health and Human Services, Office of Human Development Services (December 14, 1988). 45 CFR Part 1356, Title IV-E adoption assistance program: Nonrecurring expenses. *Federal Register, 53*, 240, 50215-50221.

Dunn, L. (1980). Guest Editorial, *Adoption Report.* Minneapolis, MN: NACAC.

Egeland, B., Sroufe, L. A., & Erickson, M. (1983). The developmental consequences of different patterns of maltreatment. *Child Abuse & Neglect, 7,* 459-469.

Fahlberg, V. I. (1991). *A child's journey through placement.* Indianapolis, IN: Perspectives Press.

Families for kids of color: A special report on challenges and opportunities (n.d.). W. W. Kellogg Foundation, P.O. Box 5196, Battle Creek, MI 49016-5196.

Finnegan, J. (1995). *Shattered dreams, lonely choices: Birthparents of babies with disabilities talk about adoption.* New York: Bergin & Garvey.

Forsythe, J. (n.d.). *Turning the tables in adoption: The adoptive parent movement.* Unpublished paper written for NACAC.

Gelles, R. J. & Straus, M. A. (1987). Is violence toward children increasing? A comparison of 1975 and 1985 national survey rates. *Journal of Interpersonal Violence, 2,* 212-222.

Gilles, T. & Kroll, J. (1992). *User's guide to PL 96-272: A summarization and codification of administrative rulings.* St. Paul, MN: NACAC.

Groze, V., Young, J., & Corcran-Rumppe, K. (n.d.). *Partners: Post adoption resources for training, networking and evaluation services: Working with special needs adoptive families in stress.* Cedar Rapids: Four Oaks.

Herman, J. L. (1981). *Father-daughter incest.* Cambridge, MA: Harvard University Press.

International Adoptions and "Reasonable Efforts," *Issues in Adoption Advocacy, 2* (1), Nov/Dec 1996, p. 2.

Keck, G. C., & Kupecky, R. M. (1995). *Adopting the hurt child.* Colorado Springs, CO: Pinon Press.

Krementz, J. (1983). *How it feels to be adopted.* New York: Alfred A. Knopf.

Kübler-Ross, E. (1969). *On death and dying.* New York: Macmillan.

Lifton, B. J. (1994). *Journey of the adopted self: A quest for wholeness.* New York: Basic Books.

Lifton, B. J. (1988). *Lost and found: The adoption experience.* New York: Harper & Row.

Mason, M. M. & Silberman, A. (Speakers) (1993). *Networking with birthparents: Seeking and finding a match.* (Cassette Recording No. 4C-93). Minneapolis, MN: Adoptive Families of America.

McFarlane, J. (1992, Jan-Feb). Self-esteem in children of color: Developmental, adoption, and racial issues. *OURS Magazine.* Minneapolis, MN: Adoptive Families of America.

McKelvey, C. A. (Spring 1994). Romania's lost children: A story of hope. *Attachments,* Spring 1994, 1-3.

Melina, L. R. (January, 1994). Transracial adoptees can develop racial identity, coping strategies. *Adopted Child, 13,* 1.

Melina, L., & Roszia, S. (1993). *The open adoption experience.* New York: HarperCollins.

North American Council on Adoptable Children (1989). *Parent group manual: Resources and ideas for adoptive parent support groups.* St. Paul: Author.

Parent Network for the Post-Institutionalized Child (Spring, 1995). *Overview: The post-institutionalized child.*

The Robins Training Group (1991). *The cultural competence continuum.* (Available from The Robins Training Group, 8306 Wilshire Blvd., Suite 701-9, Beverly Hills, CA 90211.)

Rosenthal, J. A. & Groze, V. K. (1992). *Special-needs adoption.* New York: Praeger.

Sears, W. (1990). *Nighttime parenting: How to get your baby and child to sleep.* Franklin Park, IL: La Leche League International.

U.S. Census report. (1993). *Current population reports.* Population projections of the United States by age, sex, race, and hispanic origin: 1993 to 2050.

Welch, M. G. (1978). *Holding time.* New York: Simon & Schuster.

Index

About the Authors

L. ANNE BABB is Executive Director of a nonprofit adoption advocacy center, the Family Tree Adoption and Counseling Center in Norman, Oklahoma.

RITA LAWS is Director of the Oklahoma Chapter of Adopt a Special Kid (AASK) and representative to the North American Council on Adoptable Children (NACAC).

Both authors received their M.S. degrees and Ph.D.s in psychology.